Chinese Cinema during the Era of Reform

Chinese Cinema during the Era of Reform

The Ingenuity of the System

YING ZHU

Foreword by Xie Fei

Westport, Connecticut
London

Library of Congress Cataloging-in-Publication Data

Zhu, Ying, 1965–
 Chinese cinema during the era of reform : the ingenuity of the
system / Ying Zhu ; foreword by Xie Fei.
  p. cm.
 Includes bibliographical references and index.
 ISBN 0-275-97959-8 (alk. paper)
  1. Motion pictures—China—History. 2. Motion picture industry—
China—History. I. Title.
PN1993.5.C4 Z58 2003
384'.8'0951—dc21   2002193043

British Library Cataloguing in Publication Data is available.

Library of Congress Catalog Card Number: 2002193043
ISBN: 0-275-97959-8

First published in 2003

Praeger Publishers, 88 Post Road West, Westport, CT 06881
An imprint of Greenwood Publishing Group, Inc.
www.praeger.com

Printed in the United States of America

The paper used in this book complies with the
Permanent Paper Standard issued by the National
Information Standards Organization (Z39.48–1984).

10 9 8 7 6 5 4 3 2 1

For my daughter Frances

Contents

Foreword

Much has been written in English about the politics and ideology and, to a lesser extent, the style of Chinese cinema, especially the cinemas of the Fifth Generation, and lately the underground/independent films of the younger generation. Less explored is the evolution of post–Mao Mainland Chinese cinema from pedagogy/propaganda to art to commerce. Even less noted is the similarity between Chinese cinema's current entertainment wave and its early entertainment wave from the late 1920s to the early 1930s. The mastery of both requires a thorough knowledge and understanding of not only the politics but also the economy and the culture of Chinese cinema, and most important of all, the nuts and bolts, or the daily grind, of filmmaking in China. Ying Zhu is blessed with all of these, which explains this book's richness and perceptiveness.

Most delightful to me personally is the author's willingness and ability to think outside her formal academic training, which makes the book more readable and, I think, more relevant. Here I must confess my bias as the director of a number of well-known films, as well as the mentor and advocate of the Chinese New Wave films. As a filmmaker, I naturally gravitate toward writings on film with industrial grounding and ones that are sensitive to the intricacy of filmmaking. I can certainly relate to the chaotic experience of the contemporary Chinese film community described in this book. Working in the industry, I have witnessed the rise and fall of careers and film trends. I have seen brilliant and creative people struggle to make films in an ever-changing political, cultural, and economic environment. For creative people, the difficulty of this environment seems to motivate them further to succeed and produce innovative and challenging work. My own career is an example of the constraints and opportunities of a system in transition.

My first independently directed feature, *In Our Field* (1983), lamented the loss of life and meaning in a group of educated youth laboring in the northeast wastelands of China, reenacting the traumatic experience of social injustice during the Cultural Revolution. I later participated in the cultural reflection movement by directing *A Girl from Hunan* (1986), a film that reexamines traditional culture. The only mainland urban film to win the Silver Bear at the Berlin Film Festival, *Black Snow* (1989) was made amid the widespread cynicism of the late 1980s. My somewhat pessimistic portrayal of urban life attempted to capture the feelings of alienation and existential crisis. *A Mongolian Tale* (1995) was not merely a nostalgic call for an era of simplicity and youthful idealism, it also suggested my desire to cultivate a cinema for mature audiences, age-wise and taste-wise. I have always been an avid advocate of art cinema. I still believe in the potential of a profitable art film market in China. I am not discounting popular entertainment fares as they are the foundation of any market-oriented film infrastructure. The issue becomes how to cultivate niche markets catering to various audience demographics. Diversification of both the film market and film taste seems mandatory and my hope is to nurture a working market for mature audiences of art cinema.

The Fifth Generation filmmakers have been the most successful in the global art film market, but not so good in the Chinese market. The latest generation has yet to demonstrate their ability to work within the system in order to occupy a domestic marketplace. Interestingly, both generations passed through the Beijing Film Academy during my time as chair of the Department of Directing and vice president of the academy. Of course when I started making films, investment and market were of the least concern. At the dawn of the twenty-first century, the search for audiences has brought us all together. The politics of Chinese cinema is no longer the politics of generation but the politics of the market. As the Chinese film industry struggles to maintain its place in the global cinematic landscape, the livelihood of many filmmakers is on the line. The Chinese film industry has enough talent but has yet to master the business of filmmaking. The insights offered by this book will benefit not only the scholars and fans of Chinese cinema but also the Chinese filmmakers themselves. It will remind them where they have been, and help them to contemplate what lies ahead. The book is timely and essential in this regard. As beleaguered film industries around the world confront similar issues and challenges, this book will be invaluable to other film practitioners as they develop their own strategies for surviving in the new environment.

This book provides a survey of the different generations of filmmakers active in China today and addresses the differences in perspective and approach of those generations, which deepens our understanding of the current situation and future prospects for Chinese film. The exploration of globalization and the role and function of cultural identity for a national film industry complete the picture. We shall see if a cinematic multiculturalism is at the mercy of the global juggernaut.

Xie Fei
Beijing Film Academy

Preface

Much of the inspiration for this book came from the Chinese film practitioners I have either worked with or befriended over the years. I have witnessed the coming and going of cinematic trends as well as the rise and fall of careers; I am now observing, from afar, the prolonged recession of a once prosperous film industry. Throughout, the resilience of the Chinese film practitioners never ceases to amaze me. This book is for and about them, and my gratitude should first go to them. Specifically, Professors Ni Zheng and Xie Fei at the Beijing Film Academy; Professor Zhang Tongdao at the Beijing Normal University; Wu Guangping at the journal *Film Arts*; filmmakers Zhang Junzhao, Teng Wenji, Huang Jianxing, Feng Xiaogang, and He Ping; and the head of Beijing Studio, Han Shanping deserve special credit for sharing their insights with me on the state of Chinese cinema. My friend Li Zhipu, a well-accomplished and prolific screenwriter in China, has been very kind in providing me with logistical support as has Pan Meichang, another dear friend, whose help made my trip to China productive.

Research for this book was initially funded by the Mellon Foundation. The Graduate School at the University of Texas–Austin also granted me funding for fieldwork. The funding allowed me to travel to China in the late 1990s for a series of in-depth interviews with prominent Chinese filmmakers and critics and with China's top film policy makers, which provided an empirical base for this project. I am grateful to Professor Emile McAnany, then at the University of Texas–Austin and now at the University of Santa Clara, who helped me secure the Mellon funding, and with whom I discussed the initial idea for this book. Thanks also to Professor Horace Newcomb, then at the University of Texas–Austin and now at the University of Georgia, for helping me with the funding from the Graduate School and for his unwavering academic and intellectual support. His detailed suggestions on the book at its early stages directly contributed to its current shape. Another person who merits my special tribute in making this book possible is Professor Thomas Schatz of the University of Texas–Austin. Tom offered me precise criticism of every chapter of this book throughout several revisions. No less rewarding were the many lunch meetings with him where thoughts on (academic) life in general were exchanged and free food was provided. Tom's dry sense of humor and his very direct style made our exchange all the more enjoyable. Special appreciation also goes to Professor Yvonne Chang, Professor John Downing, Professor Nikhil Sinha, and my colleague Bruce Robinson at the University of Texas–Austin, for their critical comments. This book was completed during my first year at the College of Staten Island, the City University of New York. I would like to thank my colleagues in the Department of Media Culture for providing a supportive environment. Last but not least, I would like to thank Eric Levy, my editor at Praeger, for his encouragement and editorial guidance.

Finally, thank you Andrew and Frances Hisgen for always being there for me.

1

Chinese Cinema: A Culture and Economy in Disarray

INTRODUCTION

Beginning in the mid-1980s, the Mainland Chinese film industry entered a recession that has lasted till this day. Several factors contributed to the downturn of Chinese cinema: First, China's economic reform agenda that aggressively pushes for the decentralization and privatization of the state-supported film infrastructure; second, the rise of competing entertainment options including television, video compact discs, and discotheques that have been detrimental to Chinese spectators' moviegoing impulse; and third, Hollywood's sweeping second entry into China's film market since the mid-1990s that has dramatically marginalized Chinese films' domestic market share.[1] Competing with imported blockbusters for market share, many Chinese filmmakers turned to Hollywood for possible remedies. Hollywood's institutional structure and popular narrative formula have since been taken up as models for filmmaking and marketing.[2] The Chinese film industry has been going through a series of institutional restructurings to cope with the demands of a market economy, the rise of alternative entertainment options, and the popularity of Hollywood blockbuster films. The upshot has been the commercialization and decentralization of a formerly state-subsidized film industry and the transformation to a populist film culture from an elitist one ascendant in the late 1970s. The populist film culture legitimizes, and indeed valorizes, entertainment films with commercial value. As such, the drumbeat of Chinese cinema since the late 1980s clearly champions cinema's economic value, resulting in the transition of Chinese cinema from art wave to entertainment wave.[3] The surge in domestic entertainment pictures further casts a shadow on the art cinema movement preceding it. The Chinese experimental filmmakers who made groundbreaking New Wave films such as *Yellow Earth* (Chen Kaige, 1984) and *On the Hunting Ground* (Tian

Zhuangzhuang, 1985) that utilized various narrative techniques of art film subsequently made post–New Wave films such as *Farewell My Concubine* (Chen Kaige, 1993), *The Blue Kite* (Tian Zhuangzhuang, 1993), and *Judou* (Zhang Yimou, 1990) that reprised the narrative principles of a classical continuity cinema often associated with Hollywood.[4] The arrival of a Hollywood-influenced popular entertainment wave has since taken Chinese cinema back to its commercial roots, undermining cinema's pedagogical/ideological value promoted by the state and its aesthetic value advocated by film artists.

This book explores the generative mechanisms of the transition of post–Mao Mainland Chinese cinema from pedagogy to art to commerce. Major attention will be given to Chinese cinema's transition from art to commerce since the late 1980s. It will probe the institutional and stylistic forces that have contributed to the commercialization of Chinese cinema since the late 1980s. Questions can be raised: What has contributed to the Chinese New Wave filmmakers' transition since the late 1980s from making art films to making classical films? What is the continuity and discontinuity between Chinese cinema's art film style and classical film style and what has informed such continuity and discontinuity? These questions demand a historical inquiry into the rise and fall of both Chinese cinema's entertainment wave and art wave to establish a stylistic and institutional link between the two. Therefore, a set of questions concerning factors conducive to the foregrounding of certain types of film style can be further raised about both Chinese cinema's popular entertainment wave and art wave: What has contributed to the early rise and demise and the current revival of Chinese cinema's popular entertainment wave? Likewise, what has contributed to the fashions and fads of Chinese cinema's art wave? These subquestions ultimately lead back to my central question concerning the causality of Chinese cinema's transition from art film to popular entertainment film since the late 1980s.

The formation of popular and art cinema and the transition from one to the other can be perceived in terms of China's shifting political economic milieu and hence its cultural policies that regulate the film industry and its market structure. This transition may also be discussed in relation to a Chinese film culture expressed in the form of film discourses framed by filmmakers, cultural critics, and audiences. I recognize that both the mode of production and the mode of consumption of Chinese cinema have been shaped by the narrative paradigm institutionalized by Hollywood and the industrial structure and market practices refined by Hollywood. As such, my discussion highlights the political economy and culture of Chinese cinema during the period by zeroing in on the key film reform measures and the concomitant, reform-oriented film discourse foregrounding either a populist or an elitist cinema. Equally highlighted is the stylistic metamorphosis of the Chinese Fifth Generation films from New Wave art film narration epitomized by *Yellow Earth* (Chen Kaige, 1984), *Horse Thief* (Tian Zhuangzhuang, 1986), and *One and Eight* (Zhang Junzhao, 1984) to post–New Wave classical film narration exemplified by *Farewell My Concubine* (Chen Kaige, 1993), *The Blue Kite* (Tian Zhuangzhuang, 1992), *Red Sorghum* (Zhang Yimou, 1987), and *Judou* (Zhang Yimou, 1990).[5] The discussion of the transition is extended beyond the Fifth Generation, particularly in the last chapter, to include many other commercialized filmmakers who have left their imprint in the surge of a strong popular entertainment wave influenced by Hollywood.

My elaboration on the art wave and the entertainment wave and their relation at given historical moments operates within the rather unassuming general framework of the mode of production and consumption. Mode of production may be defined as the overall structure of film production—that is, the reasons for making films, resources for film financing, division of production tasks, technology employed, delegation of responsibility and control, and finally the criteria for evaluating the finished films.[6] The concept spotlights both the political and the economic conditions of film production and the normative conceptions of film style—that is, how a particular kind of film "should" look and sound. The notion of mode of production, in my usage, implies a complex relation between production conditions and aesthetic criteria for the end products, and hence, film style should not be considered external to the mode of production as is tacitly assumed by some scholars.

While mode of production foregrounds the relations between production conditions and end products from the perspective of cultural policy, institutional organization, and market structure, mode of consumption, on the other hand, addresses such relations from the perspective of film culture shaped by professional, critical, and popular perceptions of film and filmviewing. These are the historically formulated professional, critical, and popular identifications with certain types of film narration. Broadly speaking, mode of consumption should include audience consumption patterns ranging from the reasons for watching a film to the settings of filmviewing, the affordablility and availability of a film, and finally the discourse concerning the reception of a film. While an empirical reception study would provide hard evidence concerning mode of consumption in general, such an analysis is beyond the scope of this book. Rather, I focus on film culture discernible through various film-related discourses. Defined more narrowly, this book approaches both Chinese cinema's entertainment wave and art film wave and the transition from one to the other from the perspective of film *production* and film *culture*.

Essentially, this book comprises three case studies: Chinese cinema's first formidable art wave in the mid-1980s, its transition from art wave to commercial entertainment wave since the late 1980s, and its first popular entertainment wave from the mid-1920s to the early 1930s. Here I must set forth one proviso: I do not intend to provide an exhaustive account of the highlighted periods that would require a historical narrative encompassing all aspects of cinema from aesthetics to technology, economics, sociology, and empirical audience research. Rather, attention is given first to the political, economic, and cultural factors conducive to the rise and fall of both art and entertainment films and second to the transition and convolution from art to popular film since the late 1980s. I must emphasize also that the distinction between entertainment and art films is not necessarily a stylistic rift. Indeed such stylistic continuity and discontinuity are part of the inquiry this book is undertaking. The stylistic divergence between entertainment and art cinema is dictated by their functional discrepancy. The difference between the two lies first in the former's predilection to regulate film's artistic and pedagogical concerns with the rules of the market and the latter's propensity to subjugate film's economic and/or pedagogical functions to its artistic exploration. Such a functional difference further determines the former's formulaic necessity and the latter's creative and individualistic tendency. Yet functional discrepancy does not necessarily result in stylistic rupture between art and popular entertainment films. As I will discuss later, art and entertainment films share many stylistic traits. Finally, my discussion of the Chinese film industry is strictly confined to the film industry in Mainland China. I recognize the importance of including in cinemas of Hong Kong and Taiwan in providing a more comprehensive view of Chinese cinema as a dynamic enterprise encompassing all three regions. Yet a project of such a scope is beyond the ambition of this book. So the term *Chinese film/Chinese cinema* refers only to the cinema of Mainland China.

It is commonly acknowledged among historians of Chinese cinema that the development of film production in Mainland China since its inception in 1905 has gone through the following stylistic phases bracketed broadly and somewhat conveniently by China's modernization and liberalization processes in the twentieth century: early social-problem cinema prior to the mid-1920s; popular entertainment cinema from the mid-1920s to the early 1930s; social/socialist realist cinema during the Sino–Japan War and the subsequent Chinese Civil War from the early 1930s to the late 1940s; revolutionary propaganda cinema during Mao's era from 1949 to 1976; critical realist cinema from the late 1970s to the early 1980s; the art cinema movement germinating in the late 1970s and blossoming in the mid-1980s with the arrival of the internationally acclaimed Chinese New Wave; and the entertainment wave reemerging since the mid-1980s.[7] Both the early and the current commercial entertainment waves have a strong populist undertone that advocates cinema's accessibility to the common people. Conversely, the art wave sprouting from the late 1970s and harvested in the mid-1980s carries with it an elitist overtone that champions cinema's artistic quality and filmmakers' self-expression, discounting popular taste.[8]

While taking for granted the historiography I have presented on the grounds that cultural development in a totalitarian society is closely monitored and hence closely associated with patterns in political economic change in general, I must emphasize that the trajectory of Chinese cinema is by no means an ideological and aesthetic monolith, free of internal conflicts, contradictions, and complexity. Indeed, various stylistic subtrends and countertrends have existed in all these periods. However, capturing the subtlety of cinematic evolution in the form of subtrends and antitrends is not the concern of this book. Instead, this book highlights the entertainment and art trends, including Chinese cinema's first popular entertainment wave between the mid-1920s and the early 1930s.

Indeed, the current rise of commercial entertainment film has its parallel in the early development of Chinese cinema, especially from 1926 to 1931, another period when competition from Hollywood cast a shadow on the domestic screen. The Chinese film pioneers responded by foregrounding cinema's entertainment value; and as such, Hollywood's studio model and its classical narrative paradigm were eagerly espoused as a strategic solution for winning back the domestic market. Classical Hollywood has thus become part of the Chinese cinematic heritage, or the "classical Chinese." The first entertainment wave was interrupted by the Sino–Japan War and the Chinese Civil War in the 1930s and 1940s, when cinema's pedagogical/ideological function was foregrounded to capture the Chinese public's strong nationalistic sentiment at the time. Chinese cinema's first entertainment wave was consequently condemned as escapism, along with cinema's commercial and, to a certain extent, artistic functions.

A BRIEF HISTORY OF CONTEMPORARY CHINESE FILM

One way of periodizing Chinese cinema developed by film scholars in Mainland China is to divide filmmakers into different generations based more or less on a chronological order.[9] Six generations have emerged from the 1920s to the 1990s. The first comprises film pioneers who introduced motion pictures to China during the turn of the century and who subsequently ventured into film production in the 1910s and 1920s. Exemplified by Zhang Shichuan (*Burning of the Red Lotus Temple*, 1928), Zheng Zhengqiu (*Orphan Rescues Grandfather*, 1923), and the pioneers of Chinese costume drama, the Shaw brothers, the first generation experimented with films of various styles and genres and eventually settled for commercial entertainment features in the 1920s. The second generation includes the left-wing filmmakers of the 1930s and 1940s who cultivated a realist tradition that blended classical Hollywood with the tradition of Chinese performing arts.[9] The prominent figures of this generation are Tian Han (*Three Modern Women*, 1933), Chai Chusheng (*New Women*, 1934), Sheng Xiling (*On the*

Crossroads, 1937), and Wu Yonggang (*Goddess*, 1934). The third generation consists of both the disciples of the second generation and the self-taught left-wing filmmakers of the 1940s who practiced film production in the Communist army and made political films under the party's doctrine. With Xie Jin (*Two Stage Sisters*, 1964) as its most prominent figure, this generation formed the nucleus of the newly nationalized film industry from the 1950s to the 1960s. The films of the third generation adhered to the Communist ideology and manufactured official narrative, with socialist realism as its orthodox style.

After decades of civil war and the Sino–Japan War, the disintegrated and disrupted Chinese film industry was reconsolidated and nationalized in the early 1950s under the newly established Communist regime. The mode of film production in China from the establishment of the People's Republic of China in 1949 up to the mid-1980s reflected Soviet-style centralized planning, in which the state owned and subsidized production, and the studios produced ideologically motivated films according to the state's production target; the function of such film production is propaganda-driven. The normative conceptions of propaganda cinema during Mao's era, under the rubric of "socialist realism," generally depicted exemplary characters and events rather than highly differentiated individuals. The films featured goal-oriented protagonists, most of them revolutionary-minded proletarians who engaged in some form of political struggle with unambiguous social relevance to the concerns of contemporary people. The films typically sublimated style to narrative in privileging a linear narrative trajectory with emphasis on a clear and intensified central conflict, frequently the class struggle. The films also employed extensive use of highly didactic dialogue and proscenium-style presentation that avoided naturalism. Although motivations differ, the stylistic principles and procedures do not vary drastically between socialist realism and the melodramatic conventions of classical Hollywood.

The fourth generation is the first generation of professional filmmakers who received formal film training in the late 1950s and early 1960s under the socialist educational system. Because the previous generation was still active in film production throughout the 1960s and 1970s, the fourth generation was not granted independent production opportunities until after the Cultural Revolution. Represented by Wu Yigong (*My Memories of Old Beijing*, 1983), Wu Tianming (*Old Well*, 1987), and Zhang Nuanxin (*Sacrificed Youth*, 1984), to name a few, this generation is characterized as a "transitional generation" by the Chinese film critic Ni Zhen.[10] Its overlap and competition with the older as well as the younger generation made its films eclectic in style. As suggested by Zhang Xudong, the fourth generation obtained its group identity only after the arrival of the fifth generation, the generation of filmmakers coming of age during the Cultural Revolution.[11] In general, the fourth generation, on the one hand, strove to revive Chinese cinema's pre–Cultural Revolution social realist and humanist tradition and, on the other hand, experimented with film form.

The fifth generation specifically refers to the 1982 graduating class of the Beijing Film Academy, the first class after the reopening of the academy.[12] Among the fifth generation filmmakers, Chen Kaige, Tian Zhuangzhuang, Zhang Junzhao, and Zhang Yimou were famous for their participation, in the early to mid-1980s, in making experimental art films that challenged the socialist realist tradition. I will use the capitalized term "Fifth Generation" (or Fifth G) to refer to this narrow circle of filmmakers whose formal exploration has won them global recognition. The capitalized term aims to separate the Fifth G from the fifth generation as a generic term enveloping, in addition to the aforementioned names, all the other prominent filmmakers graduating from the same academy in the same year who made more conventional films, such as Wu Ziniu (*Evening Bell*, 1988), Zhou Xiaowen (*Desperation*, 1987), Sun Zhou (*The Bloody Dusk*, 1990), and Hu Mei (*Army Nurses*, 1988). The end of Mao's era in the late 1970s witnessed a period of relatively loosened ideological grip that, together with generous funding from the state, created a window of opportunity for an unprecedented art cinema movement. The movement culminated in the mid-1980s with the arrival of the internationally acclaimed Fifth Generation New Wave cinema epitomized by *One and Eight* (Zhang Junzhao, 1984), *Yellow Earth* (Chen Kaige, 1984), and *Horse Thief* (Tian Zhuangzhuang, 1985). The New Wave took certain stylistic cues from European art cinema and departed from the established norm of Chinese cinema informed by classical Hollywood.

The sixth generation refers to a group of self-promoting young filmmakers who came of age during the post-Mao era and lived in urban centers. Under the shadow of the Fifth Generation's global recognition and the box-office pressure of a commercialized film industry, films of this generation were mostly low-budget, contemporary urban dramas reflective of a postmodern estrangement/alienation. As a marketing strategy, some of the sixth generation filmmakers made politically provocative underground films that catered to the international art film market in the hope of soliciting overseas financing and distribution. The prominent figures of this generation include Hu Xueyang (*A Lady Left Behind*, 1991), Li Xin (*Falling in Love*, 1995), and Zhang Yuan (*Beijing Bastards*, 1993). Some film scholars on Chinese cinema have argued against the "sixth generation" as a grouping tag because no consistent thematic and stylistic pattern exists among the young filmmakers. Indeed, Wang Yichuan claims that the generational paradigm as a whole is no longer relevant in the 1990s since the division among propaganda, popular, and art cinemas has been blurred. Equally crisscrossed, as Wang argues, have been the stylistic and thematic propensities that used to define each generation. Lastly, the cinematic paradigm of the Fifth Generation has been so widely circulated that virtually all prominent films made during the period bear traces of the Fifth Generation.[13]

Wang's cogent argument does not necessarily discredit the generational paradigm as a shorthand for periodization. A generational paradigm is, in fact, the foundation on which his argument is built. In the case of the sixth generation, I consider the term effective in capturing the common experience of this post–Cultural Revolution generation in their low-budget, personal approach toward filmmaking during their formative years.[14]

While dividing Chinese cinema into generations, scholars on Chinese cinema traditionally have focused on ideological analyses of film texts that foreground cinema's pedagogical value in the name of political enlightenment. Such is motivated by either the Chinese government's political agenda or film scholars' personal research agendas and political commitments. As a result, left-wing social/socialist realist cinema and some of the propaganda films produced during Mao's era have been the main focus of Chinese film criticism and history. Though art cinema has become a much discussed topic since the mid-1980s, such discussions have followed the same pattern, focusing overwhelmingly on ideological textual and contextual analyses. Less frequently addressed, from the perspective of the relationship between industrial structure, film culture, and film style, is the arrival of Chinese art cinema at a particular historical juncture that was nurtured by, simultaneously, a crumbling studio system operating under the exhausted command economy and a post–Cultural Revolution modernist film discourse. Even less frequently charted, from the same multiple perspectives, are Chinese cinema's early commercial cinema and the transition from the short-lived art cinema to the renewed popular entertainment cinema in the 1990s.[15] One goal of this book is to make up for these oversights by attending to these less examined areas and perspectives. In doing so, I hope to bring in new aspects and perspectives to the existing body of literature concerning Chinese cinema and the globalization of Hollywood. Such an objective demands an approach capable of addressing the relation between film and the production conditions of film, departing from, and hopefully complementing, the predominant research approaches to the study of national cinemas in general and Chinese cinema in particular.

In what follows, I first situate my focus and approach within relevant scholarly dialogue and then describe in more detail the structure of this book.

FROM NATIONAL CINEMA TO CHINESE CINEMA

A brief survey divides writings on Chinese cinema into film criticism and film history, with the former focusing on textual or contextual analyses of individual films or groups of films and the latter providing historical information about the development of Chinese cinema as both cultural and institutional enterprises. For the most part, the native Chinese scholars have never seriously questioned the taken-for-granted notion of Chinese cinema, though many film scholars in the West have approached the study of national cinema through what they see as a necessary first step, the conceptualization of the notion of national cinema. The necessity of terminological clarifications and paradigmatic qualifications seems to mandate such a step as a point of departure. Before I proceed to further define my research agenda, I will begin with a review of relevant literature concerning the concept of national cinema in general.

The Mobilization of the Concept of National Cinema

In conceptualizing national cinema, it is generally assumed among Western film scholars that the role of Hollywood is too decisive to be ignored in demarcating other national cinemas. Thomas Guback, for one, claims it is impossible to offer an assessment of a national film industry without taking into consideration Hollywood's export strategies and foreign policies.[16] In his research on French cinema, Richard Abel also concludes that American films determined in part what constitutes a "French cinema."[17] From the Third World, the case of Brazilian cinema is summarized by the native critic Paulo Emilio Salles Gomes as such that "American cinema so saturated the market and occupied so much space in the collective imagination . . . that it seemed to belong to us."[18] The relation between Hollywood and "the other" captured by such film scholars broaches the serious issue of how we might begin to address national cinema.

Stephen Crofts refutes the classical notion of national cinema and attempts to theorize the global range of national cinema in terms of the multiple politics of their production, distribution, and reception; their textuality; and their relations with the state and with multiculturalism. Crofts proposes a taxonomy of cinemas that divides films into seven categories:

1. European art cinemas that differ from but don't compete directly with Hollywood, and have their local market;
2. Third cinemas which differ from, don't compete directly with, but criticize Hollywood;
3. Third world and European commercial cinemas which battle against Hollywood with limited or no success;
4. Indian/Hong Kong cinemas which ignore Hollywood;
5. Anglophobe cinemas, a branch of British cinema imitating Hollywood;
6. Totalitarian cinemas with state-financed and controlled film industry;
7. Regional/ethnic cinemas.[19]

The aim of Crofts's reconceptualization is to desegregate the term *national cinema*. Even though he argues against a dualist approach, a dualism between Hollywood and the other is implicit in his framework. While other cinemas are defined against it, Hollywood is not even included in the seven categories. In other words, Hollywood is no longer a national cinema but an international one, and hence, Hollywood's historical and geolinguistic specificity is deemed insignificant. Furthermore, his taxonomy suggests the difficulty of any attempt to group films based on shifting referents. By varying among textual elements, market structure, and state policy, the referential inconsistency makes his taxonomy slippery and breakable. Examined carefully, Crofts's referents shift from a particular body of films unified in style and theme to the perceived cultural implications of imbalances between the proportion of imported and locally produced films shown to national audiences, to a particular range of "quality" local films suited to a high culture audience, and, finally, to the historical appropriation of cinema by the different subcultures of the national film audience. Yet, European commercial cinemas, for instance, from the perspective of the commercialized institutional practice, could be grouped with Hollywood, Hong Kong, and even Chinese entertainment pictures. Ultimately, Crofts's articulation of national cinema movements centers around their export strategies that foreground product differentiation and cultivate various nonmainstream distribution channels. National cinemas' cultivation of their own domestic markets is left unaddressed, leaving the impression that national cinemas' own concrete domestic markets are somehow outside the arena of a global market perceived as a unified, singular, and abstract entity. It is important to acknowledge that many of the cinematic cultural wars occur within the boundary of a nation–state or a region, overlapping and crisscrossing various distribution channels, and what motivates national film production is precisely its impulse to control its own domestic market.

Andrew Higson, on the other hand, considers the domestic market too important to be ignored in our conceptualization of national cinema.[20] In fact, he approaches the development of national cinema from within, focusing on the activity of national audiences and the conditions under which they make sense of and use the films they watch. He rejects the method of comparing and contrasting one national cinema to another, thereby establishing varying degrees of otherness, as epitomized by Crofts. He contends that such a way of defining a national cinema is premised on the semiotic principle of the production of meaning and identity through *difference*. Within this discourse the task becomes one of differentiating between a variety of apparently nationally constituted modes of cinematic practice and financially produced signs and meanings. Yet Hollywood can hardly be conceived as totally other, since much of other nations' film culture is influenced by Hollywood in terms of both narrative style and actual screen time of Hollywood films. Thus, Higson further acknowledges the paradox that for a cinema to be nationally popular it must also be international in scope, striving for the international standard set by

Hollywood. After summarizing various ways through which the term *national cinema* is mobilized, he suggests that very often the concept of national cinema is used prescriptively rather than descriptively, dictating what ought to be the national cinema, rather than describing the actual cinematic experience of popular audiences.

In what he terms a more inward-looking process, Higson further explores the cinema of a nation in relation to the nation–state's specific structure of political economy, national identity, and cultural heritage. In this way, national cinema can be defined in terms of already established discourses of national identity rather than in relation to other national cinemas. The implication here is that Hollywood is no longer the other but, rather, part of us. Higson's approach has avoided the dualism that pits the other against Hollywood. Specific aspects foregrounded within this approach are the range of films in circulation within the market of a particular nation–state, audience expectation in terms of stylistic norms, and, finally, discourses concerning both film production and reception. Higson's approach has made significant the issue of film culture, the overall institution of cinema not always addressed by other scholars.

British film scholar Geoffrey Nowell-Smith has adopted the same totalist approach to foreground the issue of film culture. Nowell-Smith forcefully argues that the main problem for the much-touted British cinema revival is that filmmaking and filmviewing are not central to British culture.[21] In other words, Britain is not a very film-oriented culture at any level, and a deeply rooted elitist view of popular culture has not been very kind to the development of entertainment films. Nowell-Smith also makes a good point that national cinema is more than national film industry. To push his argument further, a cultural-protectionist film policy motivated by a film industry's financial concerns should not blind us to the historically formulated audience expectation associated with certain cinematic norms set by Hollywood. Here Hollywood is perceived by Nowell-Smith as an intrinsic part of British cinema rather than the alien other, and vice versa.

Joining in the dialogue, from the site of Danish cinema, Mette Hjort approaches the conceptualization of national cinema by posing the question What causes the international bent of Danish cinema and how does it achieve its international recognition?[22] Hjort forcefully argues, in appropriating Gilles Deleuze and Félix Guattari's distinction between major and minor cultures, that the relative worth of cultural products is determined only partially by comparative assessments of intrinsic features such as aesthetic qualities. The salience of Hollywood in a global market must be attributed in large measure to U.S. economic, demographic, and geopolitical power as a major culture. And, consequently, cinemas of minor cultures inevitably encounter the double challenge of pleasing spectators of both major and minor cultures. To push his argument further, the Hollywood "affiliated" monolithic international spectator indifferent to alternative film style such as European art cinema, or the historical-materialist/socialist-realist cinema, makes it difficult for minor cultures to express themselves.

In defining Danish cinema, Hjort echoes Higson's culturally dependent approach to take into consideration Danish language and cultural heritage as well as Danish discourses on nationhood. The international bent of Danish cinema, the desire expressed by members of the film industry to have certain films circulate within an international public sphere, can be explained along the lines of the politics of recognition, the minor culture's need for affirmation from the major culture.[23] The strategy Danish filmmakers utilize to achieve their international recognition is called "leveraging," which skillfully balances the opaque (domestically oriented), translatable, and international (geared toward international audiences) cinematic elements. The interest of the international public is provoked not by a perception of cultural difference or specificity but by the already internationalized elements of a film. Here Hjort makes an interesting distinction between the anxieties of Third World cinema and that of Second World cinema. A politics of recognition motivated by a desire to rectify political and economic imbalances practiced by Third World cinemas is different from a politics of affirmation generated by the cultural production of small nations such as Denmark. Hence, the strategy of leveraging is associated with the latter, propelled by major cultures' perceived indifference to its products. Hjort's position on the relation between Hollywood and the other leans more toward an inward-looking perspective, yet he certainly has put an international spin on it.

Albert Moran's perspective on the same issue is premised on his claim that "New Hollywood" is more than film and America.[24] He points out that distribution remains the key sector of the motion picture industry in a globalized market and distribution has long paid little respect to the notion of nation–state. Hollywood distributes not only its own films but also marketable films from other nations/regions. With the increasing transnationalization of film production and financing, the domination of distribution outlets by the major studios and distributors, and the growth of independent producers who themselves frequently act as brokers between filmmakers and the principal distributors, the system now exists whereby national filmmaking is, through a series of commercial linkages, also a part of Hollywood. Not only in terms of coproduction, but also in terms of narrative, Hollywood was and is very much a component of other national cinemas. Historically, Hollywood has to a large extent defined the range of options for other cinemas in both economic and cultural terms. Hollywood's overseas dominance of distribution and exhibition has hampered local production and subsequently instigated state policies both protective against Hollywood imports and supportive of local production. To Moran and to me, the protective measures after the Cold War have been undertaken more for economic reasons than for cultural reasons such as lessening the "American" influence on a native culture. Moran also poses the question of whether the presence of a production sector in local culture industries is a necessary precondition for a culture to express itself.

Roy Armes posits three factors of crucial importance in our understanding of Third World cinema as caveats for studying national cinema in general. For Armes, the three factors are:

1. Cinema cannot be adequately understood on a country-by-country basis. A consideration of the whole pattern of film commerce in the capitalist world is essential if the mechanisms in operation are to be seen with real clarity.
2. The development of Hollywood and other national cinemas is mutually interdependent. While Hollywood's global dominance has stifled the growth of filmmaking in other nation-states, it has been dependent on overseas box office receipts for extra profits.
3. The extent to which the tastes of local audiences have been shaped by imports must be borne in mind.[25]

The three caveats reinforce my position on the issue of the relevance of Hollywood to the dialogue concerning national cinema—the formal and industrial paradigm of Hollywood is absolutely essential to the formation and transformation of various national cinemas. The issue really is how to conceptualize the relationship between Hollywood and the other. Is Hollywood *intrinsic*, or *extrinsic*, to the other? More specifically, should Hollywood be considered purely an external factor or part of the internal dynamic in the development of other national cinemas? Opinions are divided among various scholars. One approach, such as Crofts's, suggests a binary opposition between Hollywood and the other that insists on locating difference only in the other. A second approach, such as Hisgon's, is more culturally specific and foregrounds the specificity of any given national/regional film culture while acknowledging Hollywood's intrinsic relationship to such a culture.

Speaking from the perspective of Japanese cinema, Mitsuhiro Yoshimoto directly takes on the problem of "dualism" by introducing a debate between film scholars David Bordwell and Peter Lehman concerning the positioning of Yasojiru Ozu as being either a modernist or a classical filmmaker.[26] Yoshimoto aptly points out that their disagreement has more to do with a modernism derived from Western frameworks/theories/ideologies than with the position of Ozu from Ozu's own cultural experience. Neither critic bothers to consider what modernism might mean for the non-West. The implicit assumption is that Western theory and cultural practice are universal standards against which all texts are to be judged. Here Yoshimoto moves the dialogue beyond the concept of national cinema and into neocolonial criticism probing the theoretical assumptions and political implications of the endeavor for an all-encompassing schema concerning national cinema from the dualist perspective. Neocolonial criticism aptly cautions us about the limited applicability of a dominant film theory harvested from the narrowly confined/defined social–cultural and geopolitical experience of North America and western Europe.

Later in his article, in faulting Noel Burch for his assertion that traditional Japanese art is subversive, Yoshimoto facetiously asks what exactly traditional Japanese art subverts—the representational mode of the classical Hollywood cinema? What does traditional Japanese art have to do with Hollywood cinema? The radical European/American humanists' fascination with cultural resistance often directs them to locate only difference in cinemas of other national origins. The other is indeed burdened with being the sole bearer of difference.

On a political front, Yoshimoto divides Japanese film scholars in the United States into historians and theorists, with the former providing specific information about the cultural background of Japanese cinema and the latter constructing a theoretical framework that gives rise to new insights into Japanese cinema. He contends that such a division, extended to studies of national cinema in general, reveals an unequal power structure in "cross-cultural exchange." By designating only one direction of subject–object relation, the notion of cultural exchange elides the issue of power/knowledge. Yoshimoto observes that "when non-Western critics study English literature or French cinema, it is not called cross-cultural analysis. Whatever they say is interpreted and judged only within the context of Western discourses." In short, Yoshimoto faults the dualist position on two grounds: First, in its insistence on a binary opposition between the self and the other that locates *only* difference in the other; and second, in the polarization of Western theory and non-Western practice that subjugates the non-Western practice and consequently reproduces the relation of dominance. In his rejection of studying Asian cinema under the condition that it conforms to the field's existing priorities and agenda, William Rothman echoes Yoshimoto by arguing that "to accept the study of Asian cinema on such terms is to reject out of hand the possibility that Asian films may call for fundamentally different ways of thinking . . . if the films' different ways of thinking are to be acknowledged."[27]

Overall, the point highlighted by neocolonial critics is that the relationship between Western theory and non-Western text/practice relegated by such a theoretical underpinning is an unequal one, which at its worst reproduces a relation of domination, a serious indictment of the institutional powers of critical theory.[28] In its insistence on Hollywood as a starting point against which other national cinemas must be addressed, the dualist approach manifests the symptoms of theoreticism that attempts to generalize the experience of Western nation–states to that of all nation–states. What is missing is the historical and geolinguistic specificity of national cinemas. As Judith Mayne points out, classical Hollywood cinema has become the norm against which all other practices are measured.[29] Frequently, the very notion of an "alternative" is posed in the narrow terms of an either/or: either one is within classical discourse and therefore complicit, or one is critical of and/or resistant to it and therefore outside of it.

Different theoretical slants aside, most of the cited scholars would agree that classical Hollywood cinema has played a crucial role in the formation of any national cinema with access to it, yet it can never have complete control over how a particular national cinema is constructed. Furthermore, while Hollywood is relevant during certain periods to certain national cinemas, it should not be taken as a universal touchstone against which every nation's cinema is to be addressed. In the case of Chinese cinema, the role of the state in supporting the film industry insulated it to a great extent from the logic of comparative advantage and large-scale global enroachment between 1949 and 1984, minimizing the relevance of Hollywood to Chinese cinema during the period.

In sum, while both the dualist approach and the more culturally dependent inward-looking approach share the same assumption that Hollywood has to a great extent shaped the formation and development of other national cinemas, the two approaches differ. The former insists on Hollywood as a starting point against which other national cinemas must be addressed and differentiated. The latter insists on the specificity of the nation–state as a starting point and on Hollywood as an intrinsic rather than extrinsic part of the discourse circulating within a particular nation–state with reference to cinema's national identity. The tendency for theoreticism and its political implication as outlined by the neocolonial scholars is clearly associated with the dualist approach.

Thus far, I have discussed how the concept of national cinema(s) is mobilized by various film scholars, leaving out the interrogation of the very notion national cinema. This does not suggest that I intend to ignore the problematic nature of the phrase *national cinema*, as it often implies a monolithic cultural apparatus acting on behalf of a unified, homogeneous population within a national boundary.[30] It is clear that, while applied inclusively to refer not just to the domestic film industry but to the production sectors as the cinematic expression and imaginative projection of a national community, the term invites serious challenge. Without falling into the trap of infinite refiguration of the concept of national cinema, I hereby restrict my usage of the term to the three sectors of film production, distribution, and exhibition within the geopolitical confines of Mainland China, what are commonly acknowledged as the "Chinese domestic film industry." The designation here is economic, for it allows me to pursue an institutional approach toward Chinese cinema, a route less frequently charted by other scholars on Chinese cinema. The designation here is also operative because it provides an opportunity for me to proceed with my research without being tumbled over first by the definition of Chinese cinema as a grand cultural entity. Just as "Chinese-language cinemas" seems to be a pragmatic tag for grouping a set of research objects, the concept of Chinese domestic film industry provides me with a manageable point of departure.[31]

Chinese Cinema as a Research Topic in Mainland China

Much has been written about Chinese cinema in the West; such writings are well exposed and documented. Less known (except among the diasporatic Chinese scholars in the West and the Chinese-language-proficient Western scholars) and introduced are the lively film discourses produced by the film communities in Mainland China during the era of economic reform, especially in the 1990s.[32] It is therefore useful to provide an overview of the contemporary critical discourses on Chinese cinema written by the native Chinese film critics. Studies of pre-Mao cinema in China traditionally have focused on social realist cinema, while those of the post-Mao era focused on critical social realist and New Wave cinemas. Both types of studies have foregrounded Chinese cinema's ideological function as a form of cultural expression reflective of the complex and long-standing theme of China's nationalism and modernization. Issues such as the political and ideological undertone of a film or a group of films are the main concerns. The primary critical interest is not so much in Chinese cinema as an integrated social, economic, and aesthetic entity, but rather in its political and ideological subtext. Equipped with the globalization paradigm foregrounding the tension between global and local, film criticism in the 1990s delights in the ideological decoding and recoding of the symptoms of identity anxiety reflected in certain contemporary film texts. The intense probing of whether, in their striving for global recognition, the films made by the Fifth Generation filmmakers have lost their Chinese cultural identity is within the realm of such a critical paradigm.[33]

China's economic success in the early 1990s, coupled with post-Tiananmen restrictions on intellectual debate, has encouraged a surge of Chinese nationalism. Meanwhile, many Western postmodernist theories were introduced to China by the early 1990s, helping to advance and consolidate a growing cultural conservatism in a renewed cultural cold war with the West. Appropriating the postcolonial lexicon concerning the continuation of unequal power relations between West and East during the postcolonial era, Chinese critics have raised concerns regarding the consequences of the globalization of Chinese New Wave cinema for the future direction of Chinese cinema. Postcolonialists contend that when the physical appearance of colonialism was dismantled, it unfortunately left its psychology behind. Colonized people inevitably retained the colonizers' paradigm, perpetuating unequal power relations. Equipped with this critical lexicon, some Chinese critics fault the appropriation of "globally institutionalized" art cinema style by the internationally acclaimed Chinese Fifth Generation filmmakers. They charge that the appropriation has resulted in the deprivation of Chinese cinema's cultural identity, since the end results are films such as *Raise the Red Lantern* (Zhang Yimou, 1991) and *Farewell My Concubine* (Chen Kaige, 1993) that bear less social and cultural relevance to the Chinese audience than to the global audience.

Critical articles were published charging Chinese New Wave with selling the Chinese grotesque for international profit. Some critics pointed out that the ethnographic details such as various Chinese folk customs so fondly received by the West were mostly the New Wave filmmakers' invention.[34] Zhang Yimou and Chen Kaige's cinematic practice in the 1990s was particularly singled out for such criticism. Edward Said's concept of "Orientalism" was invoked to attack the filmmakers for exploiting a distorted depiction of China in pursuit of overseas investment and distribution. Zhang Jiwu, for one, appropriated Frederic Jameson's concept of national allegory to claim that what the Chinese Fifth Generation filmmakers had been making were in essence Westernized allegories.[35] Other native critics such as Li Xuebing argued otherwise, maintaining that the postcolonialist lexicon was itself the product of the unequal power relation referred to by the neocolonialist criticism and that the Fifth Generation films were both international and national.[36] Still others such as Wang Ning, Yan Chunjun, and Yu Ji gave a more nuanced view by suggesting a double othering process of the internationally acclaimed Chinese films, the otherness of such films to both Chinese and overseas' audiences, further echoing the neocolonialist's charge on the harmful subjugation of film analyses to Western theories.[37]

The debate, while stimulating, unfortunately falls into the prescriptive trap Andrew Higson cautioned against. Here the issue of what ought to be Chinese cinema is addressed from a political or ideological standpoint, rather than by describing the actual cinematic experience of both the filmmakers and the audiences. The development of Chinese cinema is determined not only by Chinese cultural tradition but also by the contemporary economic and political environment, domestically and globally. Chinese cinema, like Chinese culture at large, undergoes constant (re)definition and (re)adjustment in its striving for internal legitimacy and external recognition. It is not meaningful to categorize Chinese cinema in terms of the degree of Westernization or Sinonization, as the very notion and technology of motion pictures were themselves Western inventions. Elements of Westernization in the form of Western cinematic style, story structure, and techniques exist in all non-Western national cinemas during all historical periods. In this sense, cinema is inherently a global medium with an undeniable Western origin. Hence, what is at stake is Chinese filmmakers' ability to appeal to both local and global audiences by appropriating certain cinematic conventions readily accessible to the international audience. Such are also the tactics of Hollywood that are responsible, partially, for its global dominance. A closed-door film policy and practice will do more harm than good in resolving the minor (film) culture's anxiety expressed by the Chinese critics. Lastly, Chinese cinema is neither monolithic nor static. The international bent of Chinese post–New Wave film should not obscure other types of film with a strong domestic bent.

While focusing mostly on the issue of cultural identity at the level of a nation–state, issues of the identities related to ethnic minority status, sexuality, and gender have not made their way into the mainstream Chinese cultural discourse, much less film discourse at the moment. However, some Western scholars and a few Chinese scholars residing in the West have applied such identity paradigms to the analyses of Chinese cinema. Zhang Yinggin's essay, "From 'Minority Film' to 'Minority Discourse': The Questions of Nationhood and Ethnicity in Chinese Cinema," touches the issue of the homogeneous Chinese national identity propagated by the dominant discourse at the expense of internal ethnic and cultural differences.[38] The display of ethnic harmony and solidarity in such minority films, as Zhang charges, erases internal differences and tensions of ethnicity in China. Likewise, Chris Berry and Ann Kaplan have provided self-reflexive readings of Chinese cinema in terms of Western discourses on gender and sexuality. Berry's essay, "Sexual Difference and the Viewing Subject *in Li Shuangshuang* and *The In-Laws*," analyzes the deployment of gender in two popular Chinese films concerning domestic relationships.[39] Kaplan's essay, "Problematising Cross-cultural Analysis: The Case of Women in the Recent Chinese Cinema," tries to discern the patterns emerging around women directors and women spectators in Chinese cinema, again foregrounding the issue of gender.[40] In another essay, "Reading Formations and Chen Kaige's *Farewell My Concubine*," Kaplan approaches the film from her Western feminist perspective to account for the film's impact on her emotions, touching on the film's stereotypical representation of homosexuals that queer studies in the West have exposed.[41] Both Berry and Kaplan recognize the nuance involved in, and hence the limitations of, cross-cultural readings.

The standard versions of Chinese film history constructed by native Chinese film historians follow a pattern in Chinese film criticism, namely, the valuation and devaluation and the inclusion and exclusion of certain cinematic periods/movements/practices/texts dictated by certain political and cultural agendas. The standard/official historical accounts of Chinese film reflect the orthodox view of Chinese culture traditionally valorizing moralistic, or "politically progressive," cinema with pedagogical value. Several stylistic periods have been highlighted and promoted as the cinematic high points in the orthodox Chinese film history.[42] These are the politically progressive and culturally redemptive social realist films of the 1930s and 1940s and the critical realist films produced during the post–Cultural Revolution era. Certain nationalistic cinematic practices prior to the formation of the left-league movement, which advocated social realist films, were also retrospectively pulled into this narrative. Indeed for most historians, the realism associated with the left-league movement constitutes the only valuable national cinematic heritage and the realist films the most sacred cinematic products. Such a standard Chinese film history has downplayed both commercial entertainment films and art films, segregating cinema's triple function as art, commerce, and social/political discourse.

Cultural Identity within the Context of Political Economy

Overall, scholars of national cinema generally favor cinemas that are more reflective of cultural identities. Yet much of their textual analysis boils down to detecting evidence of national/cultural identity in a film, equating the desire for a national cinema independent of Hollywood with nationalism perceived as purely cultural or ideological. Less frequently addressed, traditionally, are the economic imperatives behind nationalist sentiment. At a pragmatic level, an ideological account of Chinese cinema falls short of diagnosing the economic and aesthetic problems facing the transformation of Chinese cinema, let alone prescribing possible remedies.

In the early to mid-1990s, however, critical debate attentive to the political economy of film production has emerged among Chinese native film scholars, policy makers, and industrial practitioners. It has since brought the restructuring of Chinese film industry into the forefront of the critical debate concerning Chinese cinema's cultural identity under the shadow of Hollywood. Such debates are triggered by China's overall economic reform. Since the mid-1980s, as China's economic reform policies reprising a market economy penetrated further into the cultural industries, the Chinese film industry has undergone a functional transition and a series of institutional restructurings. Film was redefined in 1984 as a *cultural industry* rather than a *propaganda institution* for the (re)enforcement of party ideology. The consequences of this functional redefinition have been sweet and sour—while enjoying a greater degree of creative autonomy, the studios, no longer qualifying for substantial government subsidies yet still overburdened by the deadweight of a Soviet-style institutional structure, have been left alone to fend for themselves in an increasingly competitive cultural market. Chinese cinema has since witnessed dramatic declines in both its audience and its flows of capital and creative forces.[43]

Meanwhile, still considered part of the propaganda machinery and hence qualifying for generous financial support from the government, the semiadvertiser-supported Chinese television has enjoyed huge gains in both its overall program ratings and its capacity to produce programming for multiple channels and longer hours. As the economic reform of decentralization and privatization penetrates into the television industry, the monopoly of the state-subsidized and state-controlled Chinese Central Television was challenged by powerful local "affiliated" stations, especially Shanghai Oriental TV, Beijing TV, and Pearl River TV in Canton. In the mid-1980s, such local stations began to produce their own popular entertainment programs, including variety shows and dramatic series, and to carry profitable dramatic programs from other local stations. Meanwhile, new distribution technologies and widespread partial deregulation have resulted in a proliferation of television channels in China. Aside from the televised film imports, Chinese domestic television is largely independent of U.S. programs. Here the Chinese language has served as a natural barrier to imported television programs. The "cultural discount," or the diminished market appeal, a television program has for audiences who speak a different language or who have difficulty accepting the values, beliefs, and institutions represented by the imported programs grants native-language programs a competitive advantage.[44] Indeed, the cultural discount is so great that sometimes the format of the program, rather than the program itself, is exported—Chinese television produces its own form of sitcom and telenovela. The language advantage guarantees Chinese television programming a potential overseas cultural-linguistic market among the diasporatic Chinese speaking populations in the United States, Canada, Australia, and some East Asia countries. Chinese television's solid domestic market and its expanding international market have attracted filmmakers. Many filmmakers consequently have turned to television for its more accessible capital and better profit.[45]

The term *crisis* has entered Chinese film discourse since the late 1980s and has caught the attention of the policy makers. The central government has introduced a series of provisional reform policies to cope with the crisis. The goal is to resuscitate the beleaguered studios not through state subsidies but through streamlining bureaucracy, eliminating waste, and further commercialization. The studios are allowed, indeed encouraged, to produce quality entertainment films with competitive market value. The early stage of institutional restructuring had been partial and haphazard, without a coherent strategy, reflecting the old Chinese saying "Crossing the river by touching the boulder." The restructuring reached its peak in 1993 when the Ministry of Radio, Film, and Television decided to decentralize its decades-long monopoly on distribution. The decentralization of distribution pushed film production further toward the market economy, since from then on the local distribution companies would no longer be held responsible for the unmarketable films produced by the big studios. The distribution reform, while inciting competition among and within the studios to produce entertainment films, did not result in pictures that performed better at the box office. Overall revenue remained slim and production capital remained remote.

To boost theater attendance, the Ministry of Radio, Film, and Television in 1994 issued a document that allowed the annual importation of ten international blockbusters, most of them big-budget, high-tech Hollywood fare. Since then, Hollywood blockbusters such as *True Lies* (James Cameron, 1994), *Forrest Gump* (Robert Zemeckis, 1994), *The Lion King* (Roger Allers and Robert Minkoff, 1994), and *Independence Day* (Roland Emmerich, 1996) have dominated the Chinese film market. These imports restored the theatergoing habits of Chinese audiences and generated huge box-office revenues. Predictably, Hollywood's strong entry into the Chinese market has sparked industrial and critical debate concerning its impact on the future direction of Chinese cinema. Hollywood's newly realized Chinese triumph is extending into television. A recent report indicates that with the creation of the movie channel on Chinese Central Television and other local stations, many college-educated viewers have turned their attention to classical Hollywood films on cable.[46]

Questions concerning how to compete with Hollywood for China's domestic market inevitably pop up. The issue has instigated a renewed sense of nationalism within the Chinese film industry and among certain segments of the Chinese intelligentsia. The nationalist sentiment is coupled with a realization of the imperative of the marketization of Chinese cinema. Debates have raged among the industrial practitioners, cultural critics, and policy makers as to whether the marketization of Chinese cinema must follow the mode of production defined by Hollywood. At the center of the debate is, once again, the question about the transnational production practice of the Chinese Fifth Generation filmmakers: What effect has the commercialization and globalization of Chinese art films had on such films' cultural identity?

Addressing the issue within a global context, the Chinese film scholar Ying Hong recognizes the economic imperative of Chinese cinema in its striving to enter the international market and to gain international recognition.[47] Ying acknowledges the necessity of absorbing foreign investment and generating overseas' box office during the period of Chinese cinema's domestic crisis in terms of scarce investment and slim audience attendance. He therefore does not simply fault the calculated globalization of Chinese New Wave for its lack of immediate cultural irrelevance to the concerns of ordinary Chinese. At the same time, Ying cautions filmmakers about the danger of Chinese cinema's international bent following certain Western standards. He suggests that going global should not mean going Western and appealing to Western standards. He further calls for a long-term ideological, cultural, artistic, and economic strategy to promote Chinese cinema in a globalized market.

Unyielding in his loathing for Hollywood's action-adventure block-busters, the prominent Chinese filmmaker and critic Xie Fei is nonetheless unequivocal in his support for the adoption of Hollywood's institutional-ized distribution system.[48] Xie is more concerned with fostering the devel-opment of art cinema by establishing a distribution network and building small theater chains for native Chinese art films. He ultimately considers the establishment of a healthy market led by a well-established distribu-tion network essential to the development of Chinese cinema. He also sug-gests the cultivation of alternative distribution channels such as home video, television broadcasting, and so on, as multiple outlets for motion pictures. In a conference organized by the Chinese film magazine *Zhong-guo yingmu* (China Screen) concerning the state of Chinese cinema in the mid-1990s, Xie further points out that the lack of serious market research and of a star system are two of the key problems facing the Chinese film industry.[49] Other film experts participating in the conference echoed his view, adding that the decades-long segregation of production, distribu-tion, and exhibition has hampered the film industry. Another prominent filmmaker and scholar, Zheng Dongtian, gives a more detailed diagnosis of the problems facing the restructuring of the film industry in its march toward marketization.[50] He comes to the same conclusion that the solution lies in an integrated operation, that is, Hollywood-style horizontal and vertical integration.

In general, film critics, filmmakers, and policy makers who approach Chinese cinema's cultural identity within the context of political economy recognize that the Chinese state-run studio system is urgently in need of structural reform.[51] Hollywood's vertically and horizontally integrated in-dustrial model is acknowledged as a viable template for the privatization and decentralization of the Chinese film industry. At the same time, film experts are aware of the danger of a speedy, wholesale Hollywoodization of Chinese film industry.[52] Instead, the institutional restructurings are to be systematic and gradual, taking into consideration the problems left from the planned economy, for example, too much overhead, lack of experience in a market economy, lack of artistic freedom.

The call for an economic restructuring of Chinese cinema, on the other hand, has generated renewed discussion concerning the functions of cin-ema. The Chinese film historian Ma Debuo proposes his periodization of Chinese cinema in terms of its functional priority.[53] The development of Chinese cinema is deftly divided into the following eight periods: primi-tive commercial cinema (1905–1931), left-wing cinema (1932–1937), realist cinema (1947–1949), propaganda cinema (1949–1976), social cinema (1980–1981), humanist cinema (1982–1986), cultural cinema (1984–1987), and the contemporary commercial cinema (1988–1990s). His periodiza-tion suggests that, though originated from commercial ventures, Chinese cinema traditionally has foregrounded either ideological/pedagogical or cultural/artistic functions and has only recently returned to its commercial roots. He considers the attention to cinema's commercial function in the 1990s encouraging. Likewise, film critic Hu Ke encourages film historians' renewed attention to early Chinese cinema from a more comprehensive approach that takes into consideration cinema's economic function long forbidden under Mao's rule.[54] Other scholars/critics/policy makers such as Zhuang Yuxing, Tuo Lake, Zheng Guoeng, and Gao Honggu, however, dispute the notion that cinema is mostly an economic entity and should therefore be regulated solely by market forces.[55] They point out the power of American ideology embedded in Hollywood films. They contend that, culturally, the hegemonic power of Hollywood imports should not be underestimated.

Overall, while the issue of cinema as first and foremost a commercial or political/cultural practice is still in debate, cinema's economic function is foregrounded. The formerly stigmatized terms such as *market, commerce*, and *profit* have regained their legitimacy in Chinese film discourse.[56] The state is urged to implement constructive film policies to tighten the regulations on importation but at the same time loosen the censorship of domestic pictures. Clearly, the discussion has moved beyond the issue of national/cultural identity and entered the context of political economy. Indeed, the development of Chinese cinema in the era of commercialization is, for the most part, driven by the imperatives of the film industry to gain both domestic and international market share, rather than by a desire to reflect or preserve Chinese cultural identity. Of course, the economic imperative does not necessarily obscure filmmakers' desire to make films with cultural significance. Yet such a desire is overshadowed by the financial reality the filmmakers face. As such, the call for the preservation of national/cultural identity is often utilized by the industry to encourage and justify the state's protective film policy in order to maintain the Chinese film industry's domestic market share. At times it has become a catchphrase for the industry's resistance not to capitalism per se but to imbalances in the global marketplace. In other words, the real conflict lies between local capitalism and transnational capitalism, as the former tries to hold onto its own territory and the latter tries to continue its global expansion. It is in this sense that the politics of national/cultural identity previously addressed from an ideological ground, while relevant to Chinese cinema, does not give much insight into the political economy of the Chinese film industry.[57] Nor does it shed much light on audience consumption patterns conducive to the issue of cultural identity in a collective sense. It does suggest, however, that the definition of a legitimately profitable national cinema is contestable among policy makers, cultural critics, and filmmakers. It is in this sense, ultimately, that the notion of national/cultural identity becomes relevant within the context of political economy.

In my view, at the core of the debates concerning the (transformation of) cultural identity of Chinese cinema in particular and national cinemas in general is the possibility of a cinematic landscape comprising cinemas of various cultural origins at both the transnational and the national/regional levels. The question becomes how to protect cinematic diversity. More specifically, What role has the state assumed, and what strategy has the industry pursued in order to compete with Hollywood for a market share? Equally important is the question of what the normative conception of a "good" film must constitute for the Chinese public and critics who evaluate the effectiveness of the efforts made by both the state and the industry. The role of state in industrial development, in general, has been explored extensively by scholars of the political economy of development in the West.[58] In a much applauded book, Peter Evans discusses the ways in which government agencies can both facilitate and hinder industrialization in contemporary developing countries.[59] Depending on the situation and the industrial sector, Evans proposes that the state plays a combination of four major roles in economic development. As custodian, it provides protection, policing, and regulation of infant industries; as midwife, it attracts private enterprises into new sectors by subsidies, tax breaks, and other devices; in the husbandry role, it teaches, cultivates, nurtures, and prods entrepreneurial forces that have been activated; and as demiurge, it becomes directly involved in productive activities that complement private investment, only to denationalize later when industries are established. Though specific to the information industries of Korea, Brazil, and India, Evans's categories are applicable to the development of Chinese industry in general and the Chinese film industry in particular. In the case of Chinese cinema, the involvement of the state has struggled to grow out of the erratic and arbitrary pattern driven by ideology. A more systematic and strategic approach at the policy level to promote national cinema from an economic standpoint has increasingly become a conscious effort by the state. Instead of hostile regulation or appropriation of private capital, the current Chinese government prefers to facilitate the emergence and maturation of private firms in the film industry to decentralize, financially, the state-run studios and production companies.

In short, the possibility of preserving cinemas of various cultural origins on the grounds of political economy and cinematic heritage has yet to be explored. Such exploration must take seriously Chinese cinema's first entertainment wave and its current transition from art cinema wave, the so-called New Wave, to yet another entertainment wave. While much critical attention has been given to the mid-1980s Chinese New Wave, few historical links have been made between New Wave and the art cinema movement preceding it, leaving the impression that the Chinese New Wave is without its own cultural heritage and beyond the confines of its own political and economic conditions. What we need is an approach that will foreground both the entertainment wave and the art wave and the current transition from the latter to the former from the perspective of the interplay among film economy, film culture, and film style. Such an approach will enable us not only to foreground the historical and geolinguistic specificity of Chinese cinema but to capture the dialogical relationships among cultural policy makers, film practitioners, and film critics who together have informed the mode of production and consumption.

From the mobilization of the concept of national cinema in general to the interrogation of the practice of Chinese cinema in particular, this literature review has covered the methodological issues pertinent to my approach toward Chinese cinema. After gauging the advantages and disadvantages of the research establishment outlined here, I now suggest an approach toward Chinese cinema's entertainment and art movements. Such an approach is directly informed by Noel Burch's notion of a mode of representation, as summarized cogently by Thomas Elsaesser:

Burch's mode of representation embraces historically pertinent media and spectacle intertexts (optical toys, dioramas, vaudeville, variety theater, operetta, stage melodrama), formal parameters (staging, shot relations, kinds of closure, editing, inserts), social parameters (spectatorial foreknowledge of story material, ethnic appeal, class and respectability, gender and morality), and finally, the recognition that changes in film style and film technique are determined by an interaction of several, often unevenly operating pressures or constraints.[60]

Burch's framework can be applied specifically to the shifting stylistic priorities of Chinese cinema. Here the pressures or constraints can be external—Hollywood so dominated the Chinese market during Chinese cinema's early development and from 1994 onward that it determines, in part, what constitutes Chinese cinema. Internally, the set of Chinese state regulations dictating film production, distribution, and exhibition shaped by China's political system also affects the normative conceptions of Chinese cinema, and so does Chinese cultural heritage in terms of classical norms of visual representation. Burch's framework foregrounds two dimensions of Chinese cinema: its textual relation with an already established discourse of Chineseness and a global cinematic paradigm; and its production relation with China's political economic system and a global capitalist system dictating the global flow of cultural products. The two dimensions form the organic parts of Chinese cinema and should not be subjected to separation. The framework "mode of representation" in my elaboration suggests a point of departure because my conceptualization of Chinese cinema attempts to unite a critical and cultural studies approach attentive to cultural products with the revised cultural industries approach attentive to the issues of policy, institution, and market.

TOWARD A SYNTHETIC APPROACH

The "cultural industries approach," that is, the revisionist political economy approach, has strong continuities with the political economy of mass communication tradition but is less deterministic than the hard-line political economy tradition rooted in the Frankfurt School in its assumptions about the social impact of the media.[61] The cultural industries approach, as articulated by John Sinclair, gives major attention to the structural formation of the market and audiovisual industries, that is, the industries' ownership and control related to state policy.[62] Of particular interest are the *effects* of regulatory regimes, modes of direct and indirect industry assistance, trade policy, and the effects of the *absence* of such intervention. While the effect of production structure on products is still a primary concern of this approach, it does seek a balance between the industrial and the cultural by taking into consideration the dynamic relation between the two. Furthermore, this approach looks to examine specific national/regional realities and their interaction with the process of globalization.

Ironically, the emergence of "cultural industries" as a category of analysis as well as criticism owns its conceptual debt to the Frankfurt School from which the cultural industries approach has attempted to maintain a methodological distance. The initial juxtaposition of the concepts "culture" and "industry" was often associated with Theodor Adorno and his colleagues at the Frankfurt School. To the Frankfurt School, the term *culture industry* was an oxymoron, intended to set up a critical contrast between the exploitative, repetitive mode of industrial mass production under capitalism and the associations of transformative power and aesthetic-moral transcendence that the concept of culture carried in the 1940s, when it still meant "high" culture. The industrialization of cultural production through the process of standardization was viewed by the Frankfurt School as an intrinsic debasement of cultural values. Adorno and Max Horkheimer's critique of culture industry was motivated by their perception that the standardized mass manufacture and marketing of cultural goods was as much an ideological as an industrial process, which had the function of stabilizing capitalism. The whole "dominant ideology thesis" influential in communication and cultural studies throughout the 1970s and beyond was the direct descendant of the Frankfurt School. The dominant ideology paradigm has since been challenged by many from both the school of "cultural studies" and the school of "political economy."[63]

From the cultural studies' standpoint, since the Frankfurt School sees industry and commerce as a stigma on all mass culture and subsumes all the cultural industries into the singular category "culture industry," it makes no attempt to distinguish between its various genres and forms and therefore provides no framework in which the actual cultural industries can be analyzed. From the standpoint of the revisionist political economy, the term is too abstract and allows no room for empirical studies of different forms of symbolic production. Attempts were made by Nicholas Garnham and others to pluralize *industry* and render *culture* into its adjectival form.[64] The new term *cultural industries* not only opens the room for empirical inquiry but also retains the critical intent of the Frankfurt School, although the tone is no longer denunciatory. Furthermore, the dominant ideology thesis has been discredited on the grounds that totalization itself should not be an objective of theoretical effort. As early as the mid-1980s, some mainstream theorists were urging a shift toward Robert Merton's "middle-range" approach from which specific empirical studies of processes could be pursued. Emile McAnany, for one, suggested a cultural industries approach in which, "instead of trying to create a theory suited to all countries and having arguments raised about the generalizability of results and the validity of the theory, the study of the growth and impact of cultural industries within each country is more appropriate."[65]

The cultural industries approach can be further fleshed out through the debate between the so-called culturalist position and the political economist position in the studies of popular culture. Cultural studies has been a much contested arena for some time. For the past decades, the spirit of cultural studies has been that of the celebratorily iconoclastic. It prides itself on its epistemological and ontological deviation from classical social science. As such, cultural studies have been charged with an inadequacy of methodological rigidity and uncertainty in terms of its research subjects and methods.[66]

The critique of culturalist positions centers around, first, cultural studies' lack of attention to cultural production and, second, its uncritical celebration of cultural practices among various "subordinated" groups. By focusing on the components of cultural products, cultural studies, as is charged, tends to ignore the conditions of cultural practice, consequently social structure, political forces, and economic dynamics are all evaporated in the process of text-only analyses. Furthermore, as is charged, the uncritical celebration of local culturalism/multiculturalism as epitomized by identity politics is naive, since localized situations are themselves shaped in fundamental but particular ways by broader, underlying social and economic dynamics.

The second point is worth elaborating here, as its subsequent call for a critical localism directs our attention to cultural studies' tendency for uncritical celebration of the marginal.[67] The warning is useful: A preoccupation with the local (pleasures and resistance from fragmented audience groups) that leaves the global outside its line of vision may be vulnerable to the manipulation of global capitalism. The struggle for meaning articulation among various local communities is really a power struggle between the old establishment and the formerly powerless groups who have acquired new power in various identity politics discourses to seek to redefine the power structure in accordance with their own interests and perceptions. Economic power struggle and political manipulation also exist within local cultures especially when earlier forms of exploitation and oppression persisting in the local team up with the imprints of modernity. In other words, there is a major difference between a diversity that is produced by social formations (particularly subordinated ones) that wish to maintain their difference from others (particularly dominant ones) and a so-called diversity that is produced by market strategies. As suggested by John Fiske, the first is diversity, for it includes differences that may be abrasive and unincorporable; the second is mere multiplicity, for its differences exist only because they are incorporable and indeed are the products of the system that incorporates them.[68]

Multiplicity is the strategy by which global marketing attempts to cope with local demands. It is an economic attempt to match products to people in such a way as to minimize differences among markets, and thus between the social formations that underlie these markets by selectively featuring inconsequential differences. This selective differentiation identifies, promotes, and rewards those characteristics of diversity that are incorporable and economically valuable, while simultaneously ignoring and discouraging those characteristics that are abrasive, oppositional, and thus resistant to incorporation. To directly apply the notion of multiplicity to our analyses of the film industry, the increasing market segmentation corresponding to a diversified audience demography in the form of various niche markets from mainstream to art film is the result of such a selective differentiation that encourages not cultural diversity but cultural commercialization. Hence, the much celebrated marginal cinemas such as art cinema and minority cinema are susceptible to the manipulation and incorporation of a global capital, and therefore, the art films and various national films, in their evasion of unincorporable cultural elements, do not necessarily reflect and celebrate real marginal cultures.

Overall, four main arguments are set forth by the revisionist political economist, or the cultural industries approach:

1. Local cultural formation is a continuous process, a site of struggle open to manipulations from the interests of global capital, national/regional politics, and various local communities.
2. The globalization of the market economy is already a fact at an economic level, yet at a cultural level, Western culture and American culture in particular, do not yet completely dominate; the outcome is still contested and hence there are opportunities to intervene.
3. While acknowledging that the mode of production is historically contingent, subject to crisis and contradictions, it nonetheless has a certain historical stability and is path-dependent because of the social investment made in its construction, the social dangers that stem from its dissolution, and, finally, the

choice of a particular set of institutions and practices cumulatively blocking off other choices.

4. It calls for a reunification of political economist and culturalist approach and deems the "divorce" between cultural studies and political economy unnecessary and harmful.[69]

Such arguments set forth by the cultural industries approach justly suggest that it is essential to move beyond national cinemas' textual elements to explore the dynamic interaction among the political, the economic, and the cultural as well as between the global and the local. Yet the cultural industries approach tends to fall short of, or deliberately shy away from, analyses of shifting formal repertoire and the discourses surrounding such shifts, which are film style and film culture in this case, both emblematic of cultural formation and transformation. In its residual disdain for qualitative textual analyses, particularly for formal analyses not directly linked to its political agenda, the cultural industries approach traditionally has been indifferent to film style, reducing the medium-specific formal parameters to nothing but the vehicle through which certain ideology is transported. Here a certain type of cultural studies and classical political economy share their precious moments of consensus. Here, too, lies the moment of contention between my focus and "theirs," so to speak, for I consider the medium-specific textuality dealing with the formation and transformation of film style essential to our understanding of the dynamic relation between production conditions and product, the larger issue at hand.

Here is, ultimately, where political economy and cultural studies might converge to strike a more synthetic approach attentive to both the economic conditions of production and the products themselves, for example, production conditions of the film industry and the films produced. Film culture manifested through film discourse—that is, critical and popular film criticism, on the other hand—adds a third dimension into the dialogue, completing the equation by introducing critical and popular evaluations of both film production and style. Thus, the reconciliation of a cultural studies approach and a political economy approach becomes the methodological platform of this book.

Lastly, the feasibility of preserving cinemas of various cultural origins on a moral and ecological ground has yet to be addressed. While an ideology-based identity politics tends to insist on cultural identity as a stable entity resistant of change, an economy-based discussion tends to frame the same issue in terms of a marketing strategy. Thus, culture seems to have lost its value without being associated with ideology or profits. I argue otherwise. I suggest that cultural identity, perceived in either economic or political terms, runs the risk of being subjugated to either the practical concerns of economy or the manipulation of politics.

Specifically, this book explores the cultural and political economic factors determinant in and contingent on the rising of Chinese cinema's art and entertainment waves. It also traces the cinematic heritage of both popular films and art films and the transition from the latter to the former since the late 1980s. It further explores the dynamic relationship between mode of production concerning film production and style and mode of consumption concerning film culture evaluating such production and style. It finally revisits the issue of Chinese cinema's cultural identity/relevance in a cinematic presentation.

Chapter 2 explores the political, economic, and cultural factors conducive to the rise of Chinese cinema's first formidable art wave. The art wave was germinated in the late 1970s as the result of China's Four Modernizations, in general, and a cinematic modernization, in particular. The wave culminated in the early 1980s with the arrival of the internationally acclaimed Fifth Generation exploration film, commonly referred to as "New Wave cinema." The art wave during the period was fostered by an apolitical cultural atmosphere abhorring pedagogical films in their association with the discredited Communist propaganda, a state-subsidized industry that shielded studios from any real financial pressure, and a modernist film discourse that encouraged the exploration of film form. The chapter also explores the stylistic principles of the New Wave and the cultural/cinematic heritage of such principles. Stylistic analyses zero in on four films emblematic of the Chinese New Wave: *One and Eight* (Zhang Junzhao, 1984), *Yellow Earth* (Chen Kaige, 1984), *On the Hunting Ground* (Tian Zhuangzhuang, 1985), and *Horse Thief* (Tian Zhuangzhuang, 1986). Among the four films, *Yellow Earth*, with its critical reputation as the consummate specimen of Chinese New Wave, receives the most extensive textual attention.

Chapter 3 focuses on the political economy and the culture of Chinese cinema from the mid-1980s to the mid-1990s by concentrating on the key film reform measures and their concomitant, reform-oriented film discourses foregrounding a populist cinema. Film criticism responded positively to the industry's institutional reform; institutional reform, on the other hand, actively sought critical opinions evaluating various reform measures. The impact of both on Chinese cinema, chiefly the commercialization and decentralization of Chinese film industry and the surge of entertainment pictures, is discussed. Both local and global factors contributed to Chinese cinema's change of direction during the period. Locally, China's economic reform policies affected the state's cultural policies and subsequently its film policies, propelling a series of reform measures aimed at the decentralization of the state-run film industry. The reform measures affected the general trend in film production and criticism during the period. Globally, the popularity of Hollywood pictures (re)defined what counted as quality films for international viewers. Likewise the industrial structure and market practice institutionalized by Hollywood has become the global norm, wiping out alternative institutional practices. My discussion of the "globalization of Hollywood" is restricted to Hollywood's dominance of China's domestic market and its influence on Chinese audience's cinematic taste.

Chapter 4 examines, economically and stylistically, the cinematic transition from New Wave art film to post–New Wave classical film of the Chinese Fifth Generation filmmakers Chen Kaige, Tian Zhuangzhuang, and Zhang Yimou.[70] Using the framework of the relationship between film style and film reform, as well as film discourse evaluating both reform and stylistic change, the chapter addresses economic and textual strategies the three filmmakers utilized to compete with Hollywood for both global and domestic market shares. At the core of the Fifth G's transition from art cinema to commercial cinema is its reprising of a classical narrative strategy. Stylistic principles of post–New Wave and its cultural/cinematic heritage are examined through formal analyses of the Fifth Generation films from the late 1980s to the mid-1990s, chiefly Chen Kaige's *Farewell My Concubine* (1993), Tian Zhuangzhuang's *The Blue Kite* (1993), and Zhang Yimou's films as a group during the period. The formal analyses do not intend to inventory all the stylistic parameters of post–New Wave but to elucidate the filmmakers' cinematic transition. The chapter also links the transition of the Fifth Generation with the Chinese film industry's general trend of commercialization. Finally, the chapter discusses the Fifth Generation filmmakers' emerging domestic bent during Chinese cinema's post-Wave era when the domestic market has demonstrated its profit potential for films with popular appeal.

Chapter 5 examines the state of Chinese cinema in the late 1990s and beyond. It presents new economic reform measures implemented by the state and carried out by the industry. It then discusses prominent cinematic trends under the rubric of Chinese cinema's commercial wave, what I term "post-Wave," the wave that has engulfed both propaganda and art cinemas. The cinematic trends addressed include films of the writer Wang Shuo, of popular genre, of the tamed Fifth Generation, of the commercialized sixth generation, and of the television-trained popular filmmakers such as Feng Xiaogang. The impact of state censorship is also explored.

Chapter 6 backtracks to explore the range of dynamics in the development of Chinese cinema's first wave of entertainment film and the industry's first institutional restructuring. A look at Chinese cinema's first commercial entertainment wave under the shadow of Hollywood-led imports can shed some light on Chinese cinema's current commercial wave under, again, Hollywood's shadow. The first entertainment wave and institutional restructuring occurred almost simultaneously from the mid-1920s to the early 1930s, and resembles Chinese cinema's current popular entertainment wave and the ongoing institutional restructurings in the

1990s. Both periods present similiar political, economic, and cultural constraints and promises. During both periods, commercialism and nationalism played significant roles in shaping the direction and duration of the entertainment wave and the institutional restructuring. Particularly relevant, and hence highlighted in my discussion, is the role of a film culture characterized by traditionalism, populism, and pragmatism in the development of the entertainment wave and the institutional restructurings. Chapter 6 finally explores the cultural and cinematic heritage of the leading popular entertainment genres during the period, the costume and martial arts–ghost dramas. Major attention is given not to the textual analyses of any particular film but to the political, economic, and cultural factors conducive to the rise and fall of the films considered as Chinese cinema's first entertainment wave. It relies on existing historical data and narratives concerning the period and films and film discourses during the period as its sources of data, insofar as they are accessible.

Chapter 7 discusses the issue of cultural identity in cinematic representation in relation to both film economy and Chinese culture at large, and examines the limitations of a liberal economic analysis in terms of its pragmatic bias that subjugates the discussion of culture to economics. It recapitulates how the modernization of the Chinese film economy and the transition of Chinese cinema from art wave to entertainment wave is both the result and the manifestation of China's shifting political, economic, and cultural orientations.

NOTES

1. Hollywood films were officially banned after the establishment of the People's Republic of China. Hollywood features entered Mainland China's market only sporadically after the Cultural Revolution. The official reintroduction of Hollywood films did not occur until 1995 when the Chinese state issued a document granting an annual importation of ten foreign films; blockbuster Hollywood fares make up a large portion of the quota.

2. The cheap Chinese knockoffs of Hollywood fares in the 1980s were mostly unremarkable. In the mid-1990s, however, the Chinese film industry beefed up its production budget, creating domestic blockbusters such as *Red Cherry* (Ye Ying, 1995), *Shanghai Triad* (Zhang Yimou, 1995), *Red River Valley* (Feng Xiaoning, 1997), and *Opium Wars* (Xie Jin, 1997). Such films have adopted, to varying degrees, Hollywood's commercial formula ranging from huge private investment to massive promotion, and to the use of star and continuity narrative structures.

3. I use art/New Wave and commercial or popular entertainment/post–New Wave interchangeably in this book.

4. See Kristin Thompson, "The Formulation of the Classical Style, 1909–1928," in *The Classical Hollywood Cinema Film Style and Mode of Production to 1960*, ed. David Bordwell, Janet Staiger, and Kristin Thompson (New York: Columbia Uni-

versity Press, 1985), 155–240. See also David Bordwell's discussion of the classical continuity framework in Chinese cinema in his essay, "Transcultural Spaces: Toward a Poetics of Chinese Film," *Post Script* 20, no. 2–3 (2001): 9–24.

5. I will discuss the generational paradigm in detail later in this chapter.

6. See the definition in Robert Allen and Douglas Gomery, eds., *Film History: Theory and Practice* (New York: Knopf, 1985), 86–87. Mode of production as both a terminology and an analytic paradigm is best exemplified in Bordwell, Staiger, and Thompson's book *The Classical Hollywood Cinema Film Style and Mode of Production to 1960.*

7. See the following historical accounts of Chinese cinema: Roy Armes, *Third World Film Making and the West* (Berkeley and Los Angeles: University of California Press, 1987); Jay Leyda, *Dianying: An Account of Films and Film Audience in China* (Cambridges: MIT Press, 1972); Li Shuyuan and Hu Jushan, *The History of Chinese Silent Cinema* (Beijing: China Film Press, 1996); and Cheng Jihua, ed., *The History of Chinese Cinema* (Beijing: China Film Press, 1980); and Paul Clark, *Chinese Cinema: Culture and Politics since 1949* (Cambridge: Cambridge University Press, 1987).

8. Throughout my book, then, I use art/elitist and popular/populist interchangeably.

9. For a more in-depth discussion, see Zhang Xudong, *Chinese Modernism in the Era of Reforms* (Durham, N.C.: Duke University Press, 1997), 215–231. Other film scholars—notably Paul Clark, *Chinese Cinema*; Chen Kaige and Tony Rayns, *King of Children and the New Chinese Cinema* (London: Faber and Faber, 1989); Nick Browne, Paul Pickowicz, Vivian Sobchack, and Esther Yau, eds. *New Chinese Cinemas: Forms, Identities, Politics* (Cambridge: Cambridge University Press, 1994); and Chris Berry, *Perspectives on Chinese Cinema* (London: BFI, 1991)—and many film critics in China have utilized, to varying degrees, such a common approach toward the periodization of Chinese cinema.

10. See Ni Zhen's discussion in "Cinema and Contemporary Life" (Dianying yu dangdai shenghuo), *Dangdai dianying* (Contemporary Film) 5, no. 2 (1985): 43–60.

11. Zhang Xudong, *Chinese Modernism in the Era of Reforms* (Durham, N.C.: Duke University Press, 1997), 224.

12. The academy was shut down during the Cultural Revolution.

13. Wang Yichuan "Chinese Cinema during the Era of Post-Generation" (Wu daiqi zhongguo dianying) *Dangdai dianying* 62, no. 5 (1994): 20–27.

14. As an example of the "antigenerational" approach, Shuqin Cui used the term *independent directors* as an alternative label to capture certain aspects of the experience of this postcultural generation of filmmakers. See Shuqin Cui, "Working from the Margins: Urban Cinema and Independent Directors in Contemporary China," *Post Script* 20, no. 2–3 (2001): 77–93.

15. Recent works such as Li Suyuan and Hu Jubin's *Chinese Silent Cinema* (Zhongguo wushen dianying) (Beijing: China Film Press, 1996); Ying Zhu's "Commercialism and Nationalism: Chinese Cinema's First Wave of Entertainment Films," *CineAction* 47 (summer 1998): 56–66; Zhang Zhen's "Bodies in the Air: The Magic of Science and the Fate of the Early 'Martial Arts' Film in China," *Post Script* 20, no. 2–3 (2001): 43–60; and articles published in China's film journals such as *Dangdai dianying* (Contemporary Film), *Dianying chuangzhuo* (Film Writing), and *Dianying yishu* (Film Art) have begun to give more attention to Chinese cinema's first commercial wave.

16. See Guback's forward to Janet Wasko's *Movies and Money: Financing the American Film Industry* (Norwood, N.J.: Ablex, 1982), xi–xv.

17. Richard Abel, "Pathe Goes to Town: French Films Create a Market for the Nickelodeon," *Cinema Journal* 35, no. 1 (1995): 3–26.

18. Paulo Emilio Salles Gomes, "Cinema: A Trajectory within Underdevelopment," in *Brazilian Cinema*, ed. Randal Johnson and Robert Stam (Rutherford, N.J.: Fairleigh Dickinson University Press, 1982), 247–265.

19. Stephen Crofts, "Reconceptualizing National Cinemas," *Quarterly Review of Film and Video* 14, no. 3 (1993): 49–67.

20. Andrew Higson, "The Concept of National Cinema," *Screen* 30, no. 4 (autumn 1989): 36–44.

21. Geoffrey Nowell-Smith, "But Do We Need It?" in *British Cinema Now*, ed. Martin Auty and Nick Roddick (London: BFI, 1985), 147–158.

22. Mette Hjort, "Danish Cinema and the Politics of Recognition," in *Post-Theory: Restructuring Film Studies,* ed. David Bordwell and Noel Carroll (Madison: University of Wisconsin Press, 1996), 520–532.

23. Hjort did not mention in this particular article the now-notorious Dogma 95 "vow of chastity," a Danish cinematic movement whose austere views are out of step with his discussion on a minor culture's need for affirmation. In 1995 the Danish filmmakers Lars von Trier and Thomas Vinterberg promulgated a list of ten principles in the hopes of rescuing world cinema from decadent bourgeois individualism. To earn the Dogma 95 seal of approval, a film must forswear such emblems of false consciousness as props, genre conventions, and "temporal and geographical alienation." Cameras must be handheld, only available light and sound may be used, and all traces of directorial personality, including the director's credit, must be expunged.

24. See Albert Moran, "Terms for Reader: Film, Hollywood, National Cinema, Cultural Identity, and Film Policy," in *Film Policy: International, National, and Regional Perspectives*, ed. Albert Moran (London: Routledge, 1996), 1–22.

25. Armes, *Third World Film Making and the West*, 40.

26. Mitsuhiro Yoshimoto, "The Difficulty of Being Radical: The Discipline of Film Studies and the Postcolonial World Order," in *Japan in the World*, ed. M. Miyoshi and H. D. Harootunian (Durham, N.C.: Duke University Press, 1993), 388–410.

27. William Rothman, "Overview: What Is American about Film Study in America?" in *Melodrama and Asian Cinema*, ed. Wimal Dissanayake (Cambridge: Cambridge University Press, 1993), 57–72.

28. A brief overview of this approach can be found in Robert Stam's "Third Cinema Revisited," in *Film Theory: An Introduction* (Malden, Mass.: Blackwell, 2000), 281–291. Ella Shohat and Robert Stam's *Unthinking Eurocentrism Multiculturalism and the Media* (New York: Routledge, 1994) provides a more in-depth discussion on the same approach.

29. Judith Mayne, *Kino and the Woman Question: Feminism and Soviet Silent Film.* (Columbus: Ohio State University, 1989), 3.

30. See Moran, "Terms for Reader."

31. While guest-editing *Post Script* (20, no. 2–3, 2001) for a theme issue on Chinese cinema, Sheldon Lu and Yeh Yueh-Yu coined the term *Chinese-language film* to designate their research objects.

32. A collection of English translations of a series of groundbreaking critical essays on Chinese cinema written in Chinese by the native Chinese film critics is provided in George Semsel, ed., *Chinese Film Theory: A Guide to the New Era* (New York: Praeger, 1990). Zha Jianying's *China Pop* (New York: Columbia University Press, 1997) and Geremie Barme's *In the Red* (New York: Columbia University Press, 2000) provide good insights into China's contemporary cultural scenes.

33. See Zhang Jiwu, "Chinese Cinema's Post New Period: The Challenge of Breaking Up" (Hou Xingshiqi zhongguo dianying: fenglie de tiaozhan), *Dangdai dianying* 62, no. 5 (1994): 4–11, and "Globalization and Chinese Cinema" (Quanqiuhua yu zhongguo dianying), *Dangdai dianying* 75, no. 6 (1996): 13–20. See also Li Xuebing, "Chen Kaige, Zhang Yimou, and Postcolonialism" (Chen Kaige, Zhang Yimou—houzhiming yujinglun de shangchuo), *Dangdai dianying* 62, no. 5 (1994): 88–90.

34. See Dai Qing, "Raised Eyebrows for Raise the Red Lantern," *Public Culture* 5 (1993): 333–337.

35. See Jiwu, "Chinese Cinema's Post New Period," and "Globalization and Chinese Cinema."

36. See Li, "Chen Kaige, Zhang Yimou, and Postcolonialism."

37. Wang Ning, "Post-Colonialism and Contemporary Chinese Cinema" (Houzhiming yujing yu zhongguo dangdai dianying), *Dangdai dianying* 68, no. 5 (1995): 32–39; Yan Chunjun "On the Topic of Post-Colonialism" (Jingyan fuhe yu duoyuan quxiang), *Dangdai dianying* 68, no. 5 (1995): 40–46; and Yu Ji, "Jottings during Evening Reading" (Yiedu Ougan), *Dangdai dianying* 68, no. 5 (1995): 47–50.

38. Zhang Yinjing, "From 'Minority Film' to 'Minority Discourse': The Questions of Nationhood and Ethnicity in Chinese Cinema," *Cinema Journal* 36, no. 3 (1997): 73–90.

39. This essay appeared in *Perspectives on Chinese Cinema*, ed. Chris Berry (London: BFI, 1991), 30–39.

40. This essay appeared in *Perspectives on Chinese Cinema*, ed. Chris Berry (London: BFI, 1991), 141–154.

41. This essay appeared in *Transitional Chinese Cinemas*, ed. Lu Sheldon (Honolulu: University of Hawaii Press, 1997), 265–276.

42. See the widely circulated and state-endorsed version of Chinese film history compiled by Cheng, *The History of Chinese Cinema*.

43. Chris Berry provides detailed statistics concerning audience attendance in his article "Market Forces: China's 'Fifth Generation' Faces the Bottom Line," in *Perspectives on Chinese Cinema*, ed. Chris Berry (London: BFI, 1991) 115. Also, according to the January 1, 1998, *China Entertainment Network News*, a China-based English newsletter delivered on-line (<newsletter@china-entertainment.net>), the total figure for national box office for 1997 was 1.56 billion yuan (US $200 million), but only 22 percent of that went to domestic films.

44. The concept of "cultural discount" is introduced by Colin Hoskins and Mirus Rolf in their coauthored essay "Reasons for the US Dominance of the International Trade in Television Programs," *Media, Culture, and Society* 10, no. 4 (1988): 499–515.

45. When I conducted my interviews with cultural critics, policy makers, and industrial practitioners in China in the summer of 1997, accomplished filmmakers— notably Zhang Junzhao (*One and Eight*, 1984), Teng Wenji (*Reverberation of Life*,

1979), Cheng Jialin (*The Last Empress*, 1985)—were all making television dramas. The only filmmakers I talked with who had not yet turned to television for profit were Huang Jianxing (*Black Cannon Incident*, 1985) and He Ping (*Red Firecrackers, Green Firecrackers*, 1994).

46. Zhang Tongdao, Liu Ningzhi, and Shong Juan, "On the Research Report on the Relationship between Film and TV" (Guanyu dianying yu dianshi guanxi de diaocha baogao), *Dianying yishu* 247, no. 2 (1996): 51–60.

47. Ying Hong, "Contemporary Chinese Cinema within the Paradigm of Globalization" (Guojihua yujingzhong de dangqian zhongguo dianying), *Dangdai dianying* 75, no. 6 (1996): 21–29.

48. See Wu Guanping's interview with Xie Fei, "Looking Out the Window of Spiritual Home" (Tiaowan zhai jingshen jiayuan de chuangqian), *Dianying yishu* 244, no. 5 (1995): 38–46. Xie expressed the same opinion in an interview I conducted with him in the summer of 1997.

49. See a special report on the conference in *Zhongguo yingmu* (China Screen) 12 (1996): 18–21.

50. Zheng Dongtian, "On Film Commodity and Industrial Structure" (Guangyu dianying shangping—gongye tixi de zhai miaoshu), *Dianying yishu* 249, no. 4 (1996): 8–11.

51. A detailed account of Chinese film's economic reform from the perspective of cultural policy can be found in Ni Zhen, ed., *Gaige yu zhongguo dianying* (Reform and Chinese Cinema) (Beijing: China Film Press, 1994). See also a group of "theme articles" on the film market in *Dangdai dianying* 72, no. 3 (1996): 32.

52. See Li Shaobai and Feng Bo, "Marching toward the Market" (Zhouxiang shichang), *Dianying yishu* 240, no. 1 (1995): 17–24.

53. Ma Debuo, "The Cycle of Cinematic Fashion" (Yingyun Huanliu), *Dianying yishu* 241, no. 2 (1995): 29–26 and 241, no. 3 (1995): 46–52.

54. Hu Ke, "Understanding Chinese Silent Cinema from Multiple Perspectives" (Chong duozhong jiaodu lijie zhongguo wusheng dianying), *Dangdai dianying* 74, no. 5 (1996): 51–59.

55. Zhuang Yuxing, "The Issue of Economy in Contemporary Mainland Chinese Cinema" (Dangdai zhongguo dalu dianying de jingji wengti), *Dangdai dianying* 72, no. 3 (1996): 17–23 and 72, no. 4 (1996): 42–48; Tuo Lake, "The Production of High Quality Films the Reality" (Jingping chuangzhu yu juanglu xianshi), *Dangdai dianying* 73, no. 4 (1996): 7–10; and Zheng Guoeng, "An Encouraging and Feasible Project" (Yige guwureng de kexing gongcheng), *Dangdai Dianying* 73, no. 4 (1996): 11–12. Gao is the chairman of the China Filmmakers' Association. He expressed his concern over the cultural impact of Hollywood during my interview with him in Beijing in the summer of 1997.

56. See articles by Shao Mujun, Ying Hong, Zhu Huijun, and Xu Zhuang in *Dianying yishu* 237, no. 2 (1996): 4–18. See also the Chinese Film Association, *Film Production and the Socialist Market Economy* (Diangying chuangzhu yu shehuizhuyi shichang jingji) (Beijing: China Film Press, 1996).

57. See Charles Taylor's writing on identity politics and multiculturalism. He recognizes the necessity of asserting one's identity on moral and ecological grounds but fails to address the political and economic imperatives behind such a need. (*Multiculturalism and "The Politics of Recognition"* [Princeton, N.J.: Princeton University Press, 1992]).

58. See the following works: Peter Evans, *Embedded Autonomy: State and Industrial Transformation* (Princeton, N.J.: Princeton University Press, 1995); Manjunath Pendakur, *Canadian Dreams and American Control: The Political Economy of the Canadian Film Industry* (Detroit: Wayne State University Press, 1990); and Peter Evans, Dietrich Rueschemeyer, and Theda Skocpol, *Bringing the State Back In* (New York: Cambridge University Press, 1985).

59. Evans, *Embedded Autonomy*.

60. Thomas Elsaesser, Introduction to *Early Cinema: Space, Frame, Narrative,* ed. Thomas Elsaesser and Adam Barker (London: British Film Institute, 1990), 406–407. See also Noel Burch, *To the Distance Observer: Form and Meaning in Japanese Cinema,* trans. Annette Michelson (Berkeley and Los Angeles: University of California Press, 1979), and *Life to Those Shadows,* trans. Ben Brewster (Berkeley and Los Angeles: University of California Press, 1990).

61. John Sinclair, "Culture and Trade: Some Theoretical and Practical Considerations," *Mass Media and Free Trade: NAFTA and the Cultural Industries,* ed. Emile McAnany and Kenton Wilkinson (Austin: University of Texas Press, 1996), 30–62.

62. Ibid., 54–55.

63. See Armand Mattelart and Jean-Marie Piemme, "Cultural Industries: The Origin of an Idea," *Cultural Industries: A Challenge for the Future of Culture* (Paris: UNESCO, 1982), 51–61. See also Nicholas Garnham, *Capitalism and Communication* (London: Sage, 1990).

64. Garnham, *Capitalism and Communication*.

65. Emile McAnany, "The Logic of Cultural Industries in Latin America: The Television Industry in Brazil," in *The Critical Communications Review*, vol. 2, *Changing Patterns of Communication Control,* ed., Vincent Mosco and Janet Wasko (Norwood, N.J: Ablex, 1984), 56–66.

66. Marjorie Ferguson and Peter Golding, eds., *Cultural Studies in Question* (London: Sage, 1997).

67. Alfred Dirlik, "The Global in the Local," in *Global Local: Cultural Production and the Transnational Imaginary,* ed. Rob Wilson and Wimal Dissanayake (Durham, N.C.: Duke University Press, 1996).

68. John Fiske, "'Global, National, Local?' Some Problems of Culture in a Postmodern World," *The Velvet Light Trap* 40 (fall 1997): 56–66.

69. Suffice it to suggest that the best of cultural studies has always accepted and practiced just this set of approaches. In that sense, some might argue that "revised political economy" is indeed cultural studies under another name, since nothing listed here has ever been "excluded" in culturalist approaches. Semantics aside, most cultural studies have suffered from the inadequacies defined by Nicholas Garnham and James Carey in their essays appearing in *Cultural Studies in Question,* ed. Marjorie Ferguson and Peter Golding (London: Sage, 1997).

70. I single out Chen, Tian, and Zhang here because they were the most influential Fifth Generation filmmakers during the period. While others such as Zhang Junzhao continue to make films, their cinematic influence, both domestically and internationally since the late 1980s, is not as significant as that of Chen, Tian, and Zhang.

2

Cinematic Modernization and Chinese Cinema's First Art Wave

INTRODUCTION

Chinese cinema's first art wave began in the late 1970s as a result of China's Four Modernizations, in general, and a cinematic modernization, in particular. The art wave culminated in the mid-1980s with the arrival of the internationally acclaimed Fifth Generation exploration film, commonly referred to as "New Wave cinema." This chapter explores the political, economic, and cultural factors conducive to the rise of the art wave. More specifically, the art wave during the period was fostered by an apolitical cultural atmosphere abhorring pedagogical films in their association with the discredited communist propaganda, a state-subsidized industry that shielded studios from any real box-office pressure, and a modernist film discourse that encouraged the exploration of film form. This chapter also explores the stylistic principles of the New Wave and the cultural/cinematic heritage of such principles. Stylistic analyses zero in on four films emblematic of the Chinese New Wave: *One and Eight* (Zhang Junzhao, 1984), *Yellow Earth* (Chen Kaige, 1984), *On the Hunting Ground* (Tian Zhuangzhuang, 1985), and *Horse Thief* (Tian Zhuangzhuang, 1986). Among the four films, *Yellow Earth*, with its critical reputation as the consummate specimen of Chinese New Wave, receives the most extensive textual attention.

THE FIFTH GENERATION

The appearance of the Fifth Generation films, particularly *One and Eight*, *Yellow Earth*, *On the Hunting Ground*, and *Horse Thief*, was treated as

A version of this chapter originally appeared in Ying Zhu, "Cinematic Modernization and Chinese Cinema's First Art Wave," *Quarterly Review of Film and Video*, 18, no. 4 (2001): 451–471. Reproduced by permission of Taylor & Francis, Inc. http://www.routledge-ny.com.

an exciting new cinematic phenomenon within the Chinese film community. Chinese critics used a variety of terms/phrases to describe the new cinematic phenomenon created by the young filmmakers, chiefly *new Chinese cinema, experimental films*, and *exploration films*. The term *Chinese New Wave* was coined by overseas critics who, with no less enthusiasm than the Chinese critics, discovered anew an alternative Chinese cinema (I will use the terms *New Wave* and *Fifth G* interchangeably here).[1] Journal articles, monographs, and books were published in the mid- to late 1980s, commenting on the exploration films.[2] While the films were endorsed enthusiastically by the reform-minded critics for their cultural reflection and their stylistic innovation, the more reserved critics expressed their concerns on such films' neither too positive nor so constructive portrayal of the Communist revolution, in particular, and Chinese history, in general, and on their perceived tendency of formalism. In general, early Chinese film discourse concerning the Fifth G was preoccupied with the films' aesthetic breakthrough, often ignoring its political-ideological challenge to official ideology and narrative. Overall, the Chinese film community warmly welcomed the arrival of the new generation filmmakers.[3] In 1986, in enthusiastic response to the new direction Chinese film had taken, a special theater was opened in Shanghai as a showcase for the art films. The theater was later closed for lack of attendance.

At its infancy, the Fifth G did not have a clear articulation of its group identity for a particular cultural and stylistic aspiration. Though sharing the leitmotiv of antitradition in its challenge of the established norms of Chinese cinema, the Fifth G's awareness of its group identity came only after the critics championed for the arrival of New Wave. What became the Chinese New Wave was the overriding style and leitmotiv of early Fifth G films, which challenged the norms of socialist realist cinema and the Communist myth manufactured within the confines of such norms. Among the New Wave filmmakers, only Zhang Yimou came from the academy's Department of Cinematography. Others were graduates of the more glamorous Directing Department. Although Zhang did not venture into directing his own films until 1987, his contribution to the New Wave establishment in the early 1980s was well acknowledged. As the director of cinematography for *One and Eight* and *Yellow Earth*, the harbingers of New Wave, Zhang's cinematic vision helped to define the Fifth G's iconoclastic spirit and style vis-à-vis Chinese cinema's socialist realist tradition. The Fifth G's formal exploration led to a thorough cinematic liberation both thematically and stylistically. Thematically, the Fifth G's grim depiction of the Sino–Japan War and the lives of ethnic minorities were out of sync with the romantic images of the Communist revolution in the films of the third and fourth generations. Stylistically, while diversity and individuality did exist, the Fifth G's striving for formal innovation earned the group its New Wave identity.

It is worth noting that the Fifth G's antiestablishment cinematic practice, while subversive of a socialist realist paradigm, submitted itself to certain stylistic norms of international art cinema. New Wave's subversion of an existent order only to search and follow a new order perceived as righteous was attributed by the Chinese film critics Yao Xiaomeng and Hu Ke to the so-called Red Guard mentality, that is, the idealism embodied in the iconoclastic Cultural Revolution that called for the total dissolution of any "regressive" political, cultural, and ideological institutions in the name of a true proletarian dictatorship considered as the consummate stage of human emancipation.[4] In other words, in its desire to subvert the existent order, the iconoclastic spirit of Mao's Cultural Revolution must, at the end, bow to the romantic and utopian notion of communism. Linking the Fifth G's red guard experience during the Cultural Revolution to its cinematic practice, Yao and Hu suggested that the Fifth G's cinematic revolution willingly subjected itself to the guidance of a higher authority, the paradigm of international art film, or the modernist film.

Sociological profiles aside, the Fifth G's adoption of certain modernist cinematic strategies might be less psychological than the term *Red Guard mentality* would like to imply. For one thing, the European and Japanese art films had been discovered with much enthusiasm by the fourth generation filmmakers and critics who championed François Truffaut, Akira Kurosawa, Ingmar Bergman, Federico Fellini, Michelangelo Antonioni, and Andrei Tarkovsky but not the masters of Hollywood, classical or modernist. The fourth generation's enthusiastic endorsement of the European and Japanese modernist films encouraged the Fifth G's anticlassical approach toward filmmaking. Indeed the formative years of the Fifth G were marked by the arrival of a modernist film discourse promoted by the fourth generation filmmakers who idolized Italian Neorealism, French New Wave, and Japanese Modernist films. The modernist film discourse had a profound impact on the development of Chinese art cinema. Interestingly, what nourished the otherwise forbidden modernist film discourse was the Four Modernizations project launched by the state and endorsed by China's cultural community.

MODERNIZATION AND CHINESE CINEMA

Launched in 1977, the Four Modernizations included the modernization of agriculture, industry, science and technology, and national defense. The project of Four Modernizations was adopted into the Chinese Communist Party's constitution at the Eleventh Congress on August 18, 1977, as the state's Ten-Year Plan. It was further endorsed by the state constitution at the Fifth National People's Congress on March 5, 1978. For the Four Modernizations to succeed, the Chinese government adopted an Open-Door

Policy to introduce to China Western science, technology, capital, and management skills. The Open-Door Policy broke the isolation of China's economic development and resulted in the rapid growth of foreign trade. The frequent contact with the West inevitably (re)introduced to China Western thoughts and cultural products. It further led to a movement for spiritual liberation that would touch China's entire cultural scene. As such, the modernization movement launched solely as an economic one soon evolved into a cultural one. Manifested in Chinese cinema was the surge of an extensive critical and theoretical debate concerning the modernization of Chinese cinema.

Meanwhile, the state-sponsored film industry was put on the defensive by the public's disgust toward the utterly routinized and, hence, monolithic Maoist propaganda films. Filmmakers had to search for a new cinematic language, which naturally led to the call for the modernization of Chinese cinema. The modernization of Chinese cinema bore the spirit of Four Modernizations, that is, the search for a Chinese alternative beyond both socialism and capitalism and the simultaneous desire to integrate into the modern world. In deriving its legitimacy from the political, cultural, and ideological momentum at the time, the modernization of Chinese cinema located its institution under the protection of the state. The modernization began with a critical examination of the established norms of Chinese cinema, most noticeably the concept of "shadowplay," the central principle of Chinese film aesthetics.

"Shadowplay" Reexamined

A Chinese term for motion picture popular in southeast China around 1920, the word *shadowplay* is the English translation of a Chinese word group, *ying* (shadow) and *xi* (play).[5] In its Chinese usage, the word *shadow* (image) modifies the word *play* (drama). The notion of shadowplay gradually evolved into a predominant theoretical framework in the 1920s. Written in the 1920s, Hou Jue's book, *Writing for Shadowplay*, was the first work that elaborated on the concept of shadowplay.[6] Other works have since been published, basically following the same vein of Hou Jue. The concept in their elaboration not only foregrounded the similarity between cinema and drama but also categorized cinema as yet another form of drama. In making "drama" the essence of motion picture and "(film) image" the means of presentation, the concept further suggested a valuation of drama over cinema. In other words, what was essential about film was not its photographic quality of light and motion but the theatrical quality of narrative. The camera functioned more as the recorder than as the participant of the drama, downplaying visual style achieved through patterned cinematic motion and stylized shot composition. What constituted a quality narrative was a tightly woven multiple-act structure much resembling the structure of a stage play. The concept of exposition, complication (crisis, conflict, obstacle, and so forth), and resolution were borrowed from stage drama and were considered the basic elements of cinema. As such, scenes, not shots, were the smallest unit of a narrative. Shadowplay further emphasized narrative efficiency over visual extravagance. Closely related to narrative efficiency was shadowplay's emphasis on film's pedagogical function. The function of Chinese cinema was to efficiently narrate stories that would enlighten the masses. Consequently, narrative must be motivated thematically rather than stylistically.

A significant adjustment occurred in the late 1950s. Xia Yan, one of the prominent left-wing screenwriters active in the 1930s and 1940s, fine-tuned the notion of shadowplay for the newly nationalized film industry.[7] Cinema's pedagogical function was linked with political propaganda that carried the voice of the socialist state.[8] Under this framework, plot, dialogue, and props must work to serve a definite ideological goal. In practice, the subject matter in Chinese film became highly selective, indeed categorical, ranging from films portraying industrial problems to films of agricultural problems, military problems, and reformation problems, to name a few. Some Chinese critics termed the framework of shadowplay an "ontology of narration," as opposed to an "ontology of cinematography" more characteristic of European cinema.[9]

The shadowplay tradition was further refined, during the Cultural Revolution, to incorporate the equally manipulative Soviet montage approach, forming the foundation for the revolutionary realist film that generally depicted exemplary characters and events rather than highly differentiated individuals. The films featured goal-oriented protagonists, most of them revolutionary-minded proletarians who engaged in some form of political struggle with unambiguous social relevance to the concerns of contemporary people dictated by the party's ideology. The films typically sublimated style to narrative in privileging a linear narrative trajectory with emphasis on a clear and intensified central conflict. The films also employed extensive use of highly didactic dialogue and proscenium-style presentation that avoided naturalism. Based on the refined model of shadowplay, Chinese cinema from the early 1950s to the late 1970s was concerned not with cinema as an art form but with its function as a tool for Communist propaganda.[10] Film criticism and theory, being dependent of the party's politicized cultural policies, were to reinforce the refined model of shadowplay.

After the end of the Cultural Revolution, as the modernization movement was extended into the cultural field, shadowplay's less cinematic and highly didactic approach was criticized. The publication of two articles in China's film journals in 1979, "Throwing Away the Walking Stick of Drama" and "On the Modernization of Cinematic Language," called into question the taken-for-granted conventions of shadowplay.[11] Written by the fourth generation film practitioners, the two articles signaled the beginning of the modernization of Chinese cinema that would lead to the arrival of Chinese New Wave. In raising an eyebrow on the notion of shadowplay, the articles foregrounded film form and called for a more cinematic approach toward filmmaking.

"Throwing Away the Walking Stick of Drama" urged the separation of cinema from the constraints of stage drama. As the author Bai Jingsheng saw it, dramatic conflict(s) revolving around plot or character so central to a stage play was at odds with a cinematic mood of presentation that valued photographic naturalism. Considering the tightly woven three-act structure too utilitarian, the author argued for the necessity of a more poetic approach that would allow unmotivated scenes and events for naturalism. Although not addressed as such, what the author ultimately criticized in this piece was Mao's socialist realist tradition manipulative of reality. Photographic naturalism was implicitly valued over socialist realism, which he saw as against the "real" realism. The article also recommended certain cinematic devices such as fast/slow motion, freeze-frame, split screen, and camera mobility as useful tools to render a film more cinematic. The article also found fault with Chinese films' "talkativeness," a trait once again associated with stage drama. Though not addressed as such, in challenging Chinese cinema's theatricality, the author essentially endorsed art film narration.

Zhang Nuanxing and Li Tuo's piece, "On the Modernization of Cinematic Language," asserted that the decades of isolation of Chinese cinema from the rest of the world had made the Chinese film community ignorant of the global cinematic achievements both in theory and in practice and had resulted in Chinese cinema's backwardness. The cinematic achievements referred strictly to the postwar European art cinemas, chiefly Italian Neorealism and French New Wave, what the author considered modernist cinema. Such modernist films were valorized for their rupture with theatrical conventions and for their bold experimentation with film form that manifested a more cinematic approach. Faulting Chinese film practitioners for their insufficient attention to film form, the article foregrounded the notion of photographic realism. André Bazin and Siegfred Kracauer, along with auteur theorists, were enthusiastically endorsed. The article made explicit Bai's call for naturalism to protect "reality" from its subordination to state and party politics. It attacked Chinese cinema's "artificiality," the antirealist tendency of the socialist realist film. As its title suggests, the article ultimately urged the modernization of Chinese cinema.

The two articles generated a heated debate about the theatricality of Chinese film and the closely related issue of realism. To most of the participants in this debate, Chinese cinema's complete submission to literature and drama and the socialist realist tradition had suppressed the exploration of film as a relatively autonomous medium. A Kracauerian notion of "physical reality" exposed by cinematography and Bazin's theory of film realism served as theoretical foundations for the reform-minded Chinese film practitioners in their pushing for the legitimacy of a cinematic realism decisively different from the socialist realism. Kracauer and Bazin's celebration of photography's power to bring into light social and historical truth also encouraged Chinese cinema's newly discovered fascination with film form. Naturalism, though not exactly the essence of Bazin's theory, was unprecedentedly valued. Therefore cinema, with its technological possibility of unveiling a "deep reality," would free the "realistic world" that had so far been imprisoned in the official version of social reality manufactured by the socialist realist films. In a similar vein, Bazin's elaboration of photographic transparency was emphasized to not only break down the official discourse but also achieve a political ambivalence, or a semantic multiplicity. As such, the montage of Sergey Eisenstein and Vsevolod Pudovkin, with its genetic link to the discredited socialist realism, was frowned upon and replaced by Bazin's long take and deep focus. The debate lasted for three years, resulting in the proposal by the veteran film critic Zhong Dianfei for a divorce of cinema from drama and of a truthful realism from socialist realism.[12]

From Classical to Contemporary Film Theories:
An Art Cinema Movement and a Modernist Paradigm

The Chinese film community's (re)discovery of classical Western theories, chiefly that of Bazin, resulted in Chinese filmmakers' fascination with film form and the notion of the auteur, which helped to rationalize their disillusionment with socialist realism and its related Soviet montage theory. Soon after the rediscovery of classical theories, Chinese cinema encountered contemporary Western film theories. The discovery of contemporary film theory would effectively link the modernization of Chinese cinema with the notion of modernist cinema.

The Chinese film community's first encounter with contemporary Western film theories occurred in 1980 when a Chinese film scholar, Li Youzheng, published an article on structuralist semiotics.[13] At the time when the Chinese film community was so preoccupied with film form and an alternative view of realism, the reception of this article was understandably lukewarm. Contemporary film theories did not make another entry into China until 1984, when the Chinese Film Artists Association invited three American film scholars to Beijing to give lectures on the development of contemporary Western cinema. The three scholars are Nick Browne of the University of California–Los Angeles, whose topic was

"Some Questions Concerning Contemporary Film Theory and the History of Western Film Theory"; Robert Rosen of the University of California–Los Angeles, whose topic was "The Social Reading of Film Texts: A Methodology"; and Beverly Houston of the University of Southern California, whose topic was "Hollywood Melodrama of the 1950s." The American scholars' lectures covered a wide range of topics, including the history of Western film theory, textual analyses from the perspective of sociology, and Hollywood melodrama of the 1950s. Inspired by the lectures, a Chinese film scholar, Cui Junyan, published an essay summarizing what he saw as the distinction between "traditional" and "modern" ideas of cinema and the difference between classical and modernist films.[14]

As defined by Cui, "modern cinema" has the following two characteristics:

One is the openness of narrative structure, the other is the suggestiveness of the content thus represented. Emphasizing participation on the audience's part is a crucial characteristic of modern western media. Modern film audiences should not be a passive consumer, but rather an active reflector in front of the screen. The mode of thinking of modern man is not only to know what has happened, but also to explore independently the internal significance of the happening.[15]

Though lacking precision in his topological description and naive in his theoretical applications, Cui's understanding of modern cinema did capture certain principles of art film style.[16] Cui's article covered, cursorily, a broad theoretical ground ranging from Bazin's cinematic ontology to Umberto Eco's and Christian Metz's film semiotics. His contribution ultimately lay in his introduction to Chinese film criticism the notion of a modern cinema that helped other critics associate the Chinese New Wave with a modernist cinema. However, Cui's notion of modern cinema had less to do with the stylistic principles of a modernist cinema advocated by Noel Burch than with the principles of art cinema summarized by David Bordwell. Yet the principles of Chinese New Wave had more to do with both Bazin's realism and Burch's modernism than with Bordwell's art film style. In its striving for photographic realism, the New Wave signaled the advent of the students of Bazin; yet in its exploration and exposition of cinema's formal possibilities, the New Wave adhered to Burch's principles. At the time, neither Cui nor the Fifth G were aware of the historical antagonism between Bazin's narrative realism and Burch's stylistic modernism. Indeed Burch's name was not mentioned at all in the discourse concerning the modernization of Chinese cinema. Yet the New Wave's refusal to subordinate formal organization to narrative demands and its foregrounding of film style captured nicely the spirit of Burch's modernist film. In this regard, the New Wave's endorsement of Bazin completely ignored his suggestion of literature and theater as models for filmmaking.

While embracing the notion of modern vis-à-vis classical cinema, Chinese film practitioners were not particularly keen on the aspect of contemporary film theories that deconstructed the photographic reality celebrated by Bazin. Shao Mujun, one of the influential film critics during the time, was skeptical about the relevance to film production in China of Metz's semiotics, Marxian–Althusserian critique of ideology, and Lacanian psychoanalysis.[17] Echoed by many at the time, his attitude reflected Chinese film theory's pragmatism, the utilitarian approach toward theoretical exploration. To Chinese film practitioners, theoretical exploration is worthwhile only when it directly addressed the practicality of film production. The Chinese film community's aversion toward Marxist-inclined contemporary film theories was also the result of their apprehension toward the much discredited term *ideology*. Highly politicized during the Cultural Revolution, the term recalled the era when the Communist Party exerted unlimited political control over film production. As noted by Nick Browne, one development in post-Revolution Chinese cinema was the emergence of a view of cinema as an autonomous art with distinctive aesthetic properties and the assertion of film's independence from any political intervention and manipulation.[18] A decade of Cultural Revolution resulted in the Chinese people's utter disillusionment with the state and its politics. Avoiding direct contact with anything vaguely political became the prevailing mood. The term *culture* understood as something that transcended politics, and the term *art*, as something autonomous, became bases for establishing an institution of culture and art as a protected regime of formal-intellectual autonomy. As such, contemporary Western theories' criticism of Bazin for his idealism in believing in cinema's power to reproduce reality was not mentioned in the discourse concerning Chinese cinema's modernization. Understandably, Chinese film practitioners at the time would not have entertained Metz's proposition that all films were woven out of codes, none of which had a privileged access to reality. Chinese film practitioners' aversion to ideological analyses would change in the late 1980s when the financially ailing industry demanded a new theoretical paradigm capable of addressing the box-office problem of Chinese cinema under Hollywood's siege.[19] Only then, contemporary theories' insistence that cinema developed within an ideology of realism and the economic milieu of capitalism would be endorsed. Paradoxically, Chinese art wave's "apolitical" approach very much resembled the Bertolt Brecht–influenced "political modernism" emerging in the late 1960s in the West, which argued that modernism could subvert orthodox conceptions of social reality. Chinese New Wave is now seen by many as a political effort to disengage the orthodox social discourse embodied by the state, in general, and the status quo of filmmaking, in particular.

As theory often preceded practice in filmmaking in China, the theoretical exploration set the stage for the arrival of Chinese film's first full-blown art cinema movement. The movement began with the fourth generation film-makers' formal experimentation with cinematic devices rarely utilized during Mao's era. Their films—such as *Reverberation of Life* (Shenghuo de chanyin; Teng Wenji, 1979), *Bitter Laughter* (Kunaoren de xiao; Yang Yanjin, 1979), and *The Alley* (Xiaojie; Yang Yanjin, 1981)—broke away from Chinese cinema's "zero-degree" style of filmmaking, foregrounding film form. Zhang Nuanxing, one of the authors of "On the Modernization of Cinematic Language," directed the highly regarded feature debut *The Drive to Win* (Sha Ou, 1981), a sports film about a woman volleyball player and coach who sacrifices all her life to gain the world championship for her team only to find that her goal cannot be achieved during her generation.[20] In this film, Zhang combined Vittorio De Sica's neorealism with Yoji Yamada's—the Japanese filmmaker then popular in China—lyricism to break away from the theatrical tradition of Chinese cinema. The film was shot entirely on location, utilizing documentary and newsreel style film techniques. Long shots and natural lighting were deployed extensively to give the film a naturalistic tone. *The Drive to Win* reflected Zhang's passion for a "documentary" depiction of the objective world in its crude, unprocessed texture and physicality, a passion later shared by the Fifth G's New Wave films such as *Yellow Earth* and *On the Hunting Ground*. Zhang also cast a professional volleyball player in the leading role, a tradition of Italian Neorealism that was praised by Bazin for its achievement of a behavioral concreteness. Zhang's second feature, *Sacrificed Youth* (1985), a film reflecting on the ancient Chinese culture, was also a critical hit, often compared with the New Wave's *Yellow Earth*.

The fourth generation's cinematic reform later shifted from film techniques to film narrative, experimenting with narrational ambiguity. The critically acclaimed film *The Alley* tried out multiple endings, one happy, one tragic, and one a mixture of both. Its reference to Akira Kurosawa's *Rashomon* (1950) was evident. Yet overall, the formal exploration of the fourth generation from the late 1970s to the early 1980s was sporadic and ad hoc, lacking a coherent central tenet. Its stylistic experimentation was somewhat mechanical, limited to the naive application of certain cinematic parameters such as rack focus, flashback/flashforward, multiple exposure, slow motion, no synchronic monologue, inserting black and white images in a color feature, using filters to manipulate color, overexposure, and so on.

As suggested by Zhang Xudong, the fourth generation's primitive cinematic exploration reflected a confusing stage in the development of Chinese cinema, a transitional period when new cinematic ideas competed with old ones for legitimacy.[21] Indeed, the turn of the 1980s was the period of cinematic confusion and confrontation between the cinematic legacy of the surviving third generation and the new cinematic aspiration of the fourth generation. As such, films made during the period were thematically and stylistically heterogeneous, ranging from humanist realist films voicing the sufferings of the Cultural Revolution (*The Legend of Tianyun Mountain*; Xie Jin, 1980) to melodramatic comedies (*They're in Love*; Qian Jiang and Zhao Yuan, 1980) to revisionist historical films (*Intimate Friends*; Xie Tieli, Chen Huaikai, and Ba Hong, 1981), to the more experimental films (*The Alley* and *Reverberation of Life*). As one film critic remarked during the period, "[W]hat is twinkling in front of me are visual images with a lost focus—they lack clarity of idea, clarity of image, and clarity of style."[22] Yet the fourth generation film's ideological and formal ambiguities not only reflected the unsettled transition in post–Cultural Revolution China, but also linked Chinese cinema's art wave with an international modernist cinema, providing a theoretical topology for the positioning of the Chinese art wave within the realm of film modernism.

It is worth noting here that Western film scholars have disputed the term *modernist* vis-à-vis *classical* as a descriptive category. While film scholars such as Noel Burch, Frederic Jameson, and Thomas Schatz endorsed such a topology in their categorization of major film trends, David Bordwell, for one, has avoided such a term on the grounds that it blurs rather than clarifies the distinction among various cinematic modes and norms, since several different sorts of film narration could be qualified as modernist.[23] In making his point, Bordwell argues that, on the one hand, art cinema narration could be called "modernist" on the basis of its generic lineage to modernist fiction and drama, and, on the other hand, historical-materialist narration could also be labeled "modernist" on the basis of the experimental works of political artists like Brecht and Sergei Tretyakov, and, on yet another ground, the parametric films, or the structuralist films, with its pedigree tracing back to the work of the Russian Formalists, might too be considered "modernist."[24] So, to Bordwell, *art cinema movement* was a more productive term to capture the leitmotiv, thematically and stylistically, of a postwar international cinematic trend inspired by concepts borrowed from modernism in theater and literature. The trend consciously positioned itself against the Hollywood establishment, the classical film narration. Semantics aside, when analyzing the Chinese New Wave, suffice it to suggest that scholars from both ends would agree on, stylistically, its departure from classical Chinese influenced by classical Hollywood and traditional Chinese visual arts. My association of the Chinese New Wave with modernist films in the West follows the conventions from the established Chinese film discourse and is restricted only to certain stylistic traits of New Wave. I will therefore use the terms *art* and *modernist* interchangeably.

Chinese cinema's art wave reached its apex in the early to mid-1980s with the arrival of the Fifth G New Wave cinema that pushed further for formal autonomy and stylistic mannerism. The surge of the New Wave was a relatively smooth one. While the New Wave's debut, *One and Eight*, was criticized by the conservative critics for its grim portrayal of the Chinese Communist Party and was banned from being exported, the Chinese public's disillusionment with political movements prevented the official press from launching a political backlash against the Fifth G.

Thematically, the New Wave was synchronous with China's overall cultural epoch at the time. More specifically, what directly influenced the New Wave was the introspective literary movement of "root-seeking" from the early to mid-1980s. Influenced by William Faulkner and Garcia Marquez, the root-seeking movement sought to understand how the Chinese culture came into being and what the origins of Chineseness are. The emotionally restrained root-seeking fictions looked for nature untamed by civilization as a salvation and a dwelling space for reflection on Chinese culture at large. Responding to such a prevailing literary mood, the New Wave's cinematic focus turned away from cosmopolitan urban centers and the cultural mainstream to the provincial hinterland and cultural margin. In doing so, the New Wave engaged itself in an anthropological observation of China and Chinese. The New Wave directly adapted fictions by root-seeking writers such as Ah Cheng (*King of Children*; Chen Kaige, 1988) and Muo Yan (*Red Sorghum*; Zhang Yimou, 1987).

While bringing literary inspiration to the New Wave, this root-seeking movement also helped foster an enthusiastic critical reception of the Fifth G film seen as the consummate example of a cinema of cultural critique. The movement further inspired a few radical critics to challenge the state-sanctioned and the public-endorsed third generation films, especially Xie Jin's shadowplay influenced melodramas (*Ah, Cradle*, 1979; *The Legend of Tianyun Mountain*, 1980; and *The Herdsman*, 1981).[25] The moralism and excessive emotions in Xie Jin's films, popular with the Chinese audiences, was compared with the classical Hollywood melodrama seen as reactionary, deceptive, and vulgar. The moralism in Xie was further charged with Confucian-style paternalism, a patriotic social hierarchy that victimized women, and with its parochial "patriotism" seen as the roadblock toward China's modernization. While attacking the Xie Jin model, the critics championed the Fifth G cinema for its radical style and its critique of traditional Chinese culture. Implicit in Chinese critics' denouncement of "the Xie Jin model" and their initial endorsement of the New Wave was their elitist attitude that defied popular taste and equated the popular with the vulgar. Such an endorsement contrasted sharply with Bazin's sanction of film's narrative propensities and mass popularity. While idolizing Bazin's realism, the critics paradoxically ignored his celebration of a film practice that derived from popular culture and appealed to a mass audience. As such, the popular reception of the New Wave was lukewarm. What sustained the Fifth G's lofty cinematic practice was the state-subsidized studio system that had long overlooked film's box-office performance.

A Centralized Studio System

The Chinese film industry was nationalized in 1953 under the direct guidance of Soviet film experts, following the Soviet-style command economy model from the mid-1950s to the late 1980s.[26] Under such an economic system, production investment was made in response to commands from planners rather than in response to market demand. Consequently, "control" by the state became the key in allocating production resources. Manifested in the film industry was the management of a nationalized studio system dictated by the central government's political agenda. The state-owned and state-subsidized production and the studios produced ideologically motivated films according to the state's production target. The function of such film production was to disseminate Communist ideology and to ensure the party's political control. In practice, the distribution of production resources and quotas, film licensing, film distribution and exhibition, and film export were all planned annually according to the party's propaganda target. The Ministry of Culture's Film Bureau was put in charge of such planning. The bureau was also responsible for regulating film studios and related institutions. Quotas were allocated to studios, the biggest ones include Changchun, Beijing, Shanghai, and August First. Production funding and targets were allocated to each studio according to the studio's production capacity and specialties.[27] Production targets referred not only to the number of films but also to the types of films being produced. Each studio maintained its full staff of actors, writers, directors, cinematographers, and technicians. The studios tended to be overstaffed, reflecting the general pattern of Chinese state-controlled enterprises.[28] Studios were generally well-equipped with 35 mm equipment. Larger studios even built their own exterior back lot generic street, the Chinese equivalent of the frontier towns in American westerns.

A system for the licensing of approved films was also promulgated in the mid-1950s. Both domestic and imported films required approval for exhibition by the Film Bureau. The bureau's Film Exhibition Management Department oversaw film distribution and exhibition. A national distribution network was established in 1950 in the form of regional film management companies in the northeast, Beijing and Shanghai, and in the south-central, southwest, and northwest military administrative regions.[29] The National Film Management Company was formed in Beijing in February 1951 to take over the duties of film distribution from the Film Bureau's distribution section. Acting as a central distribution agency overseeing film distribution at a national level, the company purchased complete film prints from studios at a rate based more on the length than on the production quality and market value of the prints. Consequently, the studios cared more about carrying out party propaganda duties than about their films' profitability. At the state level, local film bureaus established their own management organizations to control film distribution and exhibition. The central control over local activities was not always strong, and local exhibitors did take the liberty of altering the length of exhibition cycles according to the popularity of individual films. For instance, a few cinemas in Changsha managed to give the politically charged Soviet films short runs while granting entertainment-oriented domestic comedies longer runs.[30] The Shanghai Film Bureau allegedly sought to delay the reviewing of some profitable yet politically questionable films in order to grant such films an opportunity to make sufficient profits for the theaters and the studios.[31]

The nationalized studio system benefited the development of Chinese cinema from the mid-1950s to the early 1960s. It not only consolidated film technology and capital but also nourished film talent, providing a production environment free of financial constraints for the maturation of third generation filmmakers. Both the state and local governments supported mobile projection teams to bring films to long neglected places such as remote military bases, newly developed industrial areas, and impoverished rural areas. The government also subsidized film exhibition in various ethnic areas and remote mountain areas where many residents had never before encountered cinema. As a consequence, while city audiences actually might have decreased, the total film audience jumped from 47 million in 1949 to 752 million in 1953.[32] As many as one-third of the audiences were factory workers, farmers, and soldiers; the rest were students and relatively well-educated city dwellers.[33] The central government's protective film policy, though more out of political than economic concerns, kept Hollywood and West European imports at bay, keeping China's large film market exclusively for the Chinese film industry. As such, Chinese cinema witnessed a period of prosperity that lasted until the outbreak of the Cultural Revolution, which virtually collapsed film production. From 1966 to 1976, under the direct interference of Mao's wife Jiang Qing, only a handful of revolutionary films were produced, chiefly, eight model dramas (*yangbanxi*), filmed versions of eight Beijing operas with revolutionary themes.[34]

The centralized studio system resumed its function after the Cultural Revolution, with continued political control and financial subsidy from the state. The system remained intact until the mid-1980s when China's economic reform to reprise the market economy finally took off. The economic reform in the late 1970s focused on the reorientation of the central government's developmental strategy. The reorientation shifted the core development sector from heavy industry to light industry and agriculture, the bases for people's daily consumption.[35] As consumption became the new driving force for China's overall economic growth, the film industry responded by shifting its focal point from production to distribution. Recognizing film distribution and exhibition as the key to boosting film consumption, the state council approved a joint petition by the Administration of Culture and the Administration of Finance in August 1979 to allow the distribution and exhibition companies a greater profit share for future expansion. As a consequence, distribution companies were allowed to claim 80 percent of the box-office profit as an investment fee for theater renovations and expansions. In the next three years, the distribution companies invested more than 50 percent of their profit share on renovating old theaters and building new theaters as well as on updating screening equipment and recruiting more projectionists and other technicians.[36]

The profit-sharing relaxation was not extended to the production sector. The China Film Corporation (China Film, the successor of China Film Distribution and Exhibition Company) purchased original film prints from studios at a mandatory price of 900,000 yuan (US$112,500) per film, regardless of each film's individual market value. China Film provided an undiscriminating "contract" for the entire studio production at no operating costs, which worked to the studios' benefit by allowing them to sell unpopular films on the strength of the popular ones or even without the strength of the popular ones. Such a distribution system resembled the block-booking practice of Hollywood majors during the height of the studio era, except that, in the case of Chinese cinema, the studios did not need to exert any pressure to have their film distributed in a mixed package. In the 1980s, there were thirteen film studios that were entitled to produce feature films.[37] Based on production scale, their output ranged from two to sixteen films a year. In addition, some provincial-level studios previously confined to making newsreels and documentaries were venturing into producing feature films. Other film-related institutions also invested in film production. The mushrooming production ventures resulted in an increase in annual film outputs. In 1980, eighty-four features were produced, with theater attendance totaling 234 million. In 1984, the number of features produced climbed to 144, exceeding the expectations of the Film Bureau. The lack of serious competition from foreign films due to the restricted import policy and the limited entertainment options had together contributed to the popularity of domestic films.

Encouraged by the popularity of cinema and the growing wealth of the newly reformed distribution-exhibition sector, the studios lobbied for an extension of the profit-sharing policy to the production sector. The Administration of Culture issued a memorandum in 1980 requesting that China Film settle accounts with the studios according to the number of prints made for distribution rather than by paying a flat fee for original prints.[38] However, the new regulation continued to allow China Film to pay 9,000 yuan (US $1,125) per print for the first 110 copies, a number based on the average copies of each print made for the past decades. China Film must pay 99,000 yuan (US$12,375) per print only when the number of copies exceeded 110. The new accounting rule essentially gained each studio an extra 100,000 yuan (US$12,500) per year, not a sufficient amount to allow studios much commercial leeway and financial incentive to make marketable films. Still separated from the market, the studios continued to pay little attention to their films' box-office performance. While such an attitude would hurt the overall financial well-being of the industry in the long run, it did help the Fifth G's lofty cinematic exploration. It was during this optimistic period—when China's economic reform to reprise the market economy had not yet fully taken off, the central government had relaxed its political and ideological grip, and the project of Four Modernizations had led to the full-blown cinematic modernization movement—that the Chinese New Wave had a chance to flourish.[39]

CULTURAL HERITAGE, STYLISTIC PRINCIPLES, AND CHINESE REALISM OF THE NEW WAVE

Cultural Heritage

Though commonly identified for its formal innovation and its urge to transform Chinese cinema, the Fifth G did not begin with a clear articulation of a particular stylistic aspiration. The New Wave style is partly the product of critical discourses surrounding the Fifth G that helped it to define itself. The Fifth G's contingent self-positioning instead of a predefined cinematic vision made its early films a stylistic pastiche. It took stylistic cues, freely and somewhat randomly, from traditional Chinese visual arts and Western art/modernist films available to them at the time. New Wave can thus be seen as the product of its direct and indirect dialogues with cinemas of European and Japanese modernist masters and the masters of Chinese classical painting.

As suggested by Bordwell, art cinema narration takes its cue from literary modernism, which called for the aleatoric world of "objective" reality and the fleeting states that characterized "subjective" reality.[40] Such realities motivate a loosening of cause and effect, an episodic construction of the plot, and an enhancement of the film's symbolic dimension. As such, temporal manipulations in modernist/art cinema typically work on three interlocking procedural schemata: objective verisimilitude, subjective/expressive/psychological realism, and narrational commentary. The three principles at work result in modernist cinema's self-reflexivity, stylization, and a fragile plot structure. The cinematic techniques utilized to achieve objective verisimilitude are location shooting, long takes, and deep focus. Psychological realism is achieved through certain spatiotemporal "expressive" effects such as point of view shots, flash frames of a glimpsed or recalled event, flashbacks, slow motion, freeze-frames, and so on, that are expressive of character psychology. Narrational commentary are those moments in which the narrational act interrupts the transmission of story information and highlights its own role.[41] Stylistic devices frequently utilized to suggest such intrusive commentary include unusual angles and camera movement, unrealistic shift in lighting or setting, a disjunction on the sound track, and so forth. The utilization of such techniques resulted in modernist/art cinema's self-reflexivity, narrative openness and viewer's self-consciousness, and stylization as opposed to classical film's invisible narration, narrative closeness and viewers' relative passivity, and the subjugation of style to narration.[42]

Chinese New Wave selectively applied the techniques of modernist/art cinema. While the degree of appropriation in each individual film varied, the principles of art/modernist cinema contributed to Chinese New Wave's overall antinarrative approach and its pronounced mannerism. Just as the rise of French New Wave in the late 1950s and 1960s was the result of a negative response to the theatricality of the postwar French cinema, Chinese New Wave challenged Chinese cinema's own *"la tradition de la qualite,"* the shadowplay tradition. New Wave's antinarrative tendency is reflected through its plot fragmentation and minimization. It is not a coincidence that the New Wave's two signature films, *One and Eight* and *Yellow Earth*, were adaptations of poems rather than novels. The New Wave's emphasis on a minimalist acting style further distanced it from the melodramatic tradition of shadowplay and from the official-endorsed performing school of Constantin Stanislavski.

Corresponding to its antinarrative tendency is the New Wave's penchant for "parametric narration," the obsession with film form closely related to traditional Chinese landscape painting.[43] As I suggested earlier, the Chinese New Wave not only derives its stylistic cues from the heritage of world cinema but also from traditional Chinese visual arts, chiefly, the Southern School landscape painting and the Chinese New Year's folk painting. Conventions of Southern School landscape painting include multiple and parallel perspectives (as opposed to European Renaissance painting's usage of a fixed point of view with a corresponding vanishing point), shallow staging (vis-à-vis staging in depth in Renaissance painting), dwarfing of human figures by natural background, use of blank spaces, elastic framing, lack of chiaroscuro and sculptural shading, and emphasis on expressive, calligraphic contour lines.[44] In application, the horizon in Southern School landscape painting is always positioned at the very top of the frame, foregrounding the massive, dry, and flat land. By comparison, human figures are usually small, overwhelmed by the landscape. The shape of both the human figure and the landscape tends to be flat and impressionistic, as opposed to the illusion of three-dimension and verisimilitude in classical Western painting. The influence of Chinese New Year's prints came from its color system, the solid intense colors yellow, red, and black outlined in a flat and decorative fashion. As acknowledged by Zhang Yimou, the use of such colors and their decorative effect in *Yellow Earth* was derived from such a folk print tradition.[45] Both the unconventional framing and the patterned distribution of color contributed to New Wave's stylistic mannerism.

Though not influential to New Wave films, traditional Chinese painting's lack of interest in depth of the field or the illusion of depth of the field has its imprint in Zhang Yimou's post–New Wave films with their preference of shallow staging over staging in depth. Traditional Chinese painting has little concern for verisimilitude as in Renaissance painting, since it is more interested in evoking a feeling, an idea, or a state of mind than presenting reality in an objective fashion. As such, it is impressionistic and at times abstract. Such a tendency is also evident in Zhang's symbolic usage of certain props, colors, and staging.

The New Wave's appropriation of the techniques of classical Chinese painting is selective, avoiding certain techniques, chiefly, flat lighting, that were not conducive to its overall cinematic goal. Classical Chinese painting was largely indifferent to the chiaroscuro technique, which resulted in flatness in terms of both dimension and drama. To articulate space and to give a scene certain expressive quality, New Wave filmmakers, on the other hand, employed, extensively, chiaroscuro lighting to create volume and give drama to the scene. The illusion of shadow and sharp angles created by chiaroscuro lighting in the cell scenes in *One and Eight* and the cave scenes in *Yellow Earth* determined such scenes' dominant mood of anguish, contributing to the clarification, intensification, and interpretation of the scenes.

The impact of traditional Chinese painting is less apparent in *One and Eight* and Tian Zhuangzhuang's two films. While the cinematic immobility is reminiscent of classical Chinese painting, the decentered composition and incomplete framing in *One and Eight*, some of the shots even chopping off characters' half face or half nose, have more to do with the filmmakers' attempt to visualize the tortured minds of the prisoners than with their invocation of traditional Chinese painting.[46] As for Tian's films, cinematic motion is foregrounded over static framing, overshadowing the influence of any particular school of painting.

Stylistic Principles

Overall, stylistic mannerism and antinarrative tendency are evident, to a varying degree, in the New Wave's four signature films, *One and Eight*, *Yellow Earth*, *Horse Thief*, and *On the Hunting Ground*. Detailed textual analysis should help identify the New Wave style.

One and Eight. Set against the backdrop of the Sino–Japan War, *One and Eight* is a story about a wrongly accused Communist army officer, Wang Jing, who is chained with eight prisoners by a Communist army regiment and who demands and gains the freedom for the prisoners to join a fight against the Japanese. The film is concerned with both the valor of the wronged officer and the latent honor of the eight convicts. Its astonishing portrayal of the heroes at the margin and its refusal to romanticize the Communist army were aggressively out of step with the mainstream war film that often polarized good and evil and portrayed only the triumph of the Communists. The film's daring moral reflection on the meaning of being a Communist when deprived of legitimacy and credibility provoked the Film Bureau to ban its release. Promoting defeatism and valorizing the convicts were the reasons given to the filmmakers.[47]

The film's shocking effects on the film community came from its unapologetically grim images, the dark quality resulting from the filmmaker's patterned depiction of its rough-hewn characters and their harsh living conditions. Natural lighting was extensively utilized to create shadows and sharp contrasts evocative of the prisoners' highly confined psychological and physical living conditions. The dark atmosphere created by chiaroscuro lighting bore no resemblance to the mainstream Chinese war film that had traditionally fashioned flat lighting for more uplifting effects. Chiaroscuro lighting utilizing natural light went hand in hand with the film's setting, being, for the most part, in cells and darkened rooms with sometimes nothing but a few rays of sunlight coming through a few holes in the ceiling. The cinematographer, Zhang Yimou, shot most of such scenes on very fast film stock with full aperture. In a similar vein, many of the exteriors were chosen for their harsh and monochromatic landscape. The film's brutally grim and unsentimental shots were matched equally by the characters' suntanned faces, rough-hued bodies, and their brutal behavior and foul language. Dressed in dark or ocher-colored clothes, the actors were encouraged to sunbathe as much as possible to darken their skin in order to deliver realistic images of the prisoners. While the film's tonal consistency drew critical attention to its distinctive visual style, such a style was motivated less by the filmmakers' self-conscious mannerism than by the Bazinian realism. Striving for objective verisimilitude in its depiction of the lives of prisoners in the war dictated the film's deployment of certain stylistic parameters.[48]

The film's stylization focused more on acting (minimalist) and the use of color (dark) and lighting (natural) than on motion. Indeed, camera mobility was something the cinematographer avoided.[49] The emphasis on "still" was partly the result of the Fifth G's aversion to the excessive use of mobile devices and techniques in the fourth generation's exploration films. As such, still shots were emphasized over tracking shots and rack focus, and single settings over multiple ones.[50] The film worked with few exteriors and limited and highly controlled interiors, chiefly, prisoner cells and the castle where the final confrontation with the Japanese occurred. While the limited shift of setting resulted in many prolonged scenes, the spatially confined interior(s) restricted the options for blocking, both contributing

to the film's lack of vigorous cinematic motion. Ironically, the relative immobility of camera and actors created a stagelike quality characteristic of
shadowplay tradition that was supposed to be at odds with the more cinematic approach of the exploration films. The film's slow pace and its lack
of interest in romance further bore the signature marks of socialist realist
film that emphasized simple casual structure and thorough deliberation so
as to effectively convey one major theme. Its pronounced theatricality and
one-dimensional narrative make *One and Eight* more classical than radical
in its style.

Yellow Earth. This film, the New Wave's second feature, took a more
radical step in breaking away from Chinese cinema's shadowplay and socialist realist tradition. It tells a story about a Communist official's aborted
effort to "enlighten" the peasants in an isolated mountain area. The Communist official, Gu Qing, was sent to a poor mountain area by the Communist army to collect folklore during the war against the Japanese. Gu's
attempt to inject revolutionary thoughts into the minds of the local peasants was largely unsuccessful yet his presence made an impact on the
daughter, Cuiqiao, of his host family. Upon Gu's departure, Cuiqiao em-
barked on a suicidal mission sailing down the Yellow River to escape an
arranged marriage and to seek a new life. Cuiqiao's younger brother, Hanhan, helplessly watched her boat disappearing down the river. In featuring the impoverished local peasants who were resistant to change and the
frustrated Communist official who was taken aback by the degree of
poverty and resistance and who retreated to the army base, the film's narrative deconstructs the myth that the Communist ideology easily won the
hearts of the rural dwellers in China's hinterland.

Stylistically, *Yellow Earth* minimized dialogue and cinematic motion to
capture the static and reticent lifestyle of the northwestern mountain
dwellers. Restricted blocking is emphasized over free and excessive motion. Throughout the film, still images decisively outnumbered mobile
ones. The still shots exposed the detailed texture of yellow earth and its inhabitants' stagnant postures and rigid, coarse faces. A handheld camera
was used only in the waist-drum–dance and rain-prayer sequences to create the rough, unstable dancing sequence. The variations of camera angles
and distances were restricted to a minimum, as were the characters' facial
expressions and postures. There were few interiors, mostly the cave where
Gu's host family lived. The cave scenes were all shot from the same angle,
with the same distance, simulating the caves' confined space and poor visibility. Such a cinematic austerity strove to capture, realistically, the harsh
lives of the mountain dwellers. Cinematic immobility in *Yellow Earth* is motivated by both realism and symbolism. It captures the plain and static
image of the flat yellow plateau in its natural existence while simultaneously creating a monotonous atmosphere evocative of the deadweight of
poverty and history and the difficulty of change. Even when the camera

and characters were mobilized, the movements were deliberately slow and monotonous. Human figures were never allowed to enter the frame from left or right only through fade in and fade out, or simply from behind the mountain to suggest the close tie between the land and its inhabitants.[51]

Closely related to its symbolism is *Yellow Earth*'s antitheatrical tendency. As suggested by the director, the film did not attempt to tell a self-contained story from beginning to end.[52] Instead, it served to reflect, diachronically, the nation's long and difficult history. On the surface, the film tells a mainstream propaganda story about a peasant girl's attempted escape, under the influence of a Communist army officer, from an arranged marriage. Yet the film's contemplation on the ignorance and backwardness of Chinese peasants and their strength and potential rejuvenation clearly overtakes the narration of a particular story at a particular time and place. As its title suggests, the film's central character at times becomes the yellow earth plateau—the yellow earth carved mercilessly by nature is a virgin land that has nurtured and at the same time eroded the spirit of its inhabitants. The somewhat detached folk music, diegetic and nondiegetic, while suggestive of the harsh lives of the mountain dwellers, adds to the film's pensive tone. In terms of the "story" at hand, the film proceeded episodically from Cuiqiao's marriage and misfortune to the arrival of Gu and to Cuiqiao's refusal to accept the arranged marriage, and finally to Cuiqiao's escape. The four episodes had no direct causal-effect link. The film ended with Cuiqiao sailing off on the Yellow River, leaving the fate of her escape hanging in the air. Such a narrative irresolution further defied the mandatory narrative closure of a classical cinema.

The "plot" in *Yellow Earth* was minimized and fragmented further by its juxtaposition of unrelated images. Time and space are neither continuous nor coherent, free of plot constraints, at times interrupting the plot. Cuiqiao's heart-wrenching farewell to her brother was preceded by the upbeat waist-drum–dance scene in the liberated area thousands of miles away. The two sequences had no direct temporal and spatial link. Their juxtaposition is motivated by the idea-associative montage based on Lev Kuleshov's principle. Here the minimization and fragmentation of cause and effect is accompanied by the enhancement of the film's symbolic dimension through the intervention of a narrational authority. The two most talked about sequences, the waist-drum–dance sequence and the rain-prayer sequence, had no apparent temporal and spatial relation to the story. These were motivated by the filmmaker's desire to reflect on Chinese culture at large. As suggested by Chen Kaige and Zhang Yimou, the waist-drum–dance scene symbolized the positive energy of the enlightened masses in control of their own fate. Conversely, the rain-prayer scene epitomized the confused energy of the benighted village people with the mixture of their belief in a traditional idea of God's will and their struggle against fate.[53] The location of the waist-drum–dance sequence was deliberately unspecified in the film's original version in an effort to reflect on the origin and essence of traditional Chinese culture. The attempted abstraction of time and space was undone in a revised version with a subtitle clarifying the location being in Communist-controlled Yanan.

Another telling moment was the wedding scene at the beginning of the film involving a peasant girl who had no relationship with any of the other characters and did not appear again in the film. The scene was relevant, only symbolically, to Cuiqiao's own wedding. Stylistically, the two wedding sequences were executed from the same angle, with the same distance and same numbers of shots. In Cuiqiao's wedding, a long shot reveals a bridal parade zigzagging through the barren hillsides, beating drums and blowing trumpets, and all thirteen shots of the scene duplicate precisely the earlier wedding scene that opens the film. Such a patterned repetition of certain scenes and images was consistent throughout the film. The images of Cuiqiao getting water from the Yellow River, shot with a narrow-angle lens to suggest the closeness between Chuiqiao and the river, is repeated four times from the same angle and from the same distance. The intercut between the rain-prayer scene (a total of six shots) and Hanhan's running away from the praying crowd toward Gu is notably repeated, crosscutting three times with Gu's tiny image approaching from the horizon. Such patterned repetitions not only create a rhythm for the film but also insinuate the century-long unchanged rhythms of the peasants' daily routines. To paraphrase Zhang Yimou, the repetition of the same shot not only symbolizes the slow and monotonous daily drill of peasants' lives but also China's prolonged harsh history.[54]

Zhang's stylization was extended to his patterned distribution of the colors yellow, black, and red. Such color usage is influenced by Chinese New Year's folk print, which preferred solid intense colors outlined in a simple, flat, and decorative fashion. During the two wedding scenes, against the yellow (earth) background are the receiving crowds in black and the bride's wedding sedan in red. During the waist-drum–dance scene, against the same yellow background, are the drummers' black costumes and the drums laced in red silk. In the farewell scene when Cuiqiao sees Gu off, the image of Cuiqiao in red is against the yellow earth. In these sequences, color is used decoratively, with sharp contrast for visual stimulation. Zhang's penchant for intense colors is further associated with the symbolism such colors entail. A tiny black or red image placed against the massive yellow background, while motivated by aesthetic concern, also conveys the feeling of hopelessness of the impoverished peasants against the vast yellow land and their simultaneous love of, and dependence on, this silent land. Traditionally, yellow symbolizes the roots of Chinese civilization, black the suffering of the nation, and red the hope of the nation. Color is also used for idea-associative montage. While the color red in the first wedding sequence carries more or less a celebratory tone, appearing in Cuiqiao's wedding, it evokes a rather lonely and hopeless feeling. Not directly juxtaposed together, the color red in the two scenes collides, communicating the complex inner relationship and interdependence between the two events.

Stylization in *Yellow Earth* also comes from the unusual framing achieved mostly through low-angle shots that inherited classical Chinese painting's Southern School tradition. In many shots in the film, mountain and rock fill four-fifths of the frame, and the sky is allowed just the strip at the top of the screen. Human figures in the frames are consequently overwhelmed by nature. The scene in which the father and the son, accompanied by the soldier, direct the bull to plow the land is framed in such an out-of-proportion way. In this scene, the land occupied most of the frame, leaving little room for the sky. And even smaller are the three human figures lining up and moving slowly behind the bull. In the waist-drum–dance sequence, the horizon is once again high and at times simply vanishes all together, foregrounding the massive plateau with relatively insignificant human crowds. As such, the earth and the river become the focus of the shots.[55] Human figures become accessories to a nature untamed. The dwarfing of human figures resulted in ample "blank" spaces in a frame. However, such "empty" shots contain as much energy as the shots with human figures. Earth, sky, or river with no trace of, and no contact with, human beings become the Object that occupied the space in *Yellow Earth*.[56] Fixed camera position and static shots in *Yellow Earth* further evoked the eternity and solemnity of primeval nature captured in the classical Chinese landscape painting.

Yellow Earth's silent juxtaposition of images of the sensuous landscapes and numb human faces and motionless human postures created thematic ambiguity unfamiliar to the majority of Chinese patrons who had grown accustomed to the ideological certainty of socialist realist film. The film was attacked by the populist film critics and authorities for being obscure and incomprehensible to the public. It was not until its triumph at the 1985 Hong Kong Film Festival that the film began to receive more friendly responses from the Chinese critics and authorities.

On the Hunting Ground and *Horse Thief.* Often addressed together, these two films by Tian Zhuangzhuang make a radical break from Chinese cinema's theatrical tradition, opting instead for the style of cinema verité. Both films have reduced plots to the minimum: They are de-emphasized to the extent that the two films can easily pass for documentaries. Hardly a sufficient story concept for a narrative film, *On the Hunting Ground* is about life in Mongolia. It contemplates the not always harmonious relationship between nature and its human inhabitants and relates how the ancient Mongolian legal system has been rejuvenated in modern times. Likewise, *Horse Thief* "reports" the Tibetan religious life and strives for authenticity in its reporting concerning the relationship between humanity and religion. Set in the primitive landscape of Tibet, *Horse Thief*'s dwells on the enigmatic religious rituals such as the sky burial and the ghost dance. What provides the "plot" for this film is the fragmented tracing of the fatal struggle for survival of a Tibetan horse thief who was ostracized by his tribe and exiled to the wild mountains.

Objective verisimilitude and narrational commentary are the organizing principles of both films. Realism is achieved through the casting of non-professionals, location shooting, and shooting in motion. Shooting in motion captures particularly well the mobile lifestyle of the nomadic Mongolians and the Tibetans. Cinematic motions in both films utilized all the principal motions, that is, the event motion in front of the camera, camera movement, and editing. Narrational intervention was achieved through scenes that dwelled on ethnic rituals and religious artifacts which bore no direct relationship to the plot and the characters. Such scenes explored connotative, symbolic linkages between sequences or episodes. For instance, the opening scene in *Horse Thief* of the "celestial burial" and the later scene of "sunning the Buddha" interrupt the transmission of story information and highlight the director's contemplation of the cultural meanings of the rituals and religion. As a result, the dramatic components of both films are fragmented and minimized yet their historical and cultural elements become coherent and apparent, which resulted in the categorization of such films as "ethnographic" or "anthropological." Lastly, both films have adopted ambiguous endings that acknowledge the narration as both powerful and humble, for, by leaving causes dangling and questions unanswered, it respects human life's complex and ambiguous nature.

Chinese Neorealism

All four signature New Wave films have utilized, to varying degrees, the principles of modernist/art cinema narration. From *One and Eight* to *Horse Thief*, there is a progression toward de-dramatizing. While *One and Eight* is the least concerned with breaking away from classical narration's causality, *Yellow Earth* consciously distanced itself from the theatrical tradition of classical cinema. Tian Zhuangzhuang's two cinema verité films are overtly antinarrative. Though his films seem to have worked toward a total abandonment of plot and conflict, the minimization of plot is motivated more by his desire to treat his subject as an anthropological text and to give the subject a naturalistic rendition than by his interest in foregrounding the artifice of filmmaking. In other words, his antinarrative approach is motivated generically and followed the principles of Bazinian realism rather than that of art cinema narration.

Overall, New Wave films go so far as to imitate Italian Neorealism by abolishing contrived plots, doing away with professional actors, and emphasizing location shootings. The term *neorealism* in Italian cinema originally referred to what was lacking in the reactionary conventions of the Italian cinema in the 1930s, and in this sense, New Wave might be more accurately defined as Chinese Neorealism. In its socialist humanist treatment of Chinese culture and history and its artisanal approach toward cinematic experimentation, the New Wave also came to resemble the French period style of the 1930s which influenced the arrival of Italian Neorealism. Characterized as "poetic realism" by George Sadoul, a blend of lyricism and realism of French cinema from 1934 to 1940 obtained its stylistic cue from Émile Zola's literary naturalism that fashioned a naturalistic portrayal of human lives.[57] Indeed, location shooting and nonactor casting were extensively used by the influential poetic realist filmmaker Jean Renoir to make films as close as possible to a documentary.[58] Poetic realism also paid attention to film form, encouraging stylization. Furthermore, its fascination with realistic details of human life was coupled with its pensive reflection on human conditions reminiscent of socialist humanism. It is on the grounds of naturalism, stylization, and humanism that I suggest that Chinese New Wave might trace its generic roots further back to the French poetic realist cinema. Obviously lacking in the Chinese New Wave are elements of surreal fantasy and bizarre exaggeration of character typical of poetic realism. The absence of such elements can be attributed to the Chinese New Wave's lack of irony and self-reflexivity, or pure humor.

With its adherence to Bazinian realism, the Fifth G's break with classical style is not as radical as what the immediate critical response to such films suggests. While operating, to varying degrees, on art film's codified objective and subjective verisimilitude and overt narrational commentary, New Wave films do not reflect other conventions of European and American modernist cinemas, chiefly, irony and self-reflexivity. New Wave's cinematic reform focused on exploring an alternative approach toward story construction, and as such, the primacy of story is valued over the primacy of the construction of the story. In other words, the last thing the New Wave was willing to do was call attention to the filmmakers' own interventions, or to acknowledge the filmmakers' own presence, as in French New Wave and American modernist films such as *Breathless* (Jean-Luc Godard, 1959) and *Annie Hall* (Woody Allen, 1977). Such modernist elements would not appear in Chinese cinema until the mid-1990s with the arrival of Zhang Jianya and Feng Xiaogang's satirical comedies.[59] Furthermore, the characters in New Wave, while not heroic in Mao's revolutionary sense, are not goal-bereft and inscrutable, and the story it narrates, far from being the central boundary situation story typical of the institutionalized art cinema narration, is about the sufferings and the struggles of the ordinary Chinese, returning to the humanist tradition of early Chinese cinema. As such, New Wave seldom deploys certain spatiotemporal "expressive" effects such as point of view shots, flash frames of a glimpsed or recalled event, flashbacks, slow motion, and freeze-frames which strive to reflect characters' various psychological stages. In general, stories in New Wave are motivated by plot and external conflict rather than character psychology. Lastly, while conflict is generally de-dramatized and at times irreconcilable in New Wave, it is not ambiguous. The chain-gang prisoners' desire for freedom in *One and Eight* is unambiguous and is resolved in their fight against the Japanese. The peasant girl's yearning for a liberated life in *Yellow Earth* is unequivocal and is resolved by her attempted escape from her arranged marriage. While the horse thief's struggle for survival in *Horse Thief* is resolved in a more ambiguous fashion, his desire for a better and more religiously meaningful life is obvious.

While less radical in its appropriation of modernist cinematic techniques, what sets the Fifth G's four films apart from other Chinese films during the time is their subversion of classic Chinese film codes dictated by the shadowplay principles. Thematically, a cinema of ideological certainty and didacticism was replaced by a cinema of ambiguity and antipolitics. New Wave deliberately minimized dialogue and plot, seeking out, instead, subjects and perspectives that would induce ambiguity rather than ideological certainty. The typical revolutionary heroes/heroines and events in socialist realist films were replaced by marginal characters who were isolated by the mainstream. Characters such as Wang Jin and his inmate pals in *One and Eight*, the peasant girl in *Yellow Earth*, and the rough-hued herdsmen in *On the Hunting Ground* are all disenfranchised. Stylistically, the Fifth G's discontent with the cinematic status quo led it to a thorough subversion of anything conventional, including certain cinematic techniques newly utilized by the fourth generation. The cinematic immobility and the use of rough-hued character actors in *One and Eight* were a direct assault on the fourth generation's penchant for mobile cinematic techniques and its preference for handsome and well-groomed actors. In this sense, the New Wave is both a wave against the establishment of Chinese cinema and a wave for a modernist cinema.

FROM NEW WAVE TO POST–NEW WAVE

It was the fourth generation filmmakers who initiated Chinese cinema's first art wave by challenging, both in theory and in practice, Chinese cinema's shadowplay tradition and the socialist realist legacy. The art wave culminated in the mid-1980s with the arrival of the Fifth Generation New Wave films. As a group, the Fifth G pursued a distinctive cinematic style by assuming a marginal position vis-à-vis the mainstream Chinese cinema. It intentionally deviated, stylistically and thematically, from the socialist realist tradition. Thematically, New Wave strove to deconstruct the official narrative concerning Chinese history and religion. Stylistically, what became the New Wave was the assortment of antiheroes, minimal dialogue and plot, nonstar casting, long shots, location shooting, simple and sparse mise-en-scène, and harsh or remote settings. Stylistic variation among the filmmakers lay chiefly in the use of camera, with Chen and Zhang employing the static camera and Tian the fluid camera, both more or less motivated by the Bazinian realism. New Wave's stylistic eclecticism and pastiche can be traced back to its convoluted sources of influence, chiefly, certain stylistic principles of international art film and traditional Chinese landscape painting.

New Wave's challenge to the Chinese cinematic establishment was possible only after the Cultural Revolution when a relatively liberated political and cultural atmosphere prevailed. Indeed, what gave an initial impetus to the modernization of Chinese cinema was China's Four Modernizations, the economic reconstruction in agriculture, industry, military, and technology. Cinematic modernization was a cultural and ideological phenomenon rather than an economic one. Shielded by the state from real market competition, the movement was able to ignore the lukewarm reception of its experiment films by Chinese audiences.

Though the political economy of Chinese cinema during the period was conducive to the arrival of Chinese New Wave, the New Wave's stylistic deviation from the mainstream Chinese film was too radical for Chinese audiences at the time. As cited in an article by Yuan Wenshu, *Yellow Earth* had sold only thirty prints two years after its release, with an audience of 29,160,000, and a profit of 308,000 yuan (US$38,500). *One and Eight* also sold thirty prints, with an audience of 41,780,000 and a profit of 447,000 yuan (US$55,875). *Horse Thief* sold only two prints, both to China Film Corporation for reference but not for distribution. *On the Hunting Ground* fared slightly better in comparison, selling seven prints.[60] Since, in general, a typical feature in the mid-1980s needed to sell at least sixty to eighty prints to cover its production costs, all four New Wave films lost money. The lack of rapport between New Wave and Chinese audiences began to raise eyebrows among the culturally conservative critics and the fiscally conservative industrial practitioners by the late 1980s. Furthermore, the "open-door" policy endorsed by the Four Modernizations to import Western technology soon introduced to China's cultural market alternative entertainment options—discotheque, imported television programs, movies on video, and so forth—which drew a large audience away from movie theaters. From 1980 to 1983, urban film audience attendance dropped by two billion, and thus urban film release revenues fell at a rate of 25 million yuan (US$3,125,000) per year. A poll conducted by a fan club at Beijing University in February 1984 showed that filmgoing, once the number one recreational choice, had fallen to third place. Ma Qiang found that in 1984 only 26 billion tickets were sold, down 10 percent from 1980.[61] In the first quarter of 1985, the moviegoing audience was 30 percent smaller than during the same period in 1984. The result was a loss of revenue of 9.36 million yuan (US$1.17 million). Among the patrons who still preferred cinema, imported films—mostly kung fu films from Hong Kong, but including a few blockbusters from Hollywood (for example, *First Blood*; Ted Kotcheff, 1982)—became their favorite choices. As such, the Chinese film industry's rapid expansion from the late 1970s to the early 1980s came to a gradual stall. Together with the party's newly tightened ideological grip during the second half of the 1980s, New Wave's box-office crisis would contribute to its metamorphosis in the late 1980s, that is, its transition from art cinema to post–New Wave commercial entertainment cinema.

Chinese cinema's box-office decline in the face of the thriving popular culture raised serious concern among the industrial practitioners. Yuan Wenshu, the vice chairman of the China Film Association, urged filmmakers to make films appealing to ordinary people.[62] At the same time, China had been embarking on a prolonged economic reform since the late 1970s to change the Soviet-style command economy. The reform had resulted in the vigorous growth in agriculture and nonstate enterprises but had not yet changed the behavior of the state-run enterprises. The problems of low productivity and inefficiency in the state-run enterprises became apparent by the mid-1980s, which brought to light the financial crisis of the state-run film industry. As profitability became a crucial criterion for the state-dictated production target, studios could no longer ignore film's box-office performance. Meanwhile, Chinese society at large was undergoing a fundamental change. China, during the second half of the 1980s—was experiencing political unrest in the form of student demonstrations and ethnic minorities' independence demands, which resulted in the central government's tightened political and ideological control. As a result of the shifting political, economic, and cultural climate, the relatively harmonious relationship between New Wave filmmakers and the policy makers and critics came to a halt in the mid-1980s. The New Wave's lofty cinematic experimentation became the target of criticism, and its decline became imminent. A more detailed account of the political, cultural, and economic factors that have contributed to the transition of the Fifth G from New Wave to post–New Wave will be addressed in the next chapter.

NOTES

1. See Tony Rayns's discussion of new Chinese films in his book (coauthored with Chen Kaige) *King of Children and the New Chinese Cinema* (London: Faber and Faber, 1989).

2. See Shanghai Literature and Art Press, *The Anthology of Exploration Films* (Tanshuo diangying ji) (Shanghai: Literature and Art Press, 1986).

3. Ni Zhen, ed., *The Screen of Exploration* (Tanshuo de yingmu) (Beijing: China Film Press, 1994).

4. See Yao Xiaomeng, "Report on the Conference on 'New Chinese Cinema'" (Zhongguo xin dianying zuotan jiyao) *Dianying tongxun* (Film Bulletin) 12 (1988): 21–23. For more discussion see Zhang Xudong, *Chinese Modernism in the Era of Reforms* (Durham, N.C.: Duke University Press, 1997) 215–231.

5. See Zhou Jianyun and Wang Xichang's discussion in "An Introduction to Shadowplay" (Yingxi jianjie), in *Chinese Film Theory: An Anthology* (Zhongguo dianying lilu wenxuan), ed. Luo Yijun (Beijing: Culture and Art Press, 1992), 11–27.

6. Hou Jue, "On Writing for Shadowplay" (Yingxi chuangzhuo lun), in *Chinese Film Theory: An Anthology* (Zhongguo dianying lilu wenxuan), ed. Luo Yijun (Beijing: Culture and Art Press, 1992), 28–44. See also Zhong Dafeng, "Tracing the Origin of the Shadowplay Theory," *Dangdai dianying* (Contemporary Film) 4, no. 3. (1986): 36–42.

7. See Xia Yan, *Problems of Screenwriting* (Dianying juben chuangzhuo wenti) (Beijing: China Film Press, 1959).

8. Ibid.

9. See Zhong, "Tracing the Origin of the Shadowplay Theory."

10. See Hu Ke, "Contemporary Film Theory in China," *Dangdai dianying* 65, no. 2 (1995): 65–73.

11. Bai Jingshen, "Throwing Away the Walking Stick of Drama" (Diudiao xiju de guaizhang), in *A Selective Anthology of Chinese Film Theory*, ed. Luo Yijun (Beijing: China Cultural and Art Press, 1991), 3; and Zhang Nuanxing and Li Tuo, "On the Modernization of Cinematic Language," in *Chinese Film Theory: A Guide to the New Era*, ed. George Semsel, Xia Hong, and Hou Jianping (New York: Praeger, 1990), 10.

12. Zhong Dianfei, "A Letter to Ding Qiao," *Dianying tongxun* 11 (1980): 14–18.

13. Li Youzheng, "Structuralism and Film Aesthetics" (Jiegouzhuyi yu dianying meixue), *Dianying yishu yichong* (Digest of Film Translation) 3 (1980): 170–177.

14. See Cui Junyan, "Information on Modern Film Theory," *Shijie dianying* (World Cinema) 1–2 (1985): 78.

15. English translation from Zhang, *Chinese Modernism in the Era of Reforms*, 238.

16. See David Bordwell's elaboration on art film narration in his *Narration in Fiction Film* (Madison: University of Wisconsin, 1985).

17. Shao Mujun, "On *Yellow Earth*," *Guangming Daily*, 25 July 1985, p. 3.

18. Nick Browne, Introduction to *New Chinese Cinemas: Forms, Identities, Politics*, ed. Nick Browne, Paul Pickowicz, Vivian Sobchack, and Esther Yau (Cambridge: Cambridge University Press, 1994), 1–14.

19. The circulation, within the Chinese film community, of contemporary film theories epitomized by Metz's semiotics, Marxian–Althusserian critique of ideology, and Lacanian psychoanalysis will be discussed in Chapter 3.

20. She is also a professor of directing at the Beijing Film Academy.

21. Zhang, *Chinese Modernism in the Era of Reforms*.

22. See Li Xingye, "Harvests, Shortages, and Expectations: Thoughts on the Feature Movies Made in 1982," *Zhongguo dianying nianjian* (Yearbook of Chinese Cinema) (Beijing: China Film Press, 1984), 256–262.

23. Bordwell, *Narration in Fiction Film*.

24. Ibid., 310.

25. See Zhu Dake, "On the Drawbacks of Xie Jin Model" (Xie Jin dianying mu-oshi de quexian), *Wenhui bao* (Cultural Report), 18 July 1986, pp. 2–3. See also Li Jie, "Xiu Jin's Era Should End," *Wenhui bao*, 1 August 1986, p. 3.

26. While my account is mostly based on data from Chinese sources, Paul Clark's book, *Chinese Cinema: Culture and Politics since 1949* (Cambridge: Cambridge University Press, 1987) provides an English account of the process of nationalization.

27. For a more detailed account on the specialties of various studios, see George Semsel's "China," in *The Asian Film Industry*, ed. John A. Lent (London: Christopher Helm, 1990), 11–33.

28. Ibid.

29. Clark, *Chinese Cinema*, 35.

30. See *Wenyi bao* (Literature and Art Gazette) (February 1952): 37. Clark also mentioned the incident (*Chinese Cinema*, 36).

31. Ibid.

32. *Wenyi bao* 19–20 (1959): 59; and *Dazhong dianying* (Popular Film) 9 (1954): 8. See also Clark, *Chinese Cinema*, 36.

33. See *Dazhong dianying* (May 1995): 28–29. See also Clark, *Chinese Cinema*, 36.

34. For a more detailed account of the eight model dramas, see Kwok and M. C. Quiquemelle, "Chinese Cinema and Realism," in *Film and Politics in the Third World*, ed. John Downing (New York: Autonomedia, 1987).

35. See Dorothy J. Salinger, *From Lathes to Looms: China's Industrial Policy in Comparative Perspective, 1979–1982* (Stanford, Calif.: Stanford University Press, 1991).

36. According to Ni Zhen during our interview in Beijing in the summer of 1997, within the first three years of the reform, the distribution-exhibition sector accumulated almost 1 billion yuan (US$125 million) and invested roughly 500 million yuan (US$62.5 million) in expanding and strengthening the distribution-exhibition operations.

37. See Ma Qiang, "Chinese Film in the 1980s: Art and Industry," in *Cinema and Cultural Identity—Reflections on Films from Japan, India, and China*, ed. Wimal Dissanayake (New York: University Press of America, 1988), 165–173.

38. Ni Zhen, ed., *Reform and Chinese Cinema* (Gaige yu zhongguo dianying) (Beijing: China Film Press, 1994), 45–46.

39. By the mid-1980s, the transition from a command economy to a market economy was on the agenda in most manufacturing sectors. Yet since film continued to be considered part of the party's propaganda machinery rather than a state-run manufacturing enterprise, the industry's full-blown connection with a market economy would not occur until the late 1980s.

40. See Bordwell's discussion on art film narration in his *Narration in Fiction Film*.

41. Ibid., 209.

42. Thomas Schatz, *Old Hollywood/New Hollywood: Ritual, Art, and Industry* (Ann Arbor, Mich.: UMI Research Press, 1983), 217–242.

43. In reference to Noel Burch's term *parameters* for film techniques, Bordwell uses the term *parametric narration* to describe the style-centered film narration, or the so-called structuralist film which tends to foreground patterned cinematic techniques at the expense of other cinematic elements. See the chapter entitled "Parametric Narration" in Bordwell, *Narration in Fiction Film*.

44. For a more detailed discussion see Linda Ehrlich and David Desser, eds., *Cinematic Landscapes* (Austin: University of Texas, 1994).

45. See an interview with Zhang Yimou by Xiao Lu, "Zhang Yimou on the Cinematography of *Yellow Earth*," *Dianying yishu chankao zhiliao* (Film Art Reference) 15 (1984): 22.

46. Ibid.

47. Guangxi Film Studio, the studio that produced this film, was ordered to revise the film. The revised version was given fairly wide distribution in China but remained banned from export until 1987.

48. The emphasis on actors' rough image is particularly interesting, given the fact that the mainstream actors during the time were mostly clean-shaven and pale-faced. The "feminization" of male actors/characters in Chinese cinema had generated a popular outcry for "a muscular man" during the period. In its striving for Bazinian realism, *One and Eight* apparently resuscitated the muscularity of not only Chinese cinema but also Chinese men.

49. See Editorial Department of the Chinese Film Art Institution, ed. "The Cinematographers' Plan for *One and Eight*," in *On Zhang Yimou* (Beijing: China Film Press, 1994), 92–99.

50. Ibid.

51. Zhang Yimou, "Reflections on *Yellow Earth's* Cinematography," in *On Yellow Earth*, ed. Editorial Department of the Chinese Film Art Institution (Beijing: China Film Press, 1986), 285–298.

52. See Chen Kaige, "Reflections on Directing *Yellow Earth*," in *On Yellow Earth*, ed. Editorial Department of the Chinese Film Art Institution (Beijing: China Film Press, 1986), 264–284.

53. Xiao Lu, "Chen Kaige on Directing *Yellow Earth*," *Dianying yishu chankao zhiliao* 15 (1984): 11.

54. Xiao Lu, "Zhang Yimou on the Cinematography of *Yellow Earth*," *Dianying yishu chankao zhiliao* 15 (1984): 22.

55. Ibid.

56. Meng Yue, "On Chen Kaige" (Baolu de yuansheng shiji: Chen Kaige qianlun), *Dianying yishu* 4 (1990): 22.

57. George Sadoul, *The French Film* (London: Falcon, 1953).

58. Jean Renoir, *My Life and My Films*, trans. Norman Denny (New York: Atheneum, 1974).

59. I will address such films in Chapter 5.

60. Yuan Wenshu, "Film Tradition and Innovation," *Dianying yishu* 197, no. 6 (1987): 18–23.

61. Most of the statistics quoted here are from Ma, "Chinese Film in the 1980s."

62. Based on my interview with some of the Chinese film practitioners active during the time, Yuan Wenshu made such a pledge. Ding Qiao, the deputy minister of culture in charge of film production, while unwilling to endorse the term *crisis*, acknowledged that film was in danger of losing money. My interviews were conducted in Beijing in the summer of 1997.

3

Economic Reform and Populist Cinematic Revival

INTRODUCTION

This chapter focuses on the political economy and the culture of Chinese cinema from the mid-1980s to the mid-1990s by zeroing in on the key film reform measures and their concomitant, reform-oriented film discourses foregrounding a populist cinema. Film criticism responded positively to the industry's reform; and institutional reform actively sought critical opinions about concrete reform methods and pragmatic evaluation of various reform measures. The impact of both on Chinese cinema, chiefly, the marketization and privatization of the Chinese film industry and the surge of popular entertainment pictures, is discussed. Both local and global factors contributed to Chinese cinema's change of direction during the period. Locally, China's economic reform policies affected the state's cultural policies and subsequently its film policies, propelling a series of reform measures aimed at the decentralization of the state-run film industry. The reform measures affected the general trend in film production and criticism during the period. Globally, the popularity of Hollywood pictures (re)defined what counted as quality films for international spectators, incorporating Chinese audiences into the monological Hollywood audience. As such, the industrial structure and market practice institutionalized by Hollywood became the new model for the Chinese film industry.

CHINESE CINEMA IN THE ERA OF MARKETIZATION

China's economic reform since the second half of the 1980s has played a significant role in determining the parameters and possibilities of Chinese cinema as both an economically viable and a culturally motivated institution. Economic reform prior to the mid-1980s was a combination of success and failure. While considerable accomplishments were achieved in fostering the vigorous growth of the nonstate sector, the reform did not qualitatively change the behavior of state-run enterprises, which triggered a reassessment of the reform policy in terms of its direction and ultimate objective. The conservative policy makers advocated the continuing primacy of planning over key sectors of the economy while letting market forces play an increased role for less important sectors and smaller enterprises. The more radical policy makers rejected the separation of economy into different sectors with different operating mechanisms, advocating, instead, the impartial application of economic parameters to all enterprises. Such a reform would ultimately abolish mandatory planning. The then-Premier Zhao Zhiyang put together a compromised reform plan that combined elements from the two competing approaches. In practice, however, Zhao's seemingly impartial reform program was carried out in a way that radically shifted the balance of the economy toward the market sphere.[1] The key reform measures proposed by Zhao involved price reform and enterprise reform, with the former calling for a shift to full market prices and the latter challenging the inefficient bureaucratic economy. Both reform measures would profoundly affect the restructuring of the Chinese film industry. Subsequently, the period between 1984 and 1988 emerged as a productive phase for China's overall economic reform and the film industry's institutional reform.[2]

The economic reform, with its emphasis on the financial accountability of individual production units, shook the very foundation of Chinese cinema. The problems of low productivity and inefficiency in the state-run enterprises became apparent by the mid-1980s, which brought to light the financial crisis of the state-run film industry. Film reform became imperative. During the early stage of reform, Chinese cinema witnessed distressing declines in both its audience attendance and its flow of capital and creative forces. In 1984, only 26 billion tickets were sold, down 10 percent from 1980.[3] In the first quarter of 1985, the moviegoing audience was 30 percent smaller than during the same period the previous year. The result was a loss of revenue of 9.36 million yuan (US$1.17 million). All three sectors within the industry—production, distribution, and exhibition—lost money. Chinese cinema's economic crisis propelled the state to implement a series of reform measures in the hopes of resuscitating the industry.

Growing Out of a Planned Economy: Film Reform in the Second Half of the 1980s

Film reform began with distribution reform to grant local distributors more economic autonomy and, hence, financial responsibility. Under the planned economy, the state-controlled China Film Corporation (CFC) acted as the central distributor, responsible not only for distributing films to the theaters but also for paying fees to the studios, footing the bill for promotion and extra film prints. Local distributors functioned only as middlemen who passed along film prints to the theaters and turned over the box-office revenue to the CFC. With no financial responsibility save the right to share profits with the CFC, local distributors often requested more prints from the CFC to enable multiple screenings in order to gain more profit. To disperse the CFC's financial burden, the state revised its distribution policy in 1984, requiring local distributors to pay the costs for the extra prints. In allowing distributors and exhibitors a bigger share of the profits and at the same time granting them more financial responsibility, distribution–exhibition reform in the first half of the 1980s focused on encouraging the financial autonomy of local distributors and exhibitors.

Incited by the profit-sharing potential, further distribution reform was demanded by the production sector to allow studios to share profits. Under the old system, studios sold film prints outright to the CFC for a flat fee. As such, studios' profits depended on the volume of prints ordered by the CFC. Such a system was contested by the studios in the mid-1980s. The first two to challenge this system were Shanghai Film Studio and Xian Film Studio, who, in 1986, negotiated with the CFC to stop selling prints outright and to instead share in box-office receipts. Unfortunately, films from both studios failed in making real profits. The venerable Shanghai Film Studio suddenly found its feature films out of sync with audiences' shifting cinematic tastes. Xian Film Studio did produce a number of big hits yet discovered later on that the revenue from box-office returns came much more slowly than the profits from selling the prints to the CFC.

Overall, film reform during the first half of the 1980s was haphazard, lacking a coherent, long-term strategy. It reacted, passively and partially, to China's overall economic reform. In focusing solely on the distribution–exhibition sector, issues concerning production financing and production efficiency were left unaddressed. In January 1985, the China Film Bureau held a professional conference to assess the outcome of early reform measures and to hash out a more complex reform package. The goal was to revive the industry through marketization. Decentralization, price reform, and enterprise reform became the key measures. Decentralization would restrict state intervention in the film industry's microeconomic operation. Price reform would relax the planned, single-price system to allow ticket prices to adjust according to each individual film's market value. Enterprise reform would focus on streamlining the production process and granting individual production units sufficient managerial autonomy and financial incentive to increase productivity and to ultimately encourage studios to produce films with market value.

In January 1986, a structural overhaul at the state level put the Film Bureau, previously under the control of the Ministry of Culture, under the leadership of the Ministry of Radio, Film, and Television (MRFT). The restructuring attempted to consolidate and efficiently coordinate the three major sectors of China's audiovisual industry. However, the state-level institutional restructuring was not carried out at a provincial level. Power struggles and other bureaucratic bickering at the local level prevented the transition of the local Film Bureaus from the control of the local Culture Departments to the local Radio and Television Departments, creating many organizational and managerial glitches in the distribution–exhibition sector. By the end of the year, the organizational confusion, coupled with the continuing shrinkage of the domestic film market, resulted in the loss of revenue for one-third of China's distribution companies. Many distribution companies were forced to branch out, seeking compensation from alternative commercial ventures. The nationalized studios under the direct control of the central government were relatively immune from such managerial chaos.

In 1987, both the studios and the local distribution companies demanded further autonomy from the CFC in terms of overall production planning and film distribution. In their mutual attempt to dismantle the CFC's monopoly, the studios and the distribution–exhibition companies courted each other, agreeing to collaborate in film distribution. Proposals were made to allow studios to cultivate their own production/distribution/exhibition network and to grant local distribution companies the autonomy of purchasing film prints of their own selection. The proposals were deemed too radical at the time and were rejected out of hand. The achievement of the industry's own reform initiatives came down to the limited price and profit-sharing relaxation. That same year the MRFT issued "Document 975" to dismantle the mandatory price limits at both the high and low ends and to allow studios to share box-office profits with the distributors. In 1988, the symposium "Strategic Planning for the Film Industry" decided to further relax price controls on film exhibition, allowing a limited hike in ticket prices at some upscale film theaters in big urban centers. While most of the reform measures were abandoned by the end of the 1980s, price reform prevailed, raising the price tag for purchasing film prints from 9,000 yuan (US$1,125) per print in 1980 to 10,500 yuan (US$1,312.50) per print in 1989. However, instead of connecting a film's price with its market value, the price adjustment in 1989 retreated to the centralized mandatory system, contradicting the overall reform goal of marketization.

Film reform in the 1980s focused mostly on the distribution–exhibition sector, granting the distributors–exhibitors a better share of the profits and more managerial autonomy. What was left untouched by the reform in the 1980s was the mandatory block booking system that gave economic incentives to neither studios nor distributors and exhibitors. Furthermore, it created no synergy between studios and distributors–exhibitors. Since the number of prints being circulated directly affected revenues for studios, distribution companies, and theaters conflict existed between the studios who were eager to sell more prints regardless of their films' market value and the distributors–exhibitors who wanted to be more selective in their purchasing. Though in the short run, the block booking system played to the studios' advantage, it ultimately left studios with neither the motivation nor the ability to make marketable films. The one-sided reform focusing on distribution–exhibition in the 1980s reflected the policy makers' unwillingness to come to terms with the inefficient and unproductive state-run studio system, which was long out of touch with the market. Apprehensive of, as well as resistant to, a market economy, the Chinese film industry became one of the most conservative state-run enterprises in China by the late 1980s.

Chinese cinema's reluctant reform, dancing between a planned economy and a market economy, was characteristic of China's overall social and economic reform colored by the political battle between the conservatives and the reformists at the top. Premier Zhao's reform policy, combining both the planned economy and the market, proved to be problematic by the end of the decade. China experienced accelerating inflation through the early months of 1988, which led to widespread incidents of panic buying during the summer of 1988. For a few months in the summer of 1988, inflation spiraled up to annual rates approaching 50 percent. With confidence in economic policy crumbling, Zhao was pushed aside and hard-liners led by Li Peng assumed direct management of the economy. The economic downturn, together with the stalling of reforms, the emergence of an unpopular leadership, and pervasive corruption, intensified the grassroots political discontent that eventually led to the Tiananmen Square demonstration and crackdown. However, the Tiananmen crackdown in June 1989, while ending a period of gradual liberalization and inaugurating one of renewed political repression, did not mark a sustained shift in the economic arena to more conservative policies. The hard-liners initially attempted to roll back economic reforms by carrying out a program of re-control of the economy that would have reversed many of the achievements of the previous decade. But this program soon failed, and the 1989–1990 period consequently became the last time that a significant group in the Chinese leadership could plausibly argue that China needed a strengthening of the traditional planning apparatus.[4]

Toward a Market Economy: Reform in the Early 1990s

The failure of the hard-line program made it clear that there was no practical alternative to a market economy, and no coherent way to combine the market with remnants of the old planning system over the long run. By the late 1980s, a renewed search for practical reform measures was evident, and the momentum of reform accelerated through 1992. In

October 1992, the Fourteenth Party Congress declared that the objective of reform was a "socialist market economy." Socialist or not, it was the first time that the Chinese leadership had committed itself unambiguously to the transition to a market economy. The objective of reform was now shifting to dismantling the planned economy and creating a well-functioning market economy. On July 23, 1992, the State Council issued "Regulations on Transforming the Management Mechanism of State-Run Industrial Enterprises" that featured fourteen areas in which state-run enterprises were legally entitled to autonomy, including setting their own output prices, hiring and firing labor, and allocating investment finances and fixed capital.[5] The scope of planned prices for the most important commodities was reduced. Along with the consolidation of market prices, the government moved decisively to eliminate restrictions on private ownership and steadily create the conditions for a level playing field for all ownership. Consequently, the period 1992–1993 emerged as one of significant reform that was marked by further reform of the state-run enterprises, ownership reform, and rapid progress toward market prices, all three aiming at a thorough decentralization and removing interference from governments at all levels.

The newly energized economic reform propelled a thorough structural overhaul in the film industry in the early 1990s. By furthering distribution reform and finally pushing production reform into the forefront in the mid-1990s, film reform in the 1990s reflected the general trend of in-depth state-run enterprise reform, ownership reform, and marketization. The goal of distribution reform in the 1990s was even more clear than in the 1980s. It was to eliminate the multilayered distribution process under the old bureaucratic system to dredge the previously clogged distribution channel, and to encourage competition not only among the distributors–exhibitors but also among the studios. Distribution reform reached a new peak in 1993 when the MRFT issued "Document Three—Suggestions on the Deepening of Chinese Film Industries Institutional Reform" and a subsequent document ensuring the implementation of such suggestions.[6] Document Three was to carry out the state's new economic reform policy by steering film production, distribution, and exhibition toward operating under a market economy. It practically acknowledged film's economic function, endorsing a cinematic practice not necessarily in alignment with film's pedagogical function. In my interview in the summer of 1997 with Gao Jun, a manager at the Beijing Film Distribution Company, Gao attributed much of the reform progress up until 1997 to Document Three and its subsequent follow-up document. The supplemental document directly connected print prices and ticket prices with the market, decisively dismantling China Film's distribution monopoly. It also proposed measures for production reform, allowing studios to negotiate directly with local distributors on profit sharing and multiple-distribution methods. The same year, a film exchange market was established in Beijing as a permanent location for an annual production–distribution conference to simplify the distribution process by bringing together, face to face, the producers and the distributors. The exchange market, in essence, functioned as a film festival to pretest films' market value.

Continued reform of distribution eventually brought to the forefront the studios' ongoing financial trouble. The financial trouble of the state-run studios was apparent by the late 1980s. In 1989, 30 percent of the state-run studios, 23 percent of the provincial-level distribution companies, and 24 percent of the provincial theaters were losing money.[7] By the end of the year, Shanghai Film Studio was 20 million yuan (US$2.5 million) in debt, Xian Film Studio was 20 million yuan (US$2.5 million) in debt, Beijing Film Studio was 10 million yuan (US$1.25 million) in debt, and Changchun Film Studio was 30 million yuan (US$3.75 million) in debt. Studios coped with financial difficulty by producing mainly low-budget entertainment films. The consecutive decline of box-office returns since 1984 was reversed temporarily in 1991, with returns climbing back to 2,360 million yuan (US$295 million). Yet the increased box-office returns did not bring studios a boost in profits. The total revenue for all sixteen studios added up to only 179 million yuan (US$22.4 million), of which the profits were 56 million yuan (US$7 million). After the 35 million yuan (US$4.4 million) tax payment and the 8.4 million yuan (US$1.05 million) studio overhead payment, the amount left for production investment for 1992 was a slim 12.6 million yuan (US$1.57 million), enough to produce only ten small- to middle-scale feature films at an average of 1.26 million yuan (US$157,000) per picture. Yet according to the annual production target set by the state, the sixteen state-run studios were to produce a total of 120 features in 1992, which meant that another 150 million yuan (US$19 million) had to be invested from somewhere in order to meet the minimal production target.

The shortage of production capital not only affected film quantity but also quality, since any single production had to be operated at the lowest budget possible. Consequently, the most expensive production in 1992 cost only 1.5 million yuan (US$187,500) and the least expensive one 660,000 yuan (US$82,500). Although the government paid for the production of the most expensive propaganda films, which helped to alleviate the studios' financial burden since such films were part of the 120-film production target, the vicious circle of low investment and low return seriously hampered the long-term development of film production. Film production retreated to coproduction by 1993, with studios merely collecting licensing fees from overseas producers. In comparison with 1992, film exhibition in 1993 for domestic pictures dropped 50 percent, audiences dropped 60 percent, box-office returns dropped 40 percent, and distribution income dropped 40 percent. Nine out of the ten best box-office performers were coproductions, mostly with production companies from Taiwan and Hong Kong.[8]

With the studios' financial crisis exposed, a consensus emerged: Chinese cinema's state-run studio system was long overdue for a structural overhaul. Studio reform would apply equally the enterprise reform measures carried out in other state-run industrial sectors. Under the principle of providing the enterprise with increased bargaining power and decreased interference from the government, enterprise reform took to its core labor reform and ownership reform. During the 1992–1993 period, striking progress was made in making the labor system more flexible by dismantling the permanent employment system and at the same time introducing a contractual labor system. The system of linking wages to performance and profits was adopted to cover a majority of state enterprise workers. The creation of local pension funds and unemployment insurance was encouraged by the state to ensure retirees, workers from bankrupted enterprises, and the unemployed a minimum level of financial security. Under these circumstances, labor optimization programs were implemented and large numbers of redundant workers were subsequently laid off. The optimization program was also apparent in the approach to enterprise failure. A significant number of state firms were shut down. On the front of ownership reform, although a large-scale privatization of state assets had not been undertaken in the early 1990s, the larger, more modern, and more profitable state firms were increasingly "commercialized," being converted into modern corporate firms of various types, including limited-liability joint-stock companies. The smaller and less profitable state firms were allowed to be sold off by local governments. Consequently, some firms were restructured and converted rapidly to joint-stock corporations, with subsequent privatization as an option. The ability of state firms to take stakes in other firms, or create new subsidiaries, became an important part in the process by which state-owned enterprises struggled to free themselves from bureaucratic control. Several hundred "enterprise groups" were formed in an attempt to create a nucleus of large corporate groups like the Japanese *keiretsu* or Korean *chaebol*.

The same reform package was endorsed, partially, by the film industry. While the MRFT continued to maintain its control over film importation and the annual production target, individual studios implemented various reform measures, chiefly, some forms of institutional restructuring, private investment, horizontal integration, and international coproduction. Different studios applied such measures to various extents, according to what they saw as the most urgent internal problems.

In terms of institutional restructuring, Shanghai Film Studio concentrated first on dismantling the egalitarian remuneration system by dividing workers' paychecks into wages and bonuses and linking bonuses to the profitability of particular films. It then butchered the party-controlled *Nomenklatura* department, which assigned employees jobs not based on their talent but on their political background. It further discharged 15 percent of its administrative workers and encouraged its unused creative personnel to outsource their talents for financial and artistic gains. Changchun, the studio with the most severe overstaffing problem, did not focus on labor reform such as discharging the redundant labor force. It was concerned with possible labor disputes and the potentially harmful reaction of public opinion, rooted in the decades-old egalitarian system. Changchun's reform focused on managerial reform, chiefly, decentralizing the process of decision making. Considering bureaucracy of the bloated top-level management the major roadblock toward production efficiency and quality, it divided the studio into three autonomous production companies. The studio allocated an equal amount of capital to each company and equally divided the annual production target to each company. Each company, in turn, had to pay studio overhead at the rate of 25 percent of the budget for each individual film plus a 250,000 yuan (US$31,250) flat profit target regardless of the film's real box-office return.[9]

August First Studio (the Communist army film studio) also attempted a gradual transition from bureaucratic administration to a modern management system. Its contractual approach toward production was more fluid, since various creative groups were allowed to bid for each production. In other words, the studio did not arbitrarily allocate the production of films to certain creative units. It went so far as to dismantle its acting pool and contract with actors on a picture-by-picture basis. Xiaoxiang Film Studio changed its administration branch controlled by the party secretary into a business division responsible for its own financial operation, explicitly altering the branch function. It also downsized other creative branches to make the studio more productive. Beijing Film Studio divided its operation into thirteen autonomous subdivisions, independent of the studio's general managers' management control yet responsible for contributing to the studio a certain amount of revenue. It further released its acting talents' loyalty obligation to the studio and, hence, the studio's financial obligation to the talent, encouraging them to branch out and look for other means of income. Ermei Film Studio simply divided into two big production units, organizing film production around its two signature filmmakers Wang Jianxing and Han Shanping.[10] While putting the equipment and talent at their dispatch, both Wang and Han were responsible for their own production investment and a certain amount of fees to the studio.[11]

Overall, downsizing, internal restructuring, talent outsourcing, and linking bonuses with profits were the common measures the studios adopted. Experiments with horizontal expansion in the form of venturing into other audiovisual-related business were also undertaken. Some studios even went so far as to venture into alternative business such as restaurants and discotheques. The horizontal expansion, or the cultivation of a multiple-revenue system, was particularly effective in utilizing extra equipment, technology, talents, and sometimes even the exterior, back lot, or generic street temporarily not in use to produce profitable products.

The more cosmopolitan Shanghai Film Studio led the way in this regard. It ventured into the cosmetics business, using its existing talent from the makeup and costume department to design and supervise the production of brand name cosmetic products. It also produced VHS videos and made commercial spots for various clients. The more daring Shanghai Film Bureau ventured into the real estate business, renovating and expanding local cinemas and building commercial apartments. It further joined a business division under the Cultural Bureau of Haerbing, a city near Russia, and conducted border trading with the Russians. Tianshan Film Studio, located in the Ukraine-dominated Xingjiang, also conducted border trading with the Russians. Changchun Film Studio followed the Shanghai Film Bureau's suit, cultivating its own northeast-based real estate business. Pearl River Film Studio was able to keep the redundant workers under contract by assigning them to its seventeen nonfilm-related business subdivisions, which earned the studio a good name in a society still adherent to the permanent employment mentality. Beijing Film Studio's most successful business maneuver was the creation of its audiovisual department, which produced VHS and music cassettes. It also built an amusement park, a joint venture with a tourist company, with the latter providing investment capital and the studio providing its name and talent. It further ventured into animation and the software industry.

Overall, the cultivation of alternative revenues was the most successful in the film-related audiovisual sector, including making commercial spots. Due to lack of experience and overextension, the studios were less profitable in other areas such as the restaurant and hotel businesses. Extra revenues from alternative business ventures could rescue studios only when it was invested in film production. Shanghai Film Studio used profits from its audiovisual division to offset the budget shortage for feature films, which helped the studio meet the production target and further raise the morale among its employees.[12]

Xian Film Studio's reform package was the most elaborate, incorporating all the measures implemented by various other studios. It introduced a contractual unit-producer system which organized the operation of production around a single picture, a production unit, and allowed each producer sufficient autonomy and financial incentive to link film productions with market forces. In practice, the unit-producer structure on a picture-by-picture, contractual basis resembled the unit-producer system in classical Hollywood. The system emphasized efficiency of the worker in the production line and the financial responsibility of the producer, the manager of a production unit. Under this system, the producer assumed the de facto control of the management of preproduction and postproduction, replacing the director as the consummate financial czar. In some instances, an executive producer was attached to a production unit, functioning as the film's financier, or the representative financier, responsible for bringing in investment through private channels to make possible the production of feature films outside the interest of the government yet fitting the commercial or artistic agenda of the studio. The functional division of the producer and the director elevated the status of the producer, allowing the producer a lion's share of the profits, although, in practice, the producers were often intimidated by the more venerable and/or famous directors. Xian also downsized 20 percent of its administrative personnel and shrunk the studio's multiple divisions by merging and reshuffling. In turn, it created new subsidiaries, venturing into television production, a theme park, and other audiovisual-related businesses to offset the loss of revenue from film production. It also expanded into restaurants, tourism, and the investment consultant business. It further attempted to introduce a certain degree of private ownership, with primary ownership remaining with the state. The studio also divided salary into wages and bonuses, with wages accounting for 70 percent of the total income and the profit-linked bonuses 30 percent.[13]

The various reform measures, while helping to establish a market-oriented modern management system, did not solve the problem of lack of sufficient financing for film production. The sources of funding in the mid-1990s came from the state budget, overseas investments, and domestic investments from nonfilm sectors. The twenty-five state-level studios and production companies produced approximately 150 films a year, most of them state-funded, costing from 1 to 2 million yuan (US$125,000 to US$250,000) to produce. The state also set aside extra funding for the production of major propaganda films. From 1987 to 1991, six major propaganda films were produced with additional state funding totaling 10 million yuan (US$1.25 million). In the early 1990s, major propaganda films, what the Chinese film circles termed "Zhuxuanlu Dianying" (main-melody films or central message films), occupied up to 25 percent of total annual output, with 70 percent left for entertainment films and 5 percent for art films.[14] While the extra funding for propaganda films continued through the mid-1990s, the total number of films invested in by the state decreased sharply. In 1993, only 23 percent of the annual production investment came from the state budget. Studios coped with the problem by attracting investment from various private corporations who were interested in venturing into the film business. Since only the sixteen state-run studios were allowed to produce films and the distributors could only distribute studio films, an outside investor had to become attached to a studio in order to obtain the right to film production and distribution. The policy granted studios leverage in collecting a flat "management fee" of around 300,000 yuan (US$37,500) regardless of the film's profitability. If the film was profitable, studios would further bargain with the investors for a cut of the profits at the rate of 40 percent. Even though such production practice was usually termed "coproduction," in essence, the studios were "selling" production rights in the name of the management fee to wealthy investors. The investors typically borrowed the host studio's talent, equipment, and interior if necessary, which helped to pay overhead and the equipment maintenance fee. Films made in 1993 by Shanghai Film Studio were all coproductions, including joint investment and independent investment by outside investors. Other studios such as Beijing, Changchun, and Xiaoxiang also slated many such coproductions. The coproduction maneuver in the early to mid-1990s, while helping to alleviate the studios' financial problems, did not operate under the rule of a pure market economy. Rather, the studios seized the opportunity of a continued state monopoly over production and distribution rights and played the state's anti–free-market policy to their benefit.[15]

Coproduction was extended to international coproductions that used overseas' investment while employing domestic labor and facilities. International coproduction utilized studios' existing production capacity, helping to pay for the otherwise out-of-work talent and equipment. Since films of international coproduction were generally better received than the domestic coproductions by the audiences, it also created the potential for a large domestic box-office share (provided that such films would gain the approval from the always fickle Chinese censor).[16] Internationally coproduced films fared even better than foreign imports, including popular Hong Kong entertainment films. Encouraged by the popularity of the internationally coproduced films, studios welcomed any opportunity to collaborate with foreign investors and producers. Hence, the period 1992–1993 witnessed an international coproduction craze; many of the films were invested in by Hong Kong film companies who were eager to enter the huge mainland market. In 1992, the year when Chinese cinema was at its lowest ebb, the international coproductions were exceptionally active. To the overseas' investors and producers, the coproduction really came down to being able to take advantage of China's cheap labor and equipment. When a film was distributed overseas, the investors only gave the host studio a flat distribution fee. As such, while the practice of international coproduction helped keep the film production machinery running by providing employment opportunities to both the talent and the equipment during Chinese cinema's domestic crisis, and in some cases even contributed to domestic film productions by providing sufficient domestic box-office revenue, it did not help to promote Chinese cinema domestically.[17] In general, overseas investment, chiefly from Hong Kong and Taiwan, assisted the production of commercialized art films such as *Farewell My Concubine* (Chen Kaige, 1993) and *Raise the Red Lantern* (Zhang Yimou, 1991) and popular entertainment films. In an effort to expand their film's market share, the overseas investors began to venture into producing historical epics to appeal to China's more conservative rural audiences. Meanwhile, the domestic, nongovernment investment initially sponsored mostly genre films and cheap knockoffs of *Farewell My Concubine* and *Raise the Red Lantern* geared toward short-term profit. The domestic entrepreneurs soon adjusted their strategy, establishing film production companies aiming at long-term profit. Their investment became more selective, targeting filmmakers either with successful box-office records or with box-office potential. They cultivated both the art and the commercial markets by investing in experienced art and the commercial filmmakers as well as the promising sixth generation filmmakers.[18]

Film reform during the first half of the 1990s shook the very foundation of China's centralized studio system. Production reform brought to light the studios' inflated overhead and their low productivity and lack of creativity under a financially egalitarian and politically dictatorial environment. A series of policy amendments at the state-level hoped to grant more economic and creative autonomy to the studios. But the studios' problem ran deeper than what a few policy adjustments would be able to rectify. While the mandatory profit-sharing quota could be adjusted through tax reform and marketization at a macro level, the problems with a egalitarian system of remuneration and overstaffing could not be amended through a simple change of policy, since they cut deep into the complex labor relations, in particular, and human relations, in general. The problems of overstaffing, especially of administrative personnel, and the aging of creative talents and production equipment persisted. Meanwhile, the state continued to dictate production targets, refusing to relinquish control of film content. Films dealing with sensitive political subjects were sure to be banned. A young critic I interviewed in Beijing suggested that, while films of government and police corruption were main staples of Hollywood, a film about Chinese police or high-level government corruption would guarantee a ban.[19] As pointed out by Tian Zhuangzhuang, obtaining a politically safe script has become the top priority for Chinese filmmakers.[20] The limited subject options contributed to Chinese cinema's monotonous image. The film industry's structural problem during the period came down to the separation of, and the conflict between, the market-controlled distribution–exhibition and the centrally planned production. Production reform continued to lag behind the more aggressive marketization on the distribution–exhibition sectors.

Chinese Cinema and Chinese Television

While reform of vertical integration continued, a series of measures aimed at horizontal integration was carried out in the 1990s to upgrade the outdated notion of cinema which associated film exhibition mostly with movie theaters. Lack of horizontal integration prevented studios from aggressively seeking expansion into both the television and the home video markets for multiple distribution channels. While the studios' lack of control over distribution–exhibition was partially responsible for this oversight, their lack of a long-term strategy for making inroads into the television and the home video markets was also instrumental.

Chinese television began its early development in the late 1950s. The Soviet Union supplied most of the equipment and technical assistance. The development of Chinese television was interrupted first in the winter of 1960 when China broke off its relationship with the Soviet Union, which caused the Soviet Union to withdraw its economic and technological aid. Chinese television had its second setback during the Cultural Revolution when television broadcasting was partially suspended from 1966 to 1976. Chinese television resumed its full-scale operation in the late 1970s, but its popularity only began to take off in the mid-1980s. The early relationship between film and television was antagonistic, similar to that of Hollywood's major studios and U.S. network television in the 1950s. By ignoring, indeed looking down on, television in its infancy, the Chinese film industry paid a hefty price in missing the opportunity of having a stake in television's and home video's huge potential markets. Chinese television, on the other hand, quickly adopted a protective approach toward its own market, fending off film's belated inroad into television production and exhibition. The dual-track system of state-subsidized and advertiser-sponsored Chinese television put the television industry in an advantageous position in competing for audiences with the financially self-reliant film industry. Chinese television was able to purchase the right to broadcast a motion picture on television at a low price. As the commercialization of Chinese cultural industry made inroads into Chinese television, China Central Television (CCTV) was forced to increase the price they paid for the right to broadcast motion pictures, yet the increase was too small to be significant to the studios' production investments. Meanwhile, local stations were allowed to broadcast films purchased by other stations without paying royalties to the studios.

The lack of horizontal integration between film and television not only hurt the film industry but also resulted in a waste of existing studio production facilities and human resources, since the television and the video industries had to build their own production lots and cultivate their own talent pools.[21] Indeed, disdain toward producing television drama still prevailed among the big-name film directors. Teng Wenji, the venerable fourth generation director, lamented his own participation in making popular television dramas. In my interview with him in Beijing in the summer of 1997, Teng commented, somewhat sarcastically, that only a handful of directors were able to resist the financial temptation of making profitable television dramas. Only recently, in a speech to a group of film school students, Xie Jin praised Zhang Yimou for Zhang's refusal to make inroads into television drama.[22]

Policy makers were keenly aware of how home video and television had invigorated motion picture exhibition in Hollywood by enhancing the status of the theater in the distribution chain. The MRFT began to make an effort in the early 1990s to pursue such horizontal integration. In October 1993, the government-controlled CCTV, took over News Studio (NS), a state-controlled studio specializing in producing newsreels and documentaries. As a result, NS produced news for television for an extended audience. With the financial backing from CCTV, NS was able to produce feature-length documentaries for theatrical distribution. In April 1995, Science Studio (SS), a state-level studio specializing in producing films on new developments in science and technology, merged with CCTV. The merger brought to SS more production investment, expanding its audiences and production capacity. In January 1996, Shanghai Animation Studio (SAS) merged with Shanghai Television (ST). As a result, the demand for animation from the studio increased drastically. At the same time as the SAS and ST merger, CCTV launched its cinema channel, broadcasting films provided by the studios. During its best year, it brought in 600,000 yuan (US$75,000) for the film industry. In addition to bringing in extra revenue to the film studios, the cinema channel promoted cinema and exposed smaller films to a much wider audience. The cinema channel also served as an example of mutually beneficial collaboration, rather than competition, between the two industries. The cinema channel soon became the second most popular channel, reeling in substantial revenue for the film industry. Beginning in the summer of 1996, many provincial-level studios began to merge with local television stations to form film and television production centers. The mergers allowed studios to take as much as 100 million yuan (US$12.5 million) from television commercials. To cultivate various investment resources, the MRFT relaxed its film licensing in January 1997, granting provincial-level television stations and film distribution and exhibition companies the right to produce feature films. In December 1997, the state permitted the establishment of three video compact disc production lines, effectively linking film with the television, video, and music industries. The same year China Film Corporation and China Music Video Corporation launched a joint venture, Huayun Laser Disc Ltd., to put feature films on laser discs for home viewing.[23] Reform initiatives on horizontal integration worked to the film industry's benefit, ensuring a guaranteed outlet for the studios' feature films. Yet the studios continued to lag behind in feature production.

Production reform in the early 1990s did not result in pictures with better box-office performance. Chinese cinema continued to lose audiences on the theatrical front. Consequently, the overall revenues remained slim and the production funding remained meager. In the hope that attracting audiences back to the movie theaters would pave the way for the recovery of Chinese cinema, the MRFT issued yet another distribution–exhibition-centered reform measure in early 1994. The groundbreaking reform measure granted an annual importation of ten international blockbusters, most of them big-budget Hollywood films. By (re)introducing Hollywood to the Chinese market, this measure would profoundly shape the course of Chinese cinema in the second half of the 1990s.

Hollywood Reacquainted

The MRFT loosely defined the criteria for imports as reflecting up-to-date global cultural achievement and representing excellence of cinematic art and technique. The cultural achievements and artistic and technological excellency were apparently measured by either the target films' budget scale or star power or their box-office returns. Economics rather than ideology played a significant role in selecting film imports. As a result, since 1995, Hollywood's star-studded, big-budget, and high-tech blockbusters such as *Natural Born Killers* (Oliver Stone, 1995), *Broken Arrow* (John Woo, 1995), *Twister* (Jan De Bont, 1997), *Toy Story* (John Lasseter, 1995), *True Lies* (James Cameron, 1994), *Waterworld* (Kevin Reynolds, 1995), *The Bridges of Madison County* (Clint Eastwood, 1995), *Jumanji* (Joe Johnston, 1995) have entered the Chinese market. The imports generated huge box-office revenues, totaling an average of 70–80 percent of all the box-office returns in 1995. One direct impact of the ten big imports was the restoration of Chinese audiences' theatergoing habit. Going to the movies once again became one of the leading entertainment choices among the Chinese public, which, of course, benefited Chinese cinema. The returning Chinese audiences unavoidably noticed domestic pictures, discovering afresh some of China's own big-budget and/or high-tech entertainment pictures, what the Chinese called the "domestic big pictures." Such films include those of international coproductions in which the majority of creative forces are domestically based. The domestic big pictures all became top domestic blockbusters for 1995.[24] *Red Cherry's* (Ye Ying, 1995) box-office return even topped the big imports.[25] As a consequence, Chinese cinema witnessed a quick recovery in the mid-1990s. The total box-office return in 1995 witnessed a 15 percent increase from that of 1994.[26] With the popularity of ten big imports and the subsequent ten big domestic pictures, 1995 became "the year of cinema."[27]

Chinese critics attributed Chinese cinema's renewed popularity to the film industry's belated "big picture consciousness/awareness," that is, the realization of the significance of sufficient production investment in making quality films.[28] Hollywood's high-cost production values became the standard measurement for quality films for both Chinese audiences and film practitioners. As counterparts to the ten big imports, the domestic big pictures imitated their foreign rivals, creating the big-budget mentality among Chinese filmmakers. In 1995, with a budget for a single production of over 10 million yuan (US$1.25 million), four films—*In the Heat of the Sun* (Jiang Wen, 1995), *The King of Lanling* (Hu Xuehua, 1998), *Red Cherry* (Ye Ying, 1995), and *Shanghai Triad* (Zhang Yimou, 1995)—set investment records in the history of Chinese cinema.[29] Another significant contribution of the ten big imports was the introduction to the Chinese film industry of the distribution method commonly practiced in the West which divided the profit as well as the loss among the producer, the distributor, and the exhibitor. Under such a distribution system, the producer was forced to directly face the market while the distributor and the exhibitor must make every effort to promote the films. The Chinese film industry, particularly film production and distribution involving private investment, began to experiment with this new distribution method in the mid-1990s.

The film industry's replication of Hollywood's blockbuster practice alone could not explain Chinese cinema's sudden recovery in the mid-1990s. What also contributed to the recovery was a significant policy change at the beginning of 1995. The MRFT relaxed its production licensing policy in January 1995, extending the right to produce feature films from sixteen state-run studios to thirteen provincial-level studios. Furthermore, any investors outside the film industry who would cover 70 percent of the production cost were granted the right to coproduce with a studio. The MRFT also cosponsored a conference with the Film Bureau, gathering together studios and potential investors to encourage more investment in film production. Coupled with film's renewed popularity led by the big imports, the new policy attracted many private investors. Many of the years big domestic pictures were produced with the huge financial backing of the private sector.

Meanwhile, years of distribution–exhibition reform finally pushed Chinese distributors and exhibitors toward unconditionally adopting a Hollywood-style vertically integrated marketing and management system. Distributors initiated collaborations with studios, hoping to have a stake in film production. Studios directly reached out to exhibitors for the possibility of creating direct production–exhibition channels. Big theaters actively sought collaborations among themselves to establish theater chains. Vertical integration began with the establishment of distribution–exhibition networks that divided film distribution–exhibition into several geographic areas. Within each area, competition among local distributors–exhibitors in the form of various promotional packages was encouraged, further boosting films' public visibility. Film promotion actively exploited stars' on- and off-screen personae and cultivated specialty theaters, generating different crowds for different types of films. In terms of film type, the ten domestic hits of 1995 came from a diversified range, from big-budget war epics that rode the popularity of their Hollywood counterpart, for example,

Schindler's List (Steven Spielberg, 1993), to star vehicles, commercialized art films, and a sleeper dealing with contemporary social issues.

Thus, by the end of 1995, it seemed that the imports not only brought audiences back to the movie theaters but also contributed, by triggering policy changes and restoring the theatergoing habit, to the recovery of Chinese domestic film production. However, a closer examination revealed that the domestic box-office success mostly came from productions involving private investment. The majority of the state-run studios continued to fall behind in making marketable films. Two-thirds of the domestic films produced in 1995 were cheap knockoffs of Hollywood- and Hong Kong–style entertainment films. The majority of them were box-office turkeys made either by the financially ailing state-run studios or the profit-conscious private investor inexperienced in film production and distribution.

The proliferation of low-budget and low-production-value entertainment pictures not only failed to generate profits but also provoked the government's tough sanction. As risqué literature, politically explicit and exploitable artwork, and pirated rock music proliferated amid the commercialization trend, a campaign to criticize "spiritual pollution" was launched by the state in 1996 to limit cultural autonomy and regulate the cultural market. In March 1996, the MRFT held a national film workers' conference in Changsha (Changsha Meeting), the capital of Mao's birth province Hunan, addressing the MFRT's concern over the quality of Chinese cinema, particularly the low-budget entertainment films containing gratuitous sex and violence. In the Changsha Meeting, cinema's pedagogical function and social impact were once again foregrounded. The policy makers demanded that the industry produce and promote ten quality domestic pictures a year for the next five years. What counted as "quality" remained vague, prompting much discussion among the industrial practitioners. As usual, the studios practiced self-censorship, slating predominantly mainstream propaganda films. Consequently, in 1996, the hot subject for film production became biographies of various socialist heroes and model Communist members, what the Chinese film circle termed the "hero-cum-model-cum-picture." The Hollywood-influenced Chinese audiences were not thrilled by Chinese cinema's renewed passion for the socialist genre. The propaganda films were able to claim their box-office success only through the government-organized and government-sponsored public viewing. For the heavily promoted propaganda film *Kong Fansheng* (Cheng Guoxing and Wang Ping, 1996), a film featuring a contemporary Communist hero, which proudly claimed the number one box-office position among the domestic films in 1996, revenues from voluntary viewing averaged only 5 percent of the total box-office return. In urban centers such as Beijing and Shanghai, the percentage was below 1 percent. While film revenue continued to fall, the number of films produced also decreased.[30] As such, 1996 witnessed yet another downturn in Chinese cinema, causing serious doubts about whether the film market could survive without the big imports. The danger of a domestic film market dependent on foreign imports propelled the state to adopt import policies protective of domestic production. The Changsha Meeting mandated that two-thirds of the films distributed and exhibited be domestic productions. The percentage also applied to the number of times a domestic film must be screened, that is, two-thirds of screening time was reserved for domestic pictures. By allocating film quotas and mandating how many times a domestic film must be screened, film reform seemed to be taking a reverse turn in 1996. The conservative turn steered away many private investors, who, in turn, shifted their investment interest to producing more profitable television dramas. The year of cinema in 1995, hence, gave away to the year of television in 1996.

Some Chinese film critics and practitioners blamed the policy maker's politically loaded "quality-picture" demand for Chinese cinema's downturn. While some high-level administrators I interviewed in 1997 praised the March 1996 national film workers' conference, many film critics and practitioners were not thrilled by the quality-picture slogan. When I interviewed them in 1997, they either declined to comment on the conference or expressed, however reservedly, some negative opinions toward it. Others saw the studios' inability to control film distribution and exhibition as the most urgent problem. The distributors and exhibitors have gained a significant bargaining chip by taking advantage of the studios' anxiety over their films' marketability. In the extreme case, the studios were willing to accept a 28 percent share of the box-office revenue, far below the international standard of 35 percent.[31] The studios also had to pay for film prints and share promotional costs, defying the international practice in which the distributors cover the fees for film prints and promotion. Haunted by financial insecurity, studios lobbied for the right to distribute foreign films for lucrative profits. During the previous two years, the CFC assumed sole control over film. In 1996, the MRFT issued a document linking the profit from distributing imports with studios that produced quality domestic pictures. As a reward, it would allow the studios that produced popular quality films the right to distribute big imports approved by the CFC. The quota was one quality domestic film in exchange for one big import. In 1996, three big studios, Beijing, Changchun, and Shanghai, that had in the previous year produced ten domestic box-office hits, obtained the distribution rights of imports from the CFC. Among the twenty-four Hollywood imports in 1996, the three biggest—*Toy Story*, *Waterworld*, and *Jumanji*—were distributed directly by the three studios that shared the box-office returns with Hollywood and the participant theater chains. The studios thus profited from distributing these three films.

Chinese cinema's tumultuous turns in the mid-1990s indicated that an open market (to the imports) could stimulate domestic competition, indeed help to expose Chinese audiences to domestic pictures. It also indicated that the market for domestic films still had potential, but only films with relatively high production values would have a shot at the box office. Quite a few prominent Chinese filmmakers I interviewed in the summer of 1997 suggested that, government policy aside, even granted big-budget and high-tech, not many Chinese filmmakers would be able to make quality films with market appeal. Here again, what counted as quality remained vague. While some aspired to the production value of Hollywood films, others considered the diversification of film subject and type the route to quality. Still others considered a film's social and cultural relevance to contemporary Chinese audiences a crucial criteria. The consensus was that a quality film should reflect the splendor of audiovisual art and technology and at the same time be firmly rooted in Chinese culture. Indeed, one of domestic films' native attractions could rest on their cultural relevance to the Chinese audiences. The problem thus became one of the filmmakers' ability to cultivate cinematic elements firmly rooted within a given national/cultural imagination.

Yet film production during the era of reform continued to be predominantly propaganda-driven. The state continued to exercise its political censorship. Film censorship was carried out by the Propaganda Department of the Central Committee of the Chinese Communist Party; the Ministry of Radio, Film and Television; and the Chinese Film Bureau. While the MRFT and the Film Bureau controlled technological, regulatory, and administrative affairs, the party ultimately dictated film content and themes. The party committee had propaganda departments at both the state and the municipal levels to ensure that the studios in various states produced politically correct and culturally acceptable films. The standard of what was an acceptable cultural and political theme was never completely clear, shifting with the direction and force of the political winds. The studios correspondingly practiced somewhat confused, commonsensical self-censorship under the terms of an ambiguous and inconsistently applied cultural policy. The limited thematic freedom has resulted in monotonous cinematic representation and the avoidance of controversial contemporary subjects more attuned to the concerns of ordinary moviegoers. The state's ideological monopoly affected film practitioners' creative imagination and impulse, contributing to Chinese cinema's dull image. It also fostered a generation of filmmakers who were inexperienced in alternative approaches to film production. As such, even when film reform returned to the Chinese filmmakers much of the control over their creative processes and products, they had difficulty in making the transition from a cinema of propaganda to a cinema of popular appeal and commercial entertainment. In this regard, the crisis of Chinese cinema could not be resolved simply through a reform of the mode of production.[32]

Though the effectiveness of many reform measures remained obscure, what became clear by the mid-1990s, indeed since the late 1980s, was the centrality of audiences in determining the future of Chinese cinema. In its desperate search for audiences, the lofty cinematic aspiration in the early 1980s had given way to the urgent profit demand favoring popular taste. Film was considered less as an art form than a popular entertainment format. The revival of a cinematic populism seriously undermined critical and popular perceptions of art cinema. Indeed by the mid-1990s, the wave of experimental art films—such as *One and Eight* (Zhang Junzhao, 1984), *Yellow Earth* (Chen Kaige, 1985), *On the Hunting Ground* (Tian Zhuangzhuang, 1985), and *Horse Thief* (Tian Zhuangzhuang, 1986)—had become history, with its filmmakers turning to make popular films and its eulogists grappling with the ideologically and economically charged concept of popular taste. Framed as the "taste of the working class," popular taste became associated with political correctness. As such, it became most acceptable ideologically to the policy makers and most viable commercially to the industry. In this regard, the formerly renowned New Wave films failed both ideologically and economically.

As a kindred spirit, Chinese cinema's institutional restructurings developed hand in hand with a populist film culture foregrounding economy and ideology. Such a film culture began to take its shape as the state tightened its ideological grip and at the same time loosened its economic control. Discussions of the film industry's economic problems began as early as 1979 with the publication of an essay "What's Wrong with Film?" by two young filmmakers from Changchun Film Studio, Peng Ning and He Kongzhou.[33] Peng and He proposed to reform the party-dictated management and production system and to replace the old system with a more democratic one. In their plea for filmmakers' creative freedom, Peng and He argued for the idea of "the director as the center of the filmmaking group." Their focus was as much on film as an economic entity as it was on film as an autonomous art form, reflecting the period's general trend. Although it scratched only the very surface of the malady of a planned production system, the article did call attention to Chinese cinema's structural problem. Real debates on the necessity and strategy of film reform did not appear until the early 1990s. Instead, Chinese film discourse made a political turn in the late 1980s, (re)turning its focus from film art to film ideology, short-circuiting a possible progression from style to economy germinated by Peng and He's article.

Such a turn was driven first by a political movement in early 1987, the "antibourgeois liberalization" campaign. Launched by the state, the campaign was triggered by the student unrest at the end of 1986. The party accused the cultural elite of disseminating Western-style democratic thoughts considered responsible for the unrest. The students' demand for democracy was further seized upon by the party's conservative wing as an opportunity to attack the liberalization movement of the late 1970s and early 1980s. The movement was blamed for misguiding students. As the political atmosphere swung sharply toward the left, the reform-minded party general secretary, Hu Yaobang, was upstaged. The campaign against "bourgeois liberalization" did not generate real momentum among the cultural elite and the public who had grown apathetic toward any top-down political movement. But it did link, for the conservative filmmakers, critics, and policy makers, innovations in film form with other forms of political "dissidence." As such, the political validity of the New Wave cinema was challenged.[34]

A POPULIST FILM CULTURE AT THE SERVICE OF ECONOMIC REFORM

At the same time when the New Wave's political and economic validity was challenged, its cultural validity was questioned by the popular-inclined film practitioners from the perspective of a "mass culture." Wu Yigong, the head of the financially beleaguered Shanghai Film Studio and himself a well-accomplished fourth generation director, wrote an article accusing New Wave filmmakers and its supporters of failing to "serve the people" by making films beyond the comprehension of the mass audience.[35] A romantic humanist sympathy toward the so-called Xie Jin model, Wu's article vented his frustration with the New Wave's iconoclastic approach, denying any cinematic accomplishment of the previous generation and their elitist attitude toward the mass audience. The New Wave was seen as salon art neither accessible to, nor appreciated by, the public. From a semiofficial position, Wu reiterated cinema's function as a medium for connecting art with the public. An unpopular article among the younger generation of film practitioners, Wu's piece nonetheless took to its core Chinese cinema's worsening economic situation.[36] Reacting to the state's economic modernization plan, it foresaw the upcoming economic reform within the film industry. Wu was able to foreground the economy of Chinese film during the era when the term *box office* was still taboo in the culture sphere. Though Wu did not go so far as to suggest commercial success as the essential measurement evaluating a film's popular achievement, he made it clear that ignoring box-office returns would do more harm than good to the development of Chinese cinema. In hindsight, Wu presaged the arrival, in the 1990s, of a commercial culture orchestrated by the party in the service of the state's marketization agenda.

Wu's article hit hard on the New Wave's elitist cinematic view expressed, unabashedly, by Tian Zhuangzhuang. In an interview given in

1986 to the Chinese fan magazine *Popular Cinema* (Dazhong dianying), Tian declared that he was making films for audiences of the next century.[37] The remark infuriated both the socially conscious critics and ordinary film fans, providing ammunition for the attack on the New Wave filmmakers by the Politburo for their failure to serve the Party and from the audiences for their failure to serve the masses. Wu's article was a direct response to Tian's remark. Yuan Wenshu, another film practitioner active since the 1940s, echoed Wu's call that film was a popular art and that filmmakers were obligated to provide entertainment for the public. In his article, Yuan attacked Chinese New Wave's antitradition tendency and its imitation of Western modernist film techniques seen as bearing no real connection with the Chinese reality and, hence, Chinese audiences.[38] In his attack on the modernist cinema understood as "no plot, no dramatization, no characterization . . . irrationality and ambiguity," Yuan championed Chinese cinema's shadowplay tradition, which foregrounded plot and dramatic quality.[39] Yuan discussed, extensively, the relationship between film and audiences, urging filmmakers to be attentive to the popular taste. The renewed attention to popular taste brought to light film's financial accountability, which voluntarily aligned the industry with the state's overall economic reform agenda. Wu and Yuan's alignment with the state suggested the vulnerability of Chinese (film) culture under the direct influence of the state's political and economic agendas. Years of living as salaried state artists and sharing in political power had encouraged the practitioners-turned-gatekeepers to form coalitions and understandings with the state and to acutely and aptly anticipate the next shift in policy direction. The experience of living as salaried filmmakers also fostered pragmatism and opportunism within the film community. By the end of the 1980s, the transition toward a market economy became the new direction in state policy. As such, it dawned on studios and individual filmmakers that if they could not make popular films with profit then they had to rely on a limited state budget, both professionally and personally.

In the name of serving the masses, some financially attuned third and fourth generation filmmakers found legitimacy in their commercialized cinematic practices. Even the New Wave filmmakers relinquished their right to produce art with no social significance, "art for art's sake." Zhang Junzhao was the first Fifth Generation filmmaker who turned to making popular entertainment films. A newly appointed deputy head of Guangxi Film Studio, Zhang made his first entertainment film, a suspense thriller titled *The Lonely Murderer* (1987), "to earn a little money for the studio." In an interview given to *China Film News*, Zhang suggested finding a middle ground between the elite and the popular taste, calling, somewhat naively, for compromise and harmony between artists and audiences.[40] Zhang's transition from art film to entertainment film was influenced by both the studio's financial pressure and his own professional instinct. In this regard, rebellion against Chinese cinema's socialist realist tradition appeared easy in contrast to opposing commercialization and the lure of global cinematic trend. The increasing impact of the economic reforms and the development of a commercial industry meant that the market began to assume a greater role in cultural and political issues, to the extent that even ideological criticism during the period functioned to legitimize the commercial entertainment wave.

Ideological Criticism and the Entertainment Wave

Chinese cinema's strong entertainment wave and the resurgence of ideological criticism developed hand in hand. Ideological criticism was making its way back in the late 1980s. Aside from the influence of the antibourgeois liberalization movement, the resurgence of ideological criticism was affected by film critics' conversion from classical film theory to contemporary film theory, the result of direct encounters with contemporary Western film scholars. In October 1986, an American film scholar from the University of California–Los Angeles, Nick Browne, was invited to teach at Beijing Film Academy. In his thorough introduction of the history of Western film theory, Browne emphasized contemporary film theory, chiefly, semiotics, structuralism, psychoanalysis, feminism, and ideological interpretation. Though rejected by the film-form-obsessed critics from the late 1970s to the mid-1980s, contemporary Western film theories were taken more seriously in the late 1980s. The situation in film production had changed considerably by the mid-1980s. New theories were needed to make sense of the fading of Chinese New Wave and the rising of entertainment films and to assess the social implications of both trends.[41] The embrace of contemporary Western film theories in a Chinese context foregrounded the issue of ideology, downplaying such theories' ties to more traditional linguistic theories.

Ideological criticism exercised by Chinese film critics during the time strove to legitimize commercial entertainment films, contrasting sharply with Western scholars' critical stand against popular films' exploitation of the audience. Chinese film scholars such as Hao Dazheng, Chen Xihe, and Yao Xiaomeng justified popular entertainment film on the ground that it challenged both the repressive Confucian tradition and Maoist principles. Popular entertainment films were valued for their ability to entertain and to provide pleasure previously suppressed by the rigid Confucian and Maoist doctrines. Endorsed by the state in the name of serving the people, by the critics in the name of human emancipation, and by the industry in its attempt to shake off financial stress, entertainment films became the films of the mainstream by the late 1980s. The public unrest led by the university students in Beijing in the summer of 1989 interrupted the entertainment trend, briefly triggering the state to denounce the commercialized cinematic practice. Yet the deepening economic reform soon pushed the entertainment trend back to the forefront. Such attested to the very nature of Chinese film culture's dependence on the sway of the state's political and economic policy. Ideological criticism during the period was practiced in a depoliticized fashion in contrast with the more militant tone of a previous era. Nonetheless, it was shaped by China's overall political and economic milieux at the time which valued profit over pedagogy. Were it not for the state's new emphasis on the economy, ideological criticism might very well have taken a different spin, attacking popular entertainment films.

Ideological criticism was also applied to the textual analyses of individual films. Film critics followed the *Cahier du Cinema*'s model in its seminal essay "John Ford's *Young Mr. Lincoln*" to deconstruct films such as *Red Sorghum* (Zhang Yimou, 1987), *Hibiscus Town* (Xie Jin, 1986), and later, for example, *Farewell My Concubine* (Chen Kaige, 1993) and *Judou* (Zhang Yimou, 1990).[42] Hong Kong film critic Qiu Jingmei's, "*Yellow Earth*: Western Analysis and a Non-Western Text" (Huang Tudi: yixie yiyi de chansheng) became the model essay for its application of contemporary film theory to a specific Chinese film.[43] The era depicted in a film or the years when it was most popular were not important, but the times in which the rereading was done was. In the early 1990s, this led to the reexamination of auteur theory, which attributed all cinematic achievements to individual auteurs, indeed deifying them. In 1990 *Film Art* published several articles (re)evaluating the third, fourth, and fifth generation filmmakers from a critical and cultural perspective as opposed to the auteurist perspectives of the mid-1980s. The Fifth G films, particularly Chen Kaige's and Zhang Yimou's globalized post–New Wave films, caused debate concerning their authenticity in representing China and the Chinese. Ideological deconstruction of post–New Wave commercialized art films carried a strong nationalistic undertone. China's economic success in the early 1990s, coupled with post-Tiananmen restrictions on intellectual debate, has encouraged a surge of Chinese nationalism. Meanwhile, postcolonial theory was introduced to China by the early 1990s, helping to advance and consolidate a growing cultural conservatism in a renewed cultural cold war with the West.

Ideological deconstruction or (re)interpretation was also deployed to rewrite the history of Chinese cinema, questioning the taken-for-granted assumptions and presumptions about the course of Chinese film history under the guidance of Communist ideology.[44] The reconfigured film history strove to give equal attention to the formerly ignored, indeed discarded, commercial entertainment films. The venerable film journal *Contemporary Cinema* devoted a series of articles in its special issue commemorating ninety years of Chinese cinema to reevaluating Chinese cinema's early commercial wave in the 1920s. Overall, ideological criticism practiced in a depoliticized fashion aided Chinese cinema's economic reform and its commercial entertainment trend.

Institutional Criticism

As the film industry underwent further institutional restructuring in the early to mid-1990s, ideological criticism was replaced by institutional criticism concerning the economy of Chinese cinema. The close tie between academia and industry in China made the critical and professional discourses inseparable. The pragmatic slant of Chinese film criticism determined that criticism would more or less in sync with the concerns of the industry. Responding to the state and the industry's economic reform agenda, institutional criticism strove to offer strategic inputs to the industry's reform agenda.

The Chinese film community as a whole did not catch up with the reality of China's new turn in economic reform until the late 1980s. Consequently, "economic restructuring of the Chinese film industry" did not become the catchphrase in film discourse until the early to mid-1990s when Chinese cinema encountered a challenge from Hollywood's big blockbusters. Discussions on the economy of Chinese cinema went hand in hand with the reform measures in 1993, which targeted overhauling the infrastructure of Chinese cinema. The discussion progressed from vague and general terms to specific topics concerning the plausibility of a Hollywood-style institutional and market structure. Issues were raised as to whether the restructuring of the Chinese film industry must follow the mode of production defined by Hollywood. Is imitating Hollywood's big-budget, high-tech production values the route for Chinese cinema to win back its domestic market? Participants not only identified and described problems and potentials of film reform but also attempted to prescribe concrete remedies.

The achievement of early discussions was showcased in a book edited by a professor at the Beijing Film Academy, Ni Zhen, who is also a screenwriter (*Raise the Red Lantern*) and a film critic.[45] Tacitly endorsed by the policy makers, Ni's 1994 book *Reform and Chinese Cinema* offered many pragmatic solutions. After identifying external factors responsible for audience erosion such as the public's shifting cinematic taste and multiple entertainment options, the book took to its core the film industry's reluctance to examine its own internal structural problems. The chaotic stage of film industry was seen as the result of the decaying of its own internal reproductive mechanism, chiefly, the lack of collaboration among the producers, the distributors, and the exhibitors. As described in the book, on the one hand, distributors blamed the studios for Chinese cinema's slow response to audiences' shifting tastes; on the other hand, studios blamed distributors for taking away too much of the box-office revenue. Theater chains joined the suit, complaining about the unfair profit-sharing quota that left them with little cash for renovation and expansion. All three sectors came together in their denunciation of audiences' inability to appreciate real art. They also blamed alternative entertainment options and the government's restrictive film policies for their own financial crisis. All three charges fired by the industry were forcefully refuted in the book, which suggested instead that the studios' inefficiency, low productivity, and, most important, their lack of a long-term strategy to cope with the shifting entertainment climate were responsible for Chinese cinema's crisis.

The book traced the attempt at a horizontal integration that would grant feature films a special position in broadcasting and cable programming back to the mid-1980s, when the Ministry of Radio, Film, and Television was formed. It pointed out that the one-shot, top-down policy amendment that was intended to integrate film with television and radio did not bring substantial change to the segregated industry. Lack of bottom-up cooperation from local film and television/radio bureaus for the implementation of such a policy was partially responsible for the failure. The bottom-up resistance within the industry not only delayed Chinese cinema from making early inroads into television but also hampered enterprise reform within the studios. Clearly, the implementation of policy change was more difficult than the change of policy itself. The book further suggested that new policies granting more creative freedom would not reverse audience erosion. What was needed was a long-term marketing strategy that would actively cultivate niche markets by producing a diverse range of films and establishing different types of theaters tailored to audiences of varied demographic compositions.

As for production reform in particular, the book had three suggestions: First, the state should relax its control over film production rights to actively absorb alternative production investment and to foster competition among state-run studios, independent production companies, and other types of commercial production entities. The suggestion was taken up in the mid-1990s by the policy makers. Second, the industry ought to foster a variety of talent pools, cultivating especially filmmakers capable of adapting to the demand of producing market-oriented popular entertainment films. The cultivation of genre films was considered essential to the marketization of Chinese cinema. A Hollywood-style industrialized production system in the form of streamlining the production process through further specialization was valued for production efficiency and productivity over the old-style-craftsmanship approach more characteristic of Chinese film production in the 1980s. Financial incentives were considered necessary for quality productions. Large-scale production in the form of big-budget and high-tech were also endorsed as one way to improve production quality, which led to the last proposal, the proposition of the establishment of three big production centers. The third proposal suggested that studios should consolidate their production energy and activity through mergers and buy-outs to stimulate free competition within the production sector. In other words, it proposed a production restructuring at a national level.

The survival of a few stronger production companies at the expense of the weak ones was considered a necessary step toward a more organized, more productive, and more efficient feature production system. Specifically, Beijing, Shanghai, and Guangzhou, the three cosmopolitan urban centers, were singled out as feasible production centers for their leading economic and cultural status most attuned to global trends. The replacement of Changchun as a production center with Guangzhou, the capital city of Canton, which was economically and culturally more tied to Hong Kong than to the Mainland, was significant. It suggested the change of production direction from focusing on mainstream propaganda film toward the commercial entertainment film, for the party-nourished Changchun Studio was the most active in producing revolutionary films. Shanghai was the oldest film production center, attracting the largest audiences since the inception of Chinese cinema up to the establishment of the People's Republic. Shanghai was also the largest commercial center in China and was reestablishing itself as one of the largest commercial and entertainment centers in Asia. Shanghai Film Studio had been one of the most active and effective in regenerating its production mechanism. With its easy access to global capital, Shanghai would naturally play a crucial role in the future of Chinese cinema.[46] Beijing, on the other hand, was Mainland China's political and cultural center, and Beijing Film Studio was the first studio that opened its door to international coproductions. The commercial success of their coproductions such as *The Last Emperor* (Bernardo Bertolucci, 1987) and *Farewell My Concubine* enabled the studio to upgrade production equipment and expand its production capacity, making the studio one of the leading players in the industry. The number of studios were reduced by the late 1990s as the outcome of the radical restructuring beginning in the mid-1990s. The institutional restructuring at a national level essentially replaced the state monopoly with an oligopoly of a few big production enterprises centered around the three geopolitically significant urban areas.

The discussion on film reform after the arrival of Hollywood took a different turn, eliciting much comparison between Hollywood and Chinese cinema. Questions were raised as to whether the Hollywood-style institutional structure and the classical narrative paradigm should be the model for Chinese cinema in the era of popular culture and ongoing economic reform. Privatization has diminished state support for filmmakers and left them more vulnerable to imports at the moment when the new orthodoxy of global free trade has left the fragile domestic film industry unprotected.

Under such conditions, should the film industry as part of the cultural re-productive institutions be treated the same as other industrial enterprises, following the same path of commercialization and privatization? The question of what went wrong with Chinese cinema was equipped with a newly encountered globalization theory. As such, Chinese cinema's dis-concerting situation was no longer perceived as an isolated case, originat-ing solely from China's internal political and economic constraints. The globalization of Hollywood was perceived now as the trend in world cin-ema, an inevitable outcome of Hollywood's economic and ideological power that has overshadowed other national cinemas. Zhuang Yuxing compiled data illustrating the extent of Hollywood's globalization.[47] Ac-cording to his data, in 1993, eighty-eight out of the one hundred most pop-ular blockbusters internationally were Hollywood pictures, with the top twenty-six all products of Hollywood. The same year in France, Holly-wood films occupied 60 percent of the French market, with French films occupied only 0.5 percent of the U.S. market. Likewise in Germany, Hol-lywood occupied 86 percent of the domestic market. Numbers on other re-gions ranging from the former Eastern Bloc to Asia and the Middle East revealed the same trend. Its successful institutional and financial structure notwithstanding, Hollywood thrives on parading the American lifestyle so appealing to global audiences.

One of the immediate impacts of Hollywood's globalization in China, particularly the popularity of its big-budget blockbusters, was to raise the expectations for domestic film production, fostering the so-called big-budget mentality. The dangers of equating quality with budget and the inflated production investment were discussed among the big name di-rectors in a conference organized in 1997 by the magazine *China Screen*.[48] Tian Zhuangzhuang pointed out that big budget did not necessarily guar-antee big box-office return. Likewise, his contemporary, He Qun, sug-gested that big budgets did not necessarily result in quality. Jiang Wen, the director of *In the Heat of the Sun*, a big-budget film, one of the top-ten do-mestic hits of 1995, had no problem with the big-budget trend but agreed that it took certain skill to produce a big-budget film and that not every filmmaker was capable of making a blockbuster simply with lavish pro-duction investment. In other words, big-budget entailed high risk. Over-all, the participants agreed that not all the quality films needed big budgets, and while most action-adventure pictures would benefit from hefty production investment for spectacular visual effects, some small-scale films could do just as well at the box office with smaller budgets.

As Hollywood continued to make inroads into the Chinese market, many film critics and practitioners looked further into the internal prob-lems of the Chinese film industry. In his detailed economic analysis, Zheng Dongtian summarized what he saw as the unpromising outcome of Chi-nese cinema's partial reform package up until mid-1996.[49] The distribution reform at its best achieved two things: the dismantling of the monopoly of the China Film Corporation and the partial adoption of a profit-sharing distribution system. The reform failed to establish a few nationwide distribution networks since many local distributors continued to operate under the planned economy and fought hard to protect their own territory. Coupled with studios' continued blockbooking practice, the segregated system limited distribution scale and profit. The limited profit from film distribution prolonged studios' financial crisis, resulting in reduced production quantity and quality, further discouraging film distribution. The chart included in Zheng's article revealed that Chinese cinema's annual feature output was fifth in the world, lagging behind India, Hollywood, Japan, and Hong Kong; its number of movie theaters ranked seventh, its box-office revenue twelfth, and average production investment fourteenth.[50] As suggested by Zheng, the numbers revealed three things about the state of Chinese cinema: Chinese cinema's output was disproportionately small in relation to its population and huge market, and to the global market; the average Chinese film's production budget was embarrassingly small in comparison with Hollywood (1:157 as the total annual production investment and 1:52 for an average single film); and China had a limited number of theaters and few alternative outlets for feature films. Zheng proposed vertical and horizontal integration and further enterprise reform to eliminate redundant overhead. He also called for serious efforts in cultivating a pool of professional producers and financial managers. Such suggestions would not be taken up by the industry until the late 1990s.

Meanwhile, in the mid-1990s, the debate on the priority of cinema being an industrial product or an art form resurfaced. While the political legitimacy of commercial entertainment films was no longer challenged, such films' artistic quality was questioned, mostly by art filmmakers who were threatened by entertainment films' market potential.[51] The debate acknowledged Chinese cinema's peculiar boundary position regulated by the market, the celluloid technology, and party politics, the so-called one butler and three masters phenomenon.[52] Contemporary Chinese cinema was divided into three broad categories: propaganda films mandated by the state, entertainment films welcomed by the public, and art films pursued by the film artists. With the first two supported respectively by the state and the public, the last one came out the sore loser. Since the "main melody film" was untouchable, the proponents of film as first of all an art form criticized entertainment films for spreading "the religion of commodity worship."[53] They argued that cinema was a cultural rather than an economic entity, and as such the long-term success of Chinese cinema would rely more on its cultural significance and artistic achievement than on its short-term box-office gains. In my interview with the venerable art filmmaker Xie Fei (*The Black Horse*, 1997) in the summer of 1997, Xie expressed his disenchantment with mainstream Hollywood films. He considered it essential for Chinese filmmakers to portray traditional Chinese culture and to continue making small-scale art films. Xie promoted the cultivation of a distribution network and small theater chains for art films. He emphasized the importance of a diversified film market to allow different films to flourish.

The advocates of entertainment films argued otherwise. Their view was articulated nicely by a film critic, Wu Xiaoli. Wu challenged the traditional division between art and commercial film and, hence, between art and commerce, suggesting that the trend toward blurring the line between the socially critical art film and the socially conservative entertainment film was global, resulting from the neoconservative movement of the 1980s that stripped art film of its critical basis.[54] Indeed the contenders of Cannes and Oscar had grown increasingly alike; and both "art" and "commerce" had become the buzzwords for many supposedly independent or alternative film festivals, including Cannes, Berlin, Venice, and Sundance. The arrival of popular entertainment films in the 1990s simply manifested such a global trend, signaling that Chinese cinema had finally caught up with the global cinematic trend, since the late 1970s, incorporating both art and commerce. Wu positioned the ten domestic blockbusters of 1995 precisely within the blurring boundary of art and commerce. In other words, films such as *In the Heat of the Sun* and *Red Cherry* were commercial films with artistic quality, and such should be the formula for future production. In terms of Hollywood's big-budget and high-tech blockbuster, Wu speculated that what struck a chord between high-tech Hollywood fare such as *Star Wars* (George Lucas, 1977), *E.T.—The Extra-Terrestrial* (Steven Spielberg, 1982), and *Jurassic Park* (Steven Spielberg, 1993) and the Chinese audiences were not the films' spectacular special effects but the three-act plot structure. The three-act formula was also responsible for the technologically less spectacular domestic hits. In terms of domestic popular films, their social and cultural relevance to the Chinese audiences were essential to their success in competing with the more sophisticated Hollywood imports.

After the Changsha Meeting, which renewed the state's emphasis on film's ideological function, the debate took a brief detour from the discussion of art and economy to the discussion of representation. The issue of ideology was foregrounded by the supporters of the main-melody film. They claimed that Hollywood films such as *True Lies* (James Cameron, 1995) and *Forrest Gump* (Robert Zemeckis, 1994) represented, at their best, the triumph of American patriotism and capitalist ideology. Chinese cinema should not shy away from presenting China's own cultural tradition and mainstream ideology under the party's guidance.[55] A Chinese-style cinema was called forth to encourage making films suited to the Chinese audience. The call for mainstream propaganda film did not find many supporters in film circles. When I visited Beijing in the summer of 1997, quite a few film critics and filmmakers, under the conditions of anonymity, expressed their apprehension toward the state's tightened ideological control. Such a control proved to be counterproductive, and indeed short-lived, being inundated soon by the strong wave of popular culture.

Amid the strong tide of popular culture, film critics shifted their focus, relating Chinese cinema's entertainment wave in the 1990s to the surge of popular culture orchestrated by the state. By the mid-1990s, promoting and regulating the development of pop culture with its profit potential had emerged as one of the top agendas for policy makers.[56] Upon the discovery of "culture" as a site where political and economic capital can be accumulated, the state campaigned for the cultivation and consumption of popular culture. The nationwide implementation of a forty-hour work week system in the spring of 1995 made the consumption of (popular) culture all the more pertinent since it aptly linked the newly freed "double leisure day" (what we understand in the West as the weekend) with consumption. The conflation between free time and money fits the state's overall marketization agenda for it turned free time into another form of capital to be transformed into a major source of profit and tax revenues. With the media largely at the state/party's command, it does not come as a surprise that the discussions of popular culture attempted to rationalize its rise from a political, economic, and technological standpoint.

Ying Hong has said that what made the rising of popular culture possible in China in the 1990s were, first, the state's loosened ideological grip, second, China's overall economic reform and, third, technological evolution.[57] While a relaxed political environment made the commercialization of culture possible, marketization made it necessary for the cultural industry to survive, and the new distribution technology made the mass reproduction of culture feasible. Economic reform played a pivotal role in making possible the emergence of a consumer society by generating wealth among both the urban and the rural populations. The rise of a consumer society became the foundation for the consumption of, and indeed contributed to the rise of, popular culture. The rise of popular culture was characterized by Ying as the transition from a politically charged culture of enlightenment toward a commercially charged culture of entertainment, from art to industry, from depth to surface, and from the elitist to the popular. Discussions of popular culture put Chinese cinema's second wave of entertainment picture within a broader cultural sphere in contemporary China. The second entertainment wave was thus seen as reflecting Chinese audiences' changing tastes in the era of popular culture.

The second entertainment wave saw its germination in the mid-1980s, the period when New Wave made its formidable cinematic entrance. While successful critically, New Wave never reached sizable audiences. In 1985, for instance, all branches of the China Film Corporation declined to buy copies of Tian Zhuangzhuang's *On the Hunting Ground*, with the result that Inner Mongolia Film Studio sold only four prints and had to write off almost the entire cost of the production. The award-winning film *Yellow Earth*, with its international reputation, fared better, yet it was not at all popular among mainstream audiences. Beginning in the late 1980s, most studios rushed slates of down-market "entertainment" films into production. Popular genres such as crime and murder thrillers, martial arts movies, and lurid melodramas flooded the film market, many of them cheap knockoffs of Hong Kong and other Western films. The entertainment trend gained momentum in the 1990s. From 1992 to 1993, the profitable films produced by the Shanghai and the Beijing Film Studios, all of them invested in by nonstate sectors, were all popular genre films, including violence-loaded suspense thrillers, sex-loaded melodramas, tongue-in-cheek comedies, and butt-kicking martial arts films.[58] As such, the terms *suspense thriller, kung fu movie, melodrama*, and *comedy* became catchphrases for film marketing and audience identification. By the mid-1990s, all of the former New Wave filmmakers were engaged in producing such films.

As a group, entertainment pictures prior to the mid-1990s were less coherent and consistent in terms of their marketable elements. The entertainment wave entered a mature stage by the mid-1990s, following a Hollywood-style marketing strategy.[59] As indicated by the domestic hits of 1995 and 1996, popular films were mostly big-budget genre films that employed either star directors and/or star actors and adopted pre-sold commodities. While comedy and melodrama were the most popular genre vehicles, a few main-melody pictures, commercialized art films, and historical epics also commanded a certain share of the box-office return. The entertainment wave not only transformed New Wave style art film into post–New Wave popular film but also cut the throat of the government-funded propaganda film. The dismal performance of the state-sponsored propaganda films propelled the government to reevaluate such films' literary quality and production value. The problems of one-dimensional characters and/or character stereotyping, thematic simplification and overgeneralization, and the clichéd plot structure were blamed for propaganda films', indeed the majority of Chinese films', lack of emotional connection with their native audiences. The discussion shifted film discourse from economic reform back to stylistic reform, with the Fifth Generation serving as the consummate example of a commercially successful transformation from the style of New Wave to that of post–New Wave.

Overall, film criticism during the period, as in any other period, developed within the confines of the state/party's reform agenda, in general, and Chinese film's institutional restructuring, in particular. Criticism functioned to serve rather than monitor the state-orchestrated economic reform. As the market continued to assume a greater role in cultural and political issues, culture, in general, and film, in particular, parted with ideology even in the official discourse and was turned into an economic activity in itself. Manifested in film criticism was the critics' attempt to rationalize the commercial entertainment trend. Acutely anticipating a new historical development, Wu Yigong's article signaled film criticism's early turn from a discourse of modernization to the discourse of popularization. The ensuing waves of ideological and institutional criticism all strove to legitimize the popular entertainment trend and marketization. In a similiar vein, the historiography of Chinese cinema during the period called for a reevaluation of the previously condemned popular entertainment waves in the 1920s. The attempt to reassess Chinese cinema's early commercial wave was thus partly the result of the demand for a market economy. Understandably, the criticism/debate concerning the Fifth G's transition from New Wave to post–New Wave was framed from the perspective of cultural identity/authenticity rather than that of commercialization. The Fifth G was criticized not for its courting of the popular taste and its commercialized practice but for its courting of the West. In this regard, nationalism served as an ideological base for the local capitalism to compete with a global capitalism. Likewise, the caution against the big imports was aimed at Hollywood's hegemonic power textually, leaving out, indeed deeming positive, Hollywood's institutional influence. The Changsha Meeting voiced the policy makers' concern over certain popular films' risqué content and the vast majority of entertainment films' low box-office return resulting from low production quality but not over the commercial populist trend, in general. As manifested in the popularization of propaganda films, the populist trend was urged by the state in its hope for the establishment of a financially self-reliant film industry. As the state, the industry, and film discourse synergised in their marching toward marketization, concern over the state of the art film voiced by art filmmakers, self-serving or not, was largely ignored. Coupled with film practitioners' own professional instinct, the populist turn in film criticism reinforced Chinese cinema's commercial entertainment trend.

CONCLUSION

The political economy and the culture of Chinese cinema from the mid-1980s to the mid-1990s contrasted sharply with that of Chinese cinema from the late 1970s to the mid-1980s. With China's overall economic reform finally taking off, the Chinese film industry began to implement various reform packages to keep up with the state-encouraged commercialization and privatization trend. Film reform focused on institutional restructuring. Led by distribution and exhibition reform, the restructuring eventually ventured into the structural overhaul of the state-run studios, with the production sector facing the worst financial challenge among all three sectors. At times ad hoc and segmented, the production reform did have its focus, centering around enterprise reform, managerial reform, labor reform, and financial reform. The overall goal of such reform measures was marketization, the dismantling of planned production targets and mandatory price controls. In practice, deregulation and industrial consolidation became the main targets.

The achievement of Chinese cinema's institutional reform during this period was more conceptual than material. The importance of a Hollywood-style vertical and horizontal integration was realized only in theory in the early 1990s. It was not put into practice until the mid- to late 1990s, leading to a merger trend within China's audiovisual industry. Likewise, the top-down decentralization at times met bottom-up resistance, resulting in the fitful relationship between policy makers and filmmakers. As deregulation introduced imports and coproductions, the state-run, financially ailing studios were temporarily put in a disadvantaged position. The studios begged for more government regulation in the name of protecting Chinese domestic productions. The protection of the Chinese national film industry was equated with the protection of Chinese national culture. As such, regulation and deregulation weighed equally in the state's attempt to develop a semigovernment-supported and semiprivate-investment-based feature production infrastructure. Specialized theaters for popular imports were designated, to raise their ticket prices for better box-office revenue and, consequently, to limit the imports' popularity among less affluent areas. To further aid the state-run studios, the state granted them a larger share of box-office returns from domestic pictures and enacted higher taxes on coproductions and foreign imports.

Meanwhile, the consolidation of the audiovisual industry, particularly the collaboration between film and television continued and has benefited the film industry. The handover of studio management from the Ministry of Culture to the Ministry of Radio, Film, and in Television July 1986 gained the studios more than 10 million yuan (US$1.25 million) from television commercials. China Central Television's film channel paid Chinese film studios 160 million yuan (US$20 million) alone in 1998 for purchasing the rights to broadcasting feature films. The film channel also invested 17 million yuan (US$2.1 million) in coproducing motion pictures with the studios. Carried by cable with subscriptions by an estimated 30 million households, CCTV-6 aired 389 foreign films (including films from Taiwan and Hong Kong) in 1998 and planned to invest in the production of fifty to one hundred made-for-TV films in 1999. In September 1998, CCTV-6 launched a new program to showcase outstanding foreign and Chinese films. The program, *A Date with Film Classics*, showed well-known films each Saturday at 8 P.M. It premiered with a film made by a younger generation filmmaker, *This Is How Iron Is Made* (Lu Xuechang, 1995). It has featured award-winning hits such as *The Fugitive* (Andrew Davis, 1993) and *Close Encounters of the Third Kind* (Steven Spielberg, 1977). Amid the ongoing economic reform was the return of a populist cinematic view and the rise of popular culture led by Hollywood imports, both opening the flood-gates to Chinese cinema's commercial entertainment wave. Imported entertainment pictures continued to generate a sizable market share.[60] Among these, Hollywood's *Mission Impossible* (Brian De Palma, 1996), *Twister* (Jan De Bont, 1997), *Broken Arrow* (John Woo, 1995), *The Bridges of Madison County* (Clint Eastwood, 1995), and Hong Kong's *The White Golden Dragon* (Tang Jili, 1995) led China in box-office returns.[61]

Cultural development in a totalitarian society is closely monitored by and, hence, closely associated with patterns in political economic change. As the post–socialist Chinese state recast itself into a modern authority with economic development as its top agenda, its control over cultural development became ever more subtle, inviting voluntary collaborations from cultural practitioners. Chinese cultural practitioners, film practitioners in this case, willingly cooperated with the state in their search for a cinematic marketization seen as the route to rescue the financially beleaguered film industry. Thus, both the film industry and film culture positively responded to the state's economic reform agenda, pushing the popular entertainment wave to the forefront. Fostered by both political and economic concerns, a populist cinematic view effectively endorsed Chinese film's entertainment trend. Chinese cinema's institutional reform and its concomitant critical discourse actively engaged each other, nurturing a period of mutual appreciation. Together, the political economy and the culture of Chinese cinema during the period established a foundation for the surge of the popular entertainment wave.

What further fostered the wave was the impact of Hollywood's second entry into China's domestic market. Hollywood's popularity among Chinese audiences propelled Chinese cinema to adopt the narrative paradigm institutionalized by Hollywood and the industrial structure and market practices refined by Hollywood. The official and critical receptions of Hollywood-led popular imports were rather paradoxical. While crediting imports for the rejuvenation of China's domestic film market, opinions were divided on Hollywood's long-term impact on the future formation of Chinese national cinema. Given the continued failure of Chinese films to gain a strong foothold in their domestic market, Chinese film critics often adopted the rhetoric of the Americans, claiming that Chinese films have not yet attained sufficient quality. Such was the familiar tune echoed by other national/regional cinemas, including European cinema. The issue of quality shifted film industry's focus from economy to style, particularly the classical film narration perpetuated by Hollywood that had long become part of the Chinese cinematic heritage and that had struck a new chord with Chinese audiences. A populist cinematic view in the name of serving the masses-endorsed Chinese cinema's commercial trend that appropriated such a classical style. As commercial features' cultural shortcomings were excused on the basis that some films at least had to be profitable, art films' financial shortcomings were not excused by their cultural mandate and artistic successes.

Both the political economy and the culture of Chinese cinema were clearly at odds with the Chinese Fifth Generation's cinematic practice in the mid-1980s, transforming it from New Wave experimental films to post–New Wave popular films. The arrival of the post–New Wave from the perspective of the renewed popularity of a classical film style will be the focus of the next chapter.

NOTES

1. Zhao was eventually brought down by economic conservatives and political reactionaries during the height of the 1989 student movement in Beijing.

2. Barry Naughton, *Growing Out of the Plan: Chinese Economic Reform, 1978–1993* (Cambridge: Cambridge University Press, 1995).

3. Ma Qiang, "Chinese Film in the 1980s: Art and Industry," in *Cinema and Cultural Identity—Reflections on Films from Japan, India, and China*, ed. Wimal Dissanayake (New York: University Press of America, 1988), 168.

4. Naughton, *Growing Out of the Plan.*

5. Sun Yanhu, *Lectures on the Regulations for Transforming the State-Owned Industrial Enterprise Management Mechanism* (Quanmin Suoyouzhi Gongye Qiye Zhuanhuan Jingying Jizhi Tiaolie) (Beijing: Gaige, 1992).

6. Ni Zhen, ed., *Reform and Chinese Cinema* (Gaige yu zhongguo dianying) (Beijing: China Film Press, 1994), 51.

7. See Ling Lishen, "Chinese Cinema's Economic and Artistic Change in the 1990s" (Jiushi niandai zhongguo dianying de jingji biangeng he yishu fengyie), *Dianying yishu* (Film Art) 248, no. 3 (1996): 37–41. Many of the data cited in this paragraph come from Ling's article.

8. Wang Haizhou and Ni Zhen, "The Dilemma of Film Production" (Kungjing he xiwan: Zhongguo dianying zhipianyie de maodun), in *Reform and Chinese Cinema* (Gaige yu zhongguo dianying), ed. Ni Zhen (Beijing: China Film Press, 1994), 75–115.

9. Ibid.

10. Han is now the head of Beijing Film Studio.

11. Wang and Ni, "The Dilemma of Film Production."

12. Ibid.

13. Ibid.

14. Ni Zhen, "Chinese Cinema at the Dawn of 21st Century" (21 Shiji qianxi: Zhuanxingqi de zhongguo dianying), in *Reform and Chinese Cinema* (Gaige yu zhongguo dianying), ed. Ni Zhen (Beijing: China Film Press, 1994), 17.

15. Ibid.

16. See data provided by Wang and Ni in their "The Dilemma of Film Production," 87–88.

17. Beijing Film Studio generated enough revenue from its ample coproduction opportunities and was able to use the revenue alone to produce *Jinggang Mountain* (Han Shanpin, 1992), a feature film receiving good press coverage and making a profit. See Wang and Ni, "The Dilemma of Film Production."

18. Ibid.

19. The interview was conducted in Beijing in the summer of 1997. The subject wished to remain anonymous.

20. An interview with Tian Zhuangzhuang conducted by *Dianying yishu*, 266, no. 3 (1999): 17–22.

21. Deng Zhufei, "The Dawn of Audio-Visual Industries' Big Reform" (Yingshi wenhua chuzhai dabiange qianyie), *Dianying yishu* 246, no. 1 (1996): 85.

22. See the report, "Xie Jing on Contemporary Chinese Film," *World Journal*, 21 January 2000, E7.

23. Zhao Shi, "Two Decades of Film Reform" (Chuangzhao huihuan panden gaofeng), *Dianying Yishu* 264, no. 1 (1999): 4–12.

24. See "A Chart of Ten Domestic Blockbusters" (1995 nian guochan maizhuo yingpian paihangbang) compiled by *Dianying yishu* 248, no. 3 (1996): 4.

25. Pan Lujian, "Aside from *Red Cherry*'s Commercial Operation" (Hongyingtao zhai shangyie yunzhuo zhiwai), *Dianying yishu* 248, no. 3 (1996): 6.

26. Lao Mei, "Domestic Films: Dawn and Shadow" (Guochan dianying shuguang he yingying), *Dianying yishu* 247, no. 2 (1996): 44.

27. Fan Ping, "Domestic Pictures in 1997 Dare Not Entertain Bill-Sharing," *Chinese Film Market* 8 (1997): 7.

28. The term *big picture consciousness/awareness* is taken from Zhang Tongdao, "A Retro of Chinese Cinema in the 1995" (Kuayue xuanhua), *Dianying yishu* 248, no. 3 (1996): 23.

29. Zhang, "A Retro of Chinese Cinema in 1995," 23–27.

30. See Fan Jianghua, Mao Yu, and Yang Yuan, "Film Market in 1996," *Chinese Film Market* 1 (1997): 4–7.

31. Ibid.

32. The view was also expressed by a Chinese film historian, Shao Mujun, in his "Chinese Film Amidst the Tide of Reform," in *Cinema and Cultural Identity—Reflections on Films from Japan, India, and China*, ed. Wimal Dissanyake (New York: University Press of America, 1988), 199–208.

33. Peng Ning and He Kongzhou, "Why Cinema Lags Behind" (Dianying weishemuo shangbuqu), *Renming ribao* (People's Daily), 21 January 1979, 3.

34. This line of criticism was endorsed by Xia Yan, a veteran filmmaker and one-time head of the party's "underground" group in the old Shanghai film industry.

35. Wu Yigong, "We Must Become Film Artists Who Deeply Love the People," in *Perspectives on Chinese Cinema*, ed. Chris Berry (London: BFI, 1991), 133–140.

36. The article was criticized for its harsh view of art films by filmmakers who were apathetic toward the antibourgeois liberalization movement.

37. An English version of the interview can be found in Yang Ping, "A Director Who is Trying to Change the Audience: A Chat with Young Director Tian Zhuangzhuang," in *Perspectives on Chinese Cinema*, ed. Chris Berry (London: BFI, 1991), 127–129.

38. Yuan Wenshu, "Film Tradition and Innovation" (Dianying Chuantong yu gengxing), *Dianying yishu* 197, no. 6 (1987): 18–23.

39. Quoted from the English version of the same article published in *Chinese Film Theory—A Guide to the New Era*, ed. George S. Semsel, Xia Hong, and Hou Jianping (New York: Praeger, 1990), 168–178.

40. See Gao Jun, "A Changed Director, Transcription of a Dialogue with Zhang Junzhao," in *Perspectives on Chinese Cinema*, ed. Chris Berry (London: BFI, 1991), 130–132.

41. See Hu Ke, "Contemporary Film Theory in China" (Zhongguo dangdai dianying Lilun), *Dangdai dianying* (Contemporary Film) 65, no. 2 (1995): 65–73.

42. Ibid.

43. The article was published in *Dangdai dianying* 16, no. 1 (1987): 68–79. Its English version, with the author's English name Esther C. M. Yau, was collected in *Perspectives on Chinese Cinema*, ed. Chris Berry (London: BFI, 1991), 62–79.

44. See articles by Yao Xiaomeng, "The History, Narration, and Ideological Discourse of the 'Proletarian Cultural Revolution'" ("Wuchan jieji wenhuadageming" de Lishi, xushi he shixiang tixi), *Dangdai dianying* 36, no. 3 (1990): 34–35; and Yao Xiaomeng, "Early Socialist Culture and Chinese Cinema" (Zhaoqi shehui zhuyi wuhua he zhongguo dianying), *Dangdai dianying* 41, no. 2 (1991): 34–47.

45. See Ni, *Reform and Chinese Cinema*.

46. However, the current creative climate in Shanghai proved stifling, with the party maintaining an iron grip on the cultural scene. The state is acutely aware that Shanghai's social stability is paramount to the welfare of the entire nation. Shanghai has thus perfected the art of control and self-censorship. As a result, many talents have moved north, to the capital city of Beijing.

47. See Zhuang Yuxing, "The Economic Problem of Contemporary Chinese Cinema" (Dangdai zhongguo dianying de jingji wenti), *Dangdai dianying* 72, no. 3 (1996): 17–23.

48. See Gu Zhi, "Behind the Big Budget Investment of Domestic Pictures," *China Screen* 3 (1996): 2–23.

49. Zheng Dongtian, "On Film Commodity" (Dianying shangping Lun), *Dianying yishu* 249, no. 4 (1996): 8–11.

50. For detailed numbers see ibid., 9–10.

51. See debate articles on the subject published in *Dianying Yishu* 247, no. 2 (1996): 4–18.

52. Ibid.

53. Ibid.

54. Wu Xiaoli, "The Trend of Domestic Pictures Amidst World Cinema's Breakdown of Boundary" (Shijie dianying zhenghehua qushizhong de guochanpian zhong xiang), *Dianying dianshi yianjiu* (Film and TV Research) 6 (1996): 15–18.

55. See the series of short articles on the subject published in *Dangdai dianying* 73, no. 4 (1996): 4–12. In my interview in Beijing in the summer of 1997 with Gang Honggu, the former head of Guangxi Film Studio and the chair of the China Filmmakers' Association, echoed the view that mainstream Chinese cinema should represent mainstream ideology, the party's ideology.

56. Jing Wang's paper "Public Culture and Popular Culture: Urban China at the Turn of the New Century" has some interesting discussions on the phenomena. The paper was presented at the Asian Cultural Conference in 1998 organized by the Department of Asian Studies at the University of Texas–Austin.

57. Ying Hong, "Chinese Cinema in the Era of Popular Culture" (Dazhong wenhua shidai de zhongguo dianying), *Dianying yishu* 76, no. 1 (1997): 22–26.

58. Ni, *Reform and Chinese Cinema*, 81.

59. See the chart "Ten Domestic Blockbusters in 1996" (1996 Nian guochan maizhuo yingpian pai hangbang) in *Dianying yishu* 254, no. 3 (1997): 4–5.

60. Fifty-four imports (including the ten big blockbusters) in 1996 were mostly popular entertainment films from Hollywood and Hong Kong.

61. See detailed charts in Chinese Film Market 2 (1997): 27, 31, 54. The trend continued in the late 1990s, with *Titanic* (James Cameron, 1997) and *Saving Private Ryan* (Steven Spielberg, 1998) topping the box-office returns in China in 1997 and 1998.

From New Wave to Post–New Wave

INTRODUCTION

This chapter examines the Fifth Generation filmmakers' cinematic transition from New Wave art film to post–New Wave classical film. It addresses economic and textual strategies the Fifth Generation filmmakers, chiefly, Chen Kaige, Tian Zhuangzhuang, and Zhang Yimou, utilized to compete with Hollywood for both global and domestic market shares. At the core of the Fifth G's transition from art cinema to classical cinema is its reprising of a continuity narrative strategy. Stylistic principles of post–New Wave and its cultural/cinematic heritage are examined through textual analyses of the Fifth G films from the late 1980s to the mid-1990s, chiefly, Chen Kaige's *Farewell My Concubine* (1993), Tian Zhuangzhuang's *The Blue Kite* (1993), and Zhang Yimou's films as a group during the period. The textual analysis does not intend to inventory the stylistic parameters of post–New Wave but to elucidate the filmmakers' cinematic transition. This chapter also links the transition of the Fifth G with Chinese cinema's general trend of commercialization. Finally, this chapter discusses post–New Wave's emerging domestic bent since the late 1990s as the domestic market began to demonstrate its profit potential for films with popular appeal.

FROM ART TO COMMERCE: THE TRANSITION OF THE FIFTH GENERATION

The transition of Chinese film from a planned economy to a market economy and its subsequent shift from art wave to entertainment wave since the late 1980s profoundly affected the Fifth G's film practice. The commercialization of Chinese cinema and the subsequent renewal of a populist cinematic view privileging entertainment film encouraged the Fifth G's transition from the highbrow modernist cinema to the popular classical cinema. The transition from New Wave to post–New Wave was, in essence, the transition of Chinese cinema's prolonged modernization movement from the modernization of film text to that of film economy. At the core of the transition was Chinese cinema's functional shift from ontology and pedagogy to economy and entertainment. Economically, post–New Wave adopted a coproduction approach that utilized international capital, global distribution networks, and multicultural audiences. Stylistically, it adopted an approach that sought to reconcile cinema with drama, a route antithetical to the Fifth G's early aspiration of divorcing cinema from drama.

By the late 1980s, the modernist cinematic movement that demanded the separation of cinema from stage drama and literature had given way to the classical movement that reprised Chinese cinema's shadowplay principle privileging films' theatrical roots and a classical narrative formula inspired by Hollywood melodramas popular in China in the 1920–1930s. Hollywood's melodramatic formula was reappropriated and made popular again in post–Mao Mainland China by the third and fourth generation filmmakers such as Xie Jin (*Hibiscus Town*, 1986) and Wu Tianming (*Old Well*, 1987) in their sensational depictions of the anguished sufferings and uncertainties of ordinary Chinese during the Cultural Revolution. As such, "good narration," according to popular tastes, was expected to contain elements of classical narrative. The Fifth G's early obsession with formal experimentation clearly did not fit such a reemerging normative conception of good narration that privileged story over style. A cinematic transition became imminent in order for the Fifth G to survive Chinese cinema's economic reform.

Zhang Yimou's Cinematic Transition: "Bastard Films"

By the late 1980s, the New Wave's willful self-marginalization in its fascination with film form was taken by some critics as an attempt to conceal or compensate for its impotence in constructing classical narratives.[1] Doubts were expressed within film circles concerning the Fifth Generation's capability to construct classical narratives with popular appeal. The fact that most members of the Fifth G (coming of age during the Cultural Revolution) received limited traditional literary education seemed to legitimate such doubts.

The close relationship between a pragmatic film criticism and an idealistic film practice characteristic of Chinese cinema resulted in Chinese filmmakers' habitual, and indeed hyper-attentiveness to their films' critical reception. As such, the more the Fifth G was charged with narrative impotence, the more compelled its leading player, Zhang Yimou, was to demonstrate otherwise. As early as 1988, Zhang expressed in writing his concern with the critical consensus that New Wave filmmakers could not mount compelling narratives or direct professional actors.[2] He was eager to make a film that would combine the New Wave's formal experimentation with a classical plot structure. His directorial debut, *Red Sorghum* (1987), deliberately employed a popular narrative paradigm defined by goal-oriented characters who actively exert their agency to solve a clear-cut problem. The classical narrative was coupled, successfully, with his penchant for visuality, the flamboyant visual display.

Zhang made it clear that he intended to make *Red Sorghum* a "bastard film."[3] In the context of his statement, the somewhat "vulgar" term referred first to the film's story of adultery and second to the wanton assortment of stylistic and narrative devices utilized to demonstrate his ability to construct a compelling drama pleasing to popular taste. Most important, Zhang strove to foreground the love story between the two protagonists. In invoking the term *bastard*, he was not hesitant in acknowledging his pragmatism in soliciting critical approval and courting popular taste at the expense of New Wave's modernist aspiration. While recognizably New Wave in its self-reflexive visual style as opposed to the self-effacing classical style, *Red Sorghum*'s foregrounding of story over style pioneered the stylistic transition of the Fifth G from a modernist cinema toward a classical one. *Red Sorghum*'s visuality, for example, its erotic display of richly colored props and ethnographic details, contrasted sharply with *Yellow Earth*'s (Chen Kaige, 1984) more subdued visual style characteristic of Bergmanesque narrational austerity, for which Zhang served as the cinematographer. The courtship between formal extravaganza, or visuality, and dramatic tension and continuity resulted in a commercial film that begs for artistic recognition, or an art film with box-office potency. Such explains most of Zhang's films' paradoxical status as both international art cinema and domestic commercial cinema.[4] Viewed from a postmodern perspective, Zhang's films are commercialized art films whose style effectively renders artificial the division between art and commerce.[5] Such would be the case of post–New Wave, in general.

As a populist cinematic view and a concomitant entertainment wave continued to redefine the culture of Chinese cinema in the late 1980s, Zhang turned his attention to popular genre films, making an action adventure, *Codename Cougar* (1988), a story about a failed airplane hijacking involving the governments of Taiwan and Mainland China. Attempting to weave together action, political intrigue, and art to please both the critics and the public, *Codename Cougar* was another bastard film, albeit one without much commercial success.[6] Zhang's rendezvous with the male-oriented genre turned sour. Economically, the Hollywood action-adventure formula was too expensive for Zhang to replicate, and, politically, China was no place for an Oliver Stone–style political intrigue. Nonetheless, the critics generally welcomed the New Wave's venture into the popular action genre in the hope that the Fifth G might eventually reconcile art with commerce. Zhang was not alone in his new venture. In their attempt to rescue studios under box-office pressure, other New Wave directors also tried their hand at popular genre films, with limited success.[7]

Meanwhile, the critical and commercial success of *Red Sorghum* attracted investment interest from overseas. China's newly relaxed production policy made transnational coproductions possible. With financial backing from Japanese investors, the Tokuma Company, Zhang made *Judou* (1990), a rural melodrama set in feudal China, a project otherwise impossible under China's debt-ridden studio system. In *Judou,* Zhang maintained a delicate balance between his impulse for visual extravagance and a classical narrative's box-office potential.[8] The success of *Judou* won more overseas investment for Zhang and further liberated him from the constraints of domestic economics. The success of *Judou* also meant that his ability to narrate a popular drama was no longer in doubt. Freed from domestic commercial and critical concerns, Zhang's next project, *Raise the Red Lantern* (1991), displayed his formal obsession at its extreme.

A literary adaptation, *Raise the Red Lantern* is a slow-paced film about the rivalry among four women whom a wealthy man keeps in pampered imprisonment. Unchecked by Chinese critics and encouraged by the international art-film market, Zhang's stylistic excess reached its apex. Set in 1920s China, the film luxuriates in decor and landscape. Its sumptuous visual style was achieved on an impossibly thrifty 125,000 yuan (US$1 million) budget. The film's setting of a wealthy family's compound was perfect for Zhang's lavish visual display. As he plays out his melodrama, Zhang seems to wallow in nostalgia for the glamorous artifacts of a despotic past. The film spends much time lingering on exotic ethnographic details such as refined-looking furniture, utensils, food, and the erotic custom of raising the red lanterns. Each day the chamberlain will raise the red lantern in front of one of the women's houses, and that woman will be blessed with the master's favors. The ritual of raising lanterns was said to be Zhang's inventive contribution to Su Tong's original novel. The film was a global sensation, garnering a nomination for the best foreign film from Oscar in 1992. The film was also voted the best picture by Chinese audiences in 1993. The overseas critical success and domestic popular success of *Raise the Red Lantern* raised eyebrows among the Chinese critics. Though the film's physical splendor arguably underlines the sad fable of woman as ornament, its dour theme and visual extravagance was deemed, at best, reactionary and, at worst, ingratiating by some Chinese critics. Doubts were also expressed about Zhang's versatility as a filmmaker.

As if to demonstrate his versatility, Zhang took a drastic turn for his next project, *The Story of Qiuju* (1992). A cinema verité–style film set in contemporary China, *The Story of Qiuju* recounts a humorous story about a village woman's tenacious quest for justice. In this film, Zhang replaced his flamboyant visuality with a subdued depiction of village lives. Shooting on location with a smaller and more mobile camera, Zhang warmly observed the village with long takes and slow pans. The film shocked Zhang watchers for its stylistic transformation from structuralism to naturalism, which recalled Italian Neorealism.[9] To the Chinese critics, the film was a welcome sign of the prodigal son's return to the humanistic tradition of an earlier Chinese cinema. Incidentally or coincidentally, a debate was waging in the early 1990s among Chinese intellectuals concerning the loss of a humanist spirit in China's cultural landscape.[10] *The Story of Qiuju* suggested Zhang's embrace of such a humanist spirit embodied in the films of third and fourth generation filmmakers such as Xie Jin, Wu Yigong, and Wu Tianming.

Zhang's next project, *To Live* (1994), moved further toward this humanistic tradition. A "humanist spirit" was reflected in the film's tender rendition of one family's struggle over decades of turbulent Chinese political movements. Zhang expanded his focus from individuals to a family, getting in line with the Confucian emphasis on family as the central unit. Indeed, up to *To Live*, Zhang's internationally recognizable films had all featured female leads and dealt with woman's suffering in a culturally repressive Chinese society. The transformation from a woman's saga to a family's saga brought in a much broader social context with more immediate cultural relevance to the contemporary Chinese. Though covering major political events during Mao's reign, the film did little to court political controversy. As Zhang commented, in underscoring the resilience of ordinary Chinese folks, he was to make a genuinely populist film.[11] Zhang sent the film to the Cannes Festival without obtaining prior permission from the Chinese authorities, which provoked the banning of the film in China's domestic market. The fate of the film was further complicated by being associated by overseas critics with the two more politically provocative films dealing with the same period of modern Chinese history: *The Blue Kite* (Tian Zhuangzhuang, 1993) and *Farewell My Concubine* (Chen Kaige, 1993). The film made its way back to China through unofficial channels. Its popularity among Chinese patrons was attested to by Zhang's remark that upon returning to his hometown from Cannes he discovered that "everybody had seen the film."[12] The film would eventually be released in video-compact-disc format to a warm popular reception in the late 1990s.

Shying away from any potential political implication, Zhang returned to a safer historical period for his next feature *Shanghai Triad* (1995), a gangster movie set in 1930s Shanghai. Seven years after the failure of *Codename Cougar*, his first action adventure, Zhang was ready for another action genre. The gangster saga was told through the eyes of a teenage boy who arrived in Shanghai from a rural area to work for a triad boss. Upon his arrival, the boy witnessed the unfolding of a series of domestic conflicts involving women, money, and rivalry. Starting off as a gangster film about the decline of a Mafia family, Zhang's penchant for love triangles among a young woman, her old master, and her young lover turned the mob saga into a female *Godfather*. The foregrounding of female desire and sexuality was a bit of a stretch for a male genre traditionally privileging gangsters instead of their mistresses. Unlike a gangster saga of Hollywood, which centers on the male members of the gangster family, *Shanghai Triad*'s focal point is on the mistress of the triad boss, a seductive nightclub singer, Bijou, played by Gong Li. Zhang's camera constantly shifts its point of view, undermining the narrational coherence otherwise maintained by restricting the access to the story and characters to the boy's voyeuristic yet distant gaze. By switching the film's point of view between the peeping boy and the peeping God, the classical omnipresent point of view, Zhang makes arbitrary intrusions into the private life of Bijou, further altering the stylistic and thematic motifs of a classic gangster film. The Chinese film circle's critical and professional assessment of the film was lukewarm.[13] Yet the film became a hit, aided by the public's obsession with Zhang Yimou and his leading lady's love affair.[14]

The commercial success of *Shanghai Triad* underscored the significance of Zhang's second attempt to come to terms with action adventure, Hollywood's commercial staple. Once again it suggested his desire to appeal to the popular taste. Zhang was open about his contempt for an "elitist" approach still practiced by some of his contemporaries.[15] As the entertainment wave continued to grow stronger since the mid-1990s, Zhang became even less inhibited about his readiness to court popular taste. In an interview in 1997 concerning the critical assessment of his films, Zhang brushed off critical paradigms that pressed films into various "isms" and "waves."[16] He emphasized that "filmmaking was an individual activity and therefore should not be confined by 'isms' and 'waves,'" and that "a filmmaker's ultimate vindication was box-office success rather than critical acclaim."[17] From *Red Sorghum* to *Shanghai Triad*, in his quest for box-office success, Zhang had finessed a winning formula comprising thematic universality and multiplicity, theatricality, and compositional stylization and symbolism. The three components of Zhang's winning formula contributed to his (trans)cultural appeal to various audience demographics.

Thematic Universality and Multiplicity. Termed as a strategy of leveraging by Mette Hjort in his discussion of the transnational appeal of Danish cinema, cinematic multiplicity essentially combines the opaque, the translatable, and the international nature of certain cultural elements to connect with both domestic and international audiences.[18] Opaque elements are those firmly rooted within a particular cultural imagination that might not be understood by the cultural outsider, translatable elements that are understood by the outsider, and international elements that are shared transculturally. Thematic universality mostly relies on international elements for the comprehension of transnational audiences. *Red Sorghum*, Zhang's first feature, celebrated a carnivalesque spirit and the triumph of primitive passion. The theme, while refreshingly provocative to the Chinese newly liberated from Mao's rigid policing over their most intimate personal affairs, was equally appealing to the international art film circle long fascinated with the clash between nature and culture. Zhang's subsequent films *Judou*, *Raise the Red Lantern*, and *Shanghai Triad*, with their bleak and fatalistic tone, dealt specifically with female sexual transgression and the brutal punishment imposed by the patriarchy, a theme consistently appealing to the liberal-minded Western intellectuals and at the same time daring and, hence, sensational to the Chinese public. *The Story of Qiuju*, though specific to the time and space of the contemporary Chinese legal system, ultimately dealt with human relationships and the dilemma of humanly enforced regulations on human relations, another universal subplot. *To Live*'s comic depiction of ordinary folks' optimistic resilience in surviving unthinkable suffering had its appeal to both Zen Buddhism–influenced Eastern culture and Judeo-Christian–influenced Western culture. In sum, Zhang's "national allegories" were both culturally specific and cross-culturally recognizable.

The subplots in Zhang's films were not only transcultural but also ambiguous and multilayered, encouraging multiple interpretations from various political and cultural backgrounds. In the case of *Red Sorghum*, to Western eyes the symbol of red sorghum, where an illicit sexual consummation occurred, might suggest some sort of mythical oriental rituals and folk costumes and is hence culturally exotic. To the Chinese audience, it simply suggests a forbidden sexual relationship not presentable due to the censorship and is hence disgusting and exciting at the same time. To the Chinese critic, it signifies a filmmaker's profound reflection on traditional Chinese culture and grants the film much cultural and artistic significance. The same principle applies to the cinematic elements such as red lanterns in *Raise the Red Lantern*, the dye mill in *Judou*, and the puppet show in *To Live*. Both thematic universality and multiplicity contributed to Zhang's and the post–New Wave's cross-cultural appeal, in terms of the domestic and the global and the popular and the elite.

Theatricality. All of Zhang's popular films are literary adaptations, which have been the main staple for the Fifth Generation. Yet while New Wave looked to poetry for inspiration for formal experimentation, post–New Wave looked to popular novels for solid dramatic foundations. Poetry brought to cinema narrative ambiguity and reflexivity, whereas novels tend to induce narrational intensity, clarity, and continuity. Post–New Wave's reliance on popular novels suggests its predilection for a classical narrative. Zhang expressed his admiration for Steven Spielberg's "storytelling ability," a knack for constructing dramatic tales with cross-cultural appeal.[19] In preferring the classical master Spielberg over the modernist masters Ingmar Bergman and Federico Fellini, Zhang's filmmaking philosophy contrasts sharply with New Wave's antitheatrical aspiration. However, while admiring Hollywood masters for their ability to manipulate audience emotions, Zhang's narrative is a simplified Hollywood version tailored to a particular geolingustic region. To accommodate Chinese audience's melodramatic taste "contaminated" by decades of the socialist realist cinema insisting on a clear-cut central conflict and unambiguous characterization, Zhang has significantly reduced the original novels' plot complexity and thematic density. Zhang confessed that he liked "the kind of work . . . that tells a very simple, not complex, story. It is tiresome to watch a film whose meaning is unclear."[20]

With the exception of *The Story of Qiuju* and *To Live*, Zhang's simplified popular narratives generally center around a love–hate triangle, with an unambiguous central conflict and final resolution. All of Zhang's films featured goal-oriented characters, most of them simpleminded rural peasants or mundane urban dwellers who are driven by their survival instinct. If the central conflict in *Red Sorghum* was somewhat unfocused, such conflicts were much clearer in Zhang's later features. The fate of the illicit relationship between Judou and Tianqin in *Judou*, the fate of the wealthy merchant's concubines in *Raise the Red Lantern*, and the fate of a woman's quest for justice in *The Story of Qiuju*, all worked within a tightly woven three-act structure progressing from an efficient exposition through a prolonged complication to a timely climax followed by a brief resolution.

Closely related to classical narrative was Zhang's theatricality. His films tend to privilege domestic settings with few changes of location and a relatively immobile camera. Cinematic motion is achieved more by actors' blocking and performance than by camera movement. With the exceptions of *The Story of Qiuju*, which utilized a cinema-verité style for location shooting, and *To Live*'s epic style with multiple outdoor settings, Zhang's films all dwelled on a few highly controlled interiors or exteriors: the sorghum field and the winery in *Red Sorghum*, the abandoned airport in *Codename Cougar*, the dye mill in *Judou*, the quadrangle in *Raise the Red Lantern*, and, finally, the gangster's Shanghai mansion and his isolated island resort in *Shanghai Triad*. Closely related to confined settings and camera immobility, Zhang fashioned a proscenium approach that emphasizes lateral blocking over staging in depth. He shied away from mise-en-scène's staging in depth while simultaneously invoking the stylized composition achieved by lateral blocking. For the most part in Zhang's films, characters enter and exit scenes laterally, much like characters in a stage drama. Corresponding to the few changes of location is the infrequent camera movement within one shot, which leaves the burden of cinematic motion to both cutting and character movement. Zhang is not hostile to cinematic motion; rather, his movements rely heavily on the event motion in front of the camera and on the movement and rhythm established by shot sequences. As such, Zhang's formal experimentation selectively combines mise-en-scène's stylized settings and expressive lighting with Soviet montage that took cinematic motion, particularly the symbolic editing, to its core. The combination is selective because it is conditioned by Chinese cinema's shadowplay tradition that tends to de-emphasize cinematic motion invoked by the movement of camera but emphasize narrative "transparency" achieved by discreet editing and subtle camera movement. The confined indoor setting, camera immobility, and lateral blocking recall the theatricality of Chinese cinema's shadowplay tradition as well as the mise-en-scène tradition of Western cinema. The theatricality in terms of experiments in performance and mise-en-scène was the continuation of a New Wave style fashioned by Zhang as opposed to Tian Zhuangzhuang, whose New Wave films were more interested in outdoor settings with fluid camera movement. Another element unchanged in Zhang's films from New Wave to post–New Wave is his compositional stylization and symbolism.

Compositional Stylization and Symbolism. The straightforward plot progression and one-dimensional characterization in Zhang's narrative is compensated by his color motif. Zhang is particularly attentive to the use of color for setting a tone for his films. He has a penchant for the primary colors of red, blue, and yellow. Zhang's obsession with the color red, by now well-known, is played out as red sorghum in *Red Sorghum,* red dye in *Judou,* red lanterns in *Raise the Red Lantern,* and red chili peppers in *The Story of Qiuju.* Emblematic of passion and vitality, the color red also matches the earth tone in Zhang's native province of Shanxi, where red is widely used for various festivities by the native inhabitants.[21] In *The Story of Qiuju,* red is used to embellish the film's overall yellow tone evocative of human life. While the yellow corn, yellow elementary school building, yellow mountain, and yellow billboard are suggestive of the film's overall warm and earthy tone, the colorful exterior shots of hanging chili peppers and the interior shots of reddish wall hangings add variety to the earth tone. Likewise, in *Shanghai Triad,* Zhang uses deep, rich colors to create moods: blue for ominous night scenes and gold and red for the romanticized rural setting. In Shanghai, cabaret performances are depicted through a smoky haze, and the mansion occupied by the gang boss is depicted in gold colors, suggesting an opulent and sterile beauty. Zhang's color schema is matched by his equally mannered composition. Zhang often delights in the symmetrical framing of gorgeous objects, be they human or landscape. The cascading sheets of fresh-dyed silk in *Judou* cut vertical lines that divide the screen into symmetrically balanced parts. *Raise the Red Lantern* is a maze of obsessively symmetric doorways framing doorways and courtyards leading inward to other courtyards, of patterned tiles on the roof and patterned indoor decorations.

Zhang's post–New Wave formula combining thematic universality and multiplicity, theatricality, and compositional stylization and symbolism finds a perfect unity in *Judou.* The narration in *Judou* achieves the consummate balance between stylistic avant guardism and narrative conservatism.

A literary adaptation, the film is named after its female protagonist who is sold into marriage to an older man, Jinshan, but relieves her sexual frustration with Jinshan's adopted son Tianqing. Judou and Tianqing's love affair produces a son Tianbai, who is taken as Jinshan's son and later kills both his legal father in a fatalistic accident and his biological father in a fit of rage over his affair with Judou. Supremely translatable in its theme, *Judou*'s subplot examination of Chinese Confucian ethics immediately elicits the Oedipal complex, a Western allegory. In its adaptation from novel to film, the story's historical span from the Chinese Civil War to the Cultural Revolution in the original novel is changed to a more vague period, with ambiguous historical references. While its main characters wear clothing of more contemporary style, some of the costumes in the film resemble a style popular at the end of the Qing Dynasty in the late 1890s. The film's lack of historical specificity and continuity has transformed the original novel's immediate cultural relevance to the contemporary Chinese to a universal abstraction that contemplates the constraints of human civilization, in general. Historical ambiguity renders the theme universal, making it a depiction of patriarchal repression, in general, rather than merely the particular repression of Chinese Confucian culture. Such an ambiguity also encourages readings at multiple levels: the depiction of repressed sexuality can be interpreted as a critique of gender bias and the cruelty and hypocrisy of civilization.

Zhang is not unfamiliar with the famous Hollywood catchphrase *high concept*, a story summary that can be easily condensed into a single sentence for a thirty-second television spot. High concept was championed by Spielberg who commented that an idea is going to make a pretty good movie if it can be pitched in twenyty-five words or less.[22] Spielberg's vision of a marketable concept suggests a striking, easily reducible narrative. Zhang's own project choices reflect his similar vision that "the deepest truth in the world may be the simplest—it may be what can be expressed in one sentence."[23] *Judou* can indeed be condensed into a one high-concept sentence: A young woman sold to an abusive old man relieves her sexual frustration with the man's adopted son, producing a boy who grows up to kill both men. The reducibility of *Judou*'s narrative lies in both its main character and its plot structure. Judou's multiple identities as wife, lover, mother, and an individual living in feudal China are reduced to one: a lover possessed by her uncontainable sexual desire. A strong-willed yet simple-minded woman, Judou actively seeks emotional and sexual relief from her somewhat passive love interest, Tianqin. While the multiple dimensions of Judou's subjectivity in the original novel suggest a more complex social–cultural reality, such thematic complexity is not Zhang's concern, since it would only add confusion potentially harmful to the film's popular appeal. *Judou*'s condensed characterization works nicely with the equally condensed plot structure. Temporal manipulation in the film strives to efficiently advance a coherent plot by following the classical lineal fashion of exposition, complication, and resolution. The condensed narrative is easy to follow by the mainstream Chinese audience who prefers narrative simplicity rather than complexity and by the overseas art cinema patron who might not be able to savor the nuances of a foreign culture.

The story of *Judou* is primal, and so are Zhang's cinematic strategies. Everything is told through gestures and colors. Zhang remarked that *Judou* was his attempt to return to "the traditional way of making film," the melodramatic tradition of classical Chinese cinema influenced by shadowplay and Hollywood melodrama.[24] The film's scandalous subject matter and its reliance on stylized performance and emotionally charged close-ups can be traced back to early Chinese cinemas.[25] Some critics compared Zhang's foregrounding of character emotions and the relationship between characters to Chinese ancient portraiture painting that traditionally emphasized human facial expression and relations between human figures instead of human bodies and their motion.[26]

During the process of adaptation, the film's setting was shifted from an open village to a closed dye mill. The mill provides an ideal location for Zhang's stylized and colorful mise-en-scène. Zhang's fascination with primary colors and sharp geometric lines is unmistakable in *Judou*. At the mill, vertical lines are cut by red, blue, and yellow streamers of dyed cloth hung out to dry. Low-key lighting and low-angle shots render the geometric imagery visually stunning. The utilization of various color schemes to capture the story's shifting mood, or the color motif, is especially prominent. As Jenny Lau notes in her detailed textual analysis of the film, the first portion of the film is dominated by the expressionistic bright red and golden yellow, which are evocative of a positive mood in the story, while the second portion of the film is dominated by blue and dark blue, suggestive of the tragic turn the story takes.[27] Lau further observes that the contrast of bright and dark colors of the same hue also relays different messages. The same color red suggestive of positive feelings and events is cast in an unpleasant, sinister, or even monstrous dark background during the murder and the sexual abuse scenes.

Compositional symbolism achieved by color variation is enhanced by the film's symbolic staging of ethnic rituals. Zhang's stylized staging of ethnic ceremonies, on the one hand, exposes the brutality and absurdity of Confucian rituals; on the other hand, the meticulously executed scenes, such as the naming ceremony for a newborn son and the blocking of the road and coffin required of survivors to show filial piety to the dead, suggest Zhang's fascination with the formality of the folkloric festivities. The indoor setting is convenient for Zhang's proscenium approach reflected in the film's frontality, the stagelike mise-en-scène enhanced by shallow focus and lateral blocking. Tracking shots are seldom utilized and plot progression is executed primarily through cutting and fading. Overall, the spatially confined locale and the primacy of montage and performance over camera mobility foregrounds *Judou*'s melodramatic conflict. *Judou* could easily be adapted to a three-character stage play set in a dye mill. Zhang's visual style became an organic part of the narrative and served to work out, visually, the film's central conflict. In his quest for audiences, Zhang accommodated his stylistic penchant for symbolic visuality to a popular narrative structure. Throughout his career, Zhang has danced between stylistic excess and the containment of such excess by the classical narrative paradigm, with Judou achieving a perfect balance.

In seeking validation from the critics to the public, Zhang transformed New Wave elitism into post–New Wave populism, a combination of art cinema's stylistic abstraction with classical cinema's continuity conventions. This combination contributed to his films' paradoxical stature as international art cinema and domestic popular cinema. In international film circles, Zhang's auteur status resulted both from his distinctive style and from his distributors' profitable positioning of him as a politically marginalized hero in China. Zhang, however, claimed to be apolitical in his homeland and was perceived as such by his Chinese patrons fed up with films of political significance during Mao's era. Zhang's films were generally well-received by Chinese audiences. *Red Sorghum* was a box-office hit. *Judou* and *Raise the Red Lantern* were released in China after he made *The Story of Qiuju* and were warmly received by audiences.[28] His recent film, an urban comedy entitled *Staying Cool* (1997), ranked number four in domestic box-office return.[29]

Lately, freed from both critical and financial pressure, Zhang has shifted his focus from popular entertainment film to serious social drama. His two recent films, *Not One Less* (1999) and *The Road Home* (1999), tackled contemporary social issues. Produced by Guangxi Film Studio, *Not One Less* defended the right of poor Chinese kids from the countryside to a basic education. The film was distributed by Sony Pictures in the United States and Columbia in Asia and Europe. *The Road Home*, an acting debut for the now rising star Zhang Zhiyi, is a paean for the purity of love between a man and a woman from a different era.[30] The film is a direct comment on the commercialization of China. When sent to Cannes, both films received political coverage insinuating that the films carried an antigovernment undertone. Zhang promptly refuted such interpretation and withdrew the films from Cannes.[31] It is uncertain whether Zhang withdrew the films under the pressure of the Chinese government.[32] But clearly, as China's domestic film market demonstrates its huge box-office potential and at the same time the overseas market continues to be dominated by Hollywood, Zhang is shifting his focus from the limited overseas market to the domestic market. Indeed, Zhang has always wanted his films to have a local audience; and a constructive relationship with the state is conducive in this regard. Having taken care of his dual concerns for critical and popular endorsement, Zhang is ready to patch things up with the state.

At the same time, as noted by Geremie Barme, culture in China has increasingly come under the sway of a new-style leader, the party technocrat who has been cultivating a softer image than that of Mao and Deng.[33] The phase of "soft" technocratic socialism is creating a new self-censoring cultural figure, the state artist. In their common search for the market, the new state and its cultural workers and cultural consumers have measured out cultural parameters based on consensus instead of coercion. Such parameters are duly observed by filmmakers to avoid possible cultural ostracism. Zhang is no exception. From *Red Sorghum* to *The Road Home*, Zhang has leaped from commercial film to social realist film, which pushes him further back toward Chinese cinema's shadowplay tradition.

Tian Zhuangzhuang's Cinematic Transition: From Docudrama to Melodrama

Tian Zhuangzhunag's transition was the most shocking because of his very publicly known, unabashed elitist cinematic claim of "making films for the audiences of the next century."[34] As it turns out, the audiences of "the next century"—this century, that is—have moved ever farther away from anything remotely New Wave. Tian modified his claim in the mid-1990s, suggesting that his early films' antitheatrical approach was actually motivated by his desire for success in the international art film circle and therefore had nothing to do with either an elitist or a populist cinematic view.[35] Indeed, as early as in the late 1980s, Tian had quietly shifted his attention to making popular entertainment films. After his two box-office disastrous New Wave features, Tian was obliged to turn out a number of contract films. Soon after, he turned his attention to popular genre films. His popular musical *Rock-n-Roll Youth* (1988) rode the tide of the rise of rock music among urban youth. Another popular feature, *The Imperial Eunuch* (1990), catered to mainstream audiences' interest in royal gossip. Tian's populist approach reached an apex in his internationally acclaimed yet domestically banned feature *The Blue Kite*. A year after the international debut of *The Blue Kite*, Tian was banned by the Ministry of Radio, Film, and Television from film production. The ban was lifted in early 1996, and Tian was elevated to a position of authority at Beijing Film Studio in the mid-1990s. He has since devoted his energy in film packaging, matching specialty directors with niche markets. Acting more or less as a semiofficial and semi-independent agent, Tian has helped push the films of the sixth generation onto China's screen. The experience of acting as a film broker has made Tian aware of the economy of film production and distribution. For his future productions, he vowed to shy away from Chinese cinema's big-budget mentality, focusing, instead, on small productions for niche markets.[36]

The Blue Kite tells the story of an ordinary family's tragic experience in the plague years of Mao. The original script of *The Blue Kite* was returned to Tian by the censor for a rewrite. Tian hired a writer to write a different script and had it approved. But he used his original script as the shooting script. He shot the film over a three-month period during the winter of 1991–1992 as a coproduction between Beijing Film Studio and Hong Kong's Longwick Film Production Ltd. After the shooting, he showed a rough cut to the Beijing Film Studio, the Film Bureau, and the Ministry of Radio, Film and Television. A joint decision was made that since the film did not follow the approved script it should proceed no further.[37] Tian was barred from shipping the working print to Japan for postproduction as he had originally planned. Since none of the film labs in China dared touch the film, the raw prints were put on a shelf for a year. Eventually, a company in the Netherlands, Fortissimo Film Sales, picked up overseas distribution rights and completed postproduction according to Tian's remote instructions. When the film was first shown at Cannes in 1993, partisans trumpeted it as vastly superior to the more visible, co-Palme D'Or'd *Farewell My Concubine*.

Depicting an extended family caught up in the political turmoil of 1950–1960s China, *The Blue Kite* maintains the epic length and extensive cast of characters formulaic of the classical double-track narrative of "little" people living through big events. Yet the big events in *The Blue Kite* serve to dramatize the little people, not the national history. The film opens in 1953, with the marriage of lovely Chen Shujuan, a schoolteacher, and gentle Lin Shaolong, a librarian. The two celebrate not only their love but also the dawn of a true People's Republic. The couple soon have a son, Tietou. The story was told from the viewpoint of the mischievous Tietou who, as the film progresses, grows from an energetic, impish toddler into a pubescent brat. The plot follows Tietou's childhood during the years 1953–1967 when China was caught up in the Rectification Movement and Anti-Rightist Campaign, then the Great Leap Forward, then the Cultural Revolution.

Throughout, Tian's narrative is a carefully plotted one, with many humorous and ironic incidents and coincidences. The progress of the story follows a rigorously constructed plot structure that highlights, chronologically, three marriages of Tietou's mother. After the birth of Tietou came the Rectification Movement of 1957 when citizens were urged to "let a hundred schools of thought contend." A colleague of Tietou's father innocently implicates him in criticism of their work conditions. When the official policy reverts back to thought control, the father is banished to a labor camp, later to be killed by a falling tree. The informer helps the widow and becomes rather sympathetic, eventually winning the woman's love and marrying her. The second husband dies from a liver ailment aggravated by the rampant malnutrition of the early 1960s. The boy's mother is courted next by a high-ranking bureaucrat, who marries her and transports her to a bourgeois villa. Yet during the frenzy of the Cultural Revolution, Shujuan's third husband is humiliated and beaten by the righteous Red Guard. Though the mother's powerful, exasperated ties to her son (their mutual dependency and love) form the emotional spine of the film, there are also a dozen sharply etched minor characters filling in the background of this broad-canvassed domestic narrative. The narrative deftly covers a family with its run of exemplary bad luck: Tietou's uncle is going blind, and the uncle's girlfriend, the star of an army theater troupe, is sent to jail because she refuses an order to have sex with political leaders; meanwhile, Tietou's aunt is also implicated in the never-ending political movements, and Tietou's grandmother is heartbroken. The convoluted plot structure was the opposite of Tian's plotless, documentary-style New Wave films *Horse Thief* and *On the Hunting Ground.* The detached attitude, with "something emotionally lacking," in Tian's early films had given way to the melodramatic depiction of human suffering.[38]

The appropriation of a classical cinematic paradigm was achieved through rigid and, at the same time, elaborate formal parameters. The setting in *The Blue Kite* is shifted from an uncontrolled, naturalistic cinematic space to a confined indoor mise-en-scène. Most of the action in the film happens in and around a courtyard in Beijing, the Dry Well Lane. Such a confined cinematic space keeps the overarching narrative focused. The film also contains many elaborate moments that call for elaborate crane shots and convoluted montage. The death of Tietou's uncle, for example, uses an elaborate crane shot accompanied by a blue light raking across the set. Yet *The Blue Kite* also displays much stylistic restraint, foregrounding dramatic conflict over cinematic style. The framing, camera movements, and cuts in the film serve to give us the information we need without drawing attention to themselves. As such, long shots and shots for their formal beauty in Tian's New Wave films are replaced by medium and close-up shots and shots that advance the story.[39]

The film further contains many understated moments that defied melodramatic conventions. Its overall quiet, subdued, and realistic mood is more in line with the approach of humanist realism than with that of melodrama. The film warmly observes the rhythms of Tietou's extended family—the meals and arguments, the worries about money, and the sweet moments when a put-upon mom finds bliss playing with her bright child. While humor, irony, and observant detail make the film closer to Zhang's *To Live* than to Chen's *Farewell My Concubine*, certain keyed-up segments in *The Blue Kite* recall Chen's melodramatic devices. Overall, though, the film's meditative, subtle, psychological complexity diverged from Chen's epic-prone and Zhang's visually splashy styles. It is commonly acknowledged within the

Chinese film circle that Tian has always been something of a renegade, hard to classify.

From *Horse Thief* to *The Blue Kite*, Tian's ethnographic, semidocumentary approach with its mysterious, haunting, rigorous manner similar to an avant-garde aesthetics is replaced by a classical approach in favor of the rigidity of the plot structure and an understated formal style. *The Blue Kite* attested to Tian's serious attempt to reconcile with classical narrative he so despised earlier. Due to his lack of follow-up products, Tian's transition from New Wave to post–New Wave was least commented on by critics. Yet Tian's populist cinematic bent was more decisive, apparent from his popular genre films since the late 1980s.

Chen Kaige's Cinematic Transition: Concubine Film

It took half a decade after the release of Tian Zhuangzhuang's *Rock-N-Roll Youth* and Zhang Yimou's *Red Sorghum* for Chen Kaige to come to terms with a populist cinematic practice. His transition from New Wave to post–New Wave filmmaker was marked by the critical and popular success of *Farewell My Concubine.* The Golden Globe Award and the best foreign film nomination for the Oscar aside, the film was the biggest international art house box-office success in 1993.[40] Banned and then unbanned in China for its treatment of homosexuality and the brutality of the Cultural Revolution, the popular reception of *Farewell My Concubine* after it was distributed in China was positive.[41]

In *Farewell My Concubine*, Chen abandoned New Wave's modernist bent and turned to the melodramatic conventions of the classical Chinese/Hollywood. From *Yellow Earth* to *Farewell My Concubine*, the normative conceptions of how a film should look and sound clearly changed for Chen. Such a change could be attributed partly to a changed mode of production that legitimized a populist cinematic theme and a classical style. Yet the changed mode of production alone could not account for the stylistic variations within a classical approach. What is responsible for the stylistic variation among post–New Wave's three formidable figures is their individualized cinematic conceptions and practices shaped by their personal experiences. A look at the production history of *Farewell My Concubine* can help to untangle the complex creative dynamics involving Chen's personal condition and the conditions of Hong Kong/Mainland China production alliances.

Farewell My Concubine was a coproduction between Hong Kong–based Tomson Films and Beijing Film Studio. When Hsu Feng, the head of Tomson Films, first approached Chen with an adaptation project featuring a homoerotic story of the linked destinies of two Beijing opera stars, the idea of adapting a popular Hong Kong novel did not quite click for

Chen.[42] Historically, the colonized Hong Kong was looked down on by Chinese intellectuals as a cultural wasteland—the much marginalized British colony could not possibly produce any authentic cultural products that would carry historical significance. Still longing for a perfect match between an avant-garde cinema and an enlightened audience, Chen was shopping around for a more weighty project than the adaptation seemed to promise.[43]

Chen, however, could not spurn the overtures of a powerful Hong Kong producer. For one thing, his filmmaking had suffered a setback since *Yellow Earth*. He had made two flops since then. With their intellectually and philosophically inclined themes and minimal storylines, both *King of Children* (1988) and *Life on a String* (1991) were disasters critically and commercially. The austerity of Chen's philosophical probing became so unbearable, the critics at Cannes went so far as to give *King of Children* the "Golden Alarm Clock" for the most boring picture of the year. At the same time, Chen was witnessing, perhaps quite bitterly, his former cinematographer, Zhang Yimou, appearing as a rising star at international film festivals. Comments began to circulate that what made *Yellow Earth* a breakthrough for Chinese cinema was really its captivating visual image credited more to Zhang's imagination than to Chen's vision. The critical and commercial success of *Red Sorghum* added more pressure to Chen but at the same time suggested to him the possibility of a Chinese film that could not only bridge the gap between art and commerce but also generate cross-cultural appeal.

Chen seemed to have few choices but to accept Hsu's offer. What finally connected Chen with Hsu was the latter's self-claimed aspiration to make a globalized commercial movie that would also be culturally valuable.[44] Chen later told a reporter from the *World Press Review* that *Farewell My Concubine* was a commercial project with an intellectual soul.[45] Chen accepted Hsu's offer with three story changes. He added a section about the Cultural Revolution to make the epic more weighty, with a broader scale. Chen also beefed up the weak female character, a saucy prostitute who stirred up trouble and teased out the sexual ambiguities between the two leading men. As it turned out, some of the film's most moving and commercial moments were those depicting the bitter jealousy between her and the male characters. Finally, Chen had one of the male characters commit suicide instead of leaving for Hong Kong with his buddy after the Cultural Revolution.[46] The suicidal ending, along with the newly defined political edge and the presence of a stronger female character who further complicated the gay theme, made the story more melodramatic than its novel counterpart.

Budgeted at 500,000 yuan (US$4 million), *Farewell My Concubine* was considered a luxurious project compared to the 12,500 yuan (US$100,000) budget for the average Chinese film.[47] With a pre-sold commodity, the popular novel, on hand, Chen brought in established stars for the project. While the internationally acclaimed leading lady, Gong Li, would boost the film's appeal to the West, the leading man, Leslie Cheung, a Hong Kong pop singer and movie icon in the Far East, would secure audiences in Hong Kong, Taiwan, Mainland China, Singapore, and Japan. Shot on location in Beijing, Chen's film exceeded both budget and schedule. The movie's final price tag was roughly 625,000 yuan (US$5 million).[48] But the film came out a critical and commercial hit.

Farewell My Concubine differs decisively from Chen's early films. Thematically, the film moved away from New Wave's preoccupation with Chinese culture at large toward individuals' repressed emotions and sexual passion. Chen tackled, persistently, the theme of Chinese culture in all the films he made up to *Farewell My Concubine*. *Yellow Earth* served as a profoundly ambiguous and multilayered contemplation on China's revolution and Chinese civilization. *The Big Parade* (1985) examined relations between the minimal individual and the massive collective so blurred in the Chinese consciousness. *King of Children* raised philosophical issues on how children become part of a culture and what education could do to their and to China's future. *Life on a String* contemplated Chinese culture at its most fundamental level. *Farewell My Concubine* was the first film in which Chen began to focus on the fate of individuals rather than the nation. Spanning a half century of Chinese history from the era of the warlords in the 1920s to the end of the Cultural Revolution in the 1960s, *Farewell My Concubine* charted the tale of a love triangle that began in the harsh confines of an all-male Beijing Opera School where young Dieyi was being trained to take on female roles and his pal Xiaolou the leading-man parts. The boyish devotion, on Dieyi's part, soon turned into a homosexual crush and prevailed even after Xiaolou married a prostitute from the House of Blossoms bordello. Chen is outspoken about his emerging new thematic concerns in *Farewell My Concubine*, resulting partially from his own attempt to come to terms with popular taste, and partially from his Hong Kong investor and American distributor's interest in the picture's box-office potential.[49] Cinematic elements such as Chinese homosexuality, the exquisite Beijing Opera School, and the violent Cultural Revolution were at once culturally specific and cross-culturally translatable.

Stylistically, *Farewell My Concubine* moved away from Chen's early cinematic austerity that insisted on minimal dialogue and unconvoluted plot structure, nonstar casting, long shots instead of close-ups, location shooting, static camera movement, and simple and sparse mise-en-scène. The static long shots of the distant ravines and slopes of the Loess Plateau, the silent, expressionless soldier, and the muted peasants in *Yellow Earth* were replaced in *Farewell My Concubine* with elaborate long takes and close-ups of expressive faces for dramatic tension, the crucial component of a classical, communicative narrative.[50] Shots in *Farewell My Concubine* are not only tighter and shorter but also packed with more expressive images than in Chen's early films. The sexual articulation is delivered mainly through close-ups, the expressive gaze among the three main characters, and the star actors Gong Li, Lesley Chang, and Zhang Fengyi. Emotions are not only highlighted through expressive close-ups but are externalized through elaborating actions. Anguish is, hence, expressed in violence and love in lovemaking. At the beginning of the movie, Dieyi's mother, a prostitute unable to raise the child herself, deposits him at the Beijing Opera School. Informed that the school cannot take in a boy who has six fingers on one hand, she quickly chops off the extra finger. As opposed to the long takes in *Yellow Earth*, the images here are brief: swinging knife, crying child, bloody hand, new pupil at the school. Tragic materials are externalized through fast-paced actions and montage, contrasting sharply with Chen's New Wave films.

It is not without significance that the setting in *Farewell My Concubine* is shifted from the harsh, wild landscape in remote villages of Chen's early films to a soft, refined stage of an urban city. A well-decorated in-studio mise-en-scène superseded sparse natural settings. Large crowds of extras on massive sets are meticulously blocked to re-create the mood and ambiance of Beijing and the Beijing opera from a different era. The focused foregrounds and the neatly timed background actions are executed through subtle camera movement and decoupage. The highly elaborate narrative schema functions to unobtrusively sustain the viewer's attention. Meanwhile, the presence of the colorful Beijing opera granted Chen ample opportunity for a flamboyant visual exhibition, since a rich panoply of color and pageantry goes well with the characteristics of the school. The colorful mise-en-scène resembles Zhang Yimou's style more than that of Chen's New Wave style.

Farewell My Concubine returned to a cinematic convention that had historically combined the two seemingly antagonistic production conceptions and practices, one driven by profit, in the tradition of Hollywood melodrama, one driven by moral mission, in the tradition of Chinese shadowplay. The sentimentality and moralization of shadowplay tradition coincides nicely with Hollywood-finessed melodrama. Both shadowplay and classical Hollywood championed continuity editing for narrative coherence. They both fashioned a goal-oriented protagonist, although what counted as heroic differed based on different ideology. They both emphasized the sublimation of style to narrative and, hence, the primacy of a narrative over the primacy of a narrator. *Farewell My Concubine*'s reprising of classical Hollywood and classical Chinese signaled Chen's shift from experimental cinema to commercial cinema.

Chen's willful commercialization became more evident in his subsequent films, *Temptress Moon* (1996) and *The Emperor and the Assassin* (1999). *Temptress Moon*, a sexual intrigue about love and betrayal set in

1920s Shanghai, narrates a story about a callous gigolo's sexual dance with the female head of an opium-dazed family he is supposed to seduce. As convention has it, the woman he sets out to seduce, played by Gong Li, is his childhood love interest. The assignment opens a Pandora's box of unresolved childhood conflicts for the smooth urban hustler played by Leslie Cheung. With an investment of 50 million yuan (US$6.25 million), *Temptress Moon* has all the ingredients of Hollywood-perfected melodrama. The most expensive Asian film ever produced, *The Emperor and the Assassin* is a historical epic revolving around Ying Zheng, the ruthless third-century B.C. ruler who became China's first emperor after conquering and forcibly unifying the country's seven kingdoms. The conquest was achieved through a staggering loss of life. At the end, Ying Zheng's united China lasted only fifteen years. The film's production scale and its blood-soaked narrative skein of backstabbing imperial politics, murderous betrayals, and mass slaughter closely resemble one of Cecil DeMille's grandiose melodramatic epics. As Stephen Holden puts it nicely, "in its blend of pomp, suds, swashbuckling action and moralizing (about the price of power and imperial ambition), the movie conveys the sweep of history with a capital H(ollywood)."[51] The plot in *The Emperor and the Assassin* progresses in a straightforward way. The stunning scenery and battle sequences more often than not overshadow the development of characters. Both *Temptress Moon* and *The Emperor and the Assassin* followed the same international coproduction and distribution strategy, featured globally recognizable stars, and narrated visually and thematically provocative stories set in China's past.

From *Yellow Earth* to *The Emperor and the Assassin*, Chen's status as one of the pioneers of Chinese modernist cinema has changed to being one of the masters of classical cinema. What is at stake in Chen's cinematic transition is the globalization of post–New Wave, that is, the cross-cultural appeal of the commercialized Fifth G. The declining domestic film market forced the Fifth G filmmakers to branch out and test the global market. The extent of U.S. dominance in audiovisual markets on a global scale further compelled New Wave filmmakers to adopt the structural and textual strategies of Hollywood for their films' cross-cultural appeal.

COMPETITIVE STRATEGIES AND CROSS-CULTURAL APPEAL OF THE POST–NEW WAVE

As suggested by Michael Porter, to achieve and sustain a competitive edge in an increasingly globalized cultural market, national/regional cultural industries often employ certain production strategies, typically those of cost leadership, marketing focus, and product differentiation.[52] Applied to Chinese post–New Wave, a cost leadership strategy was achieved through coproductions financed by overseas investors that exploited local Chinese resources at a considerably lower cost. A marketing focus strategy was achieved by aiming for niche markets, the international art-house theaters, and the domestic mainstream theaters. A strategy of product differentiation was achieved through producing films with a distinct Chinese origin while retaining an international appeal through the foregrounding of certain cinematic elements cross-culturally recognizable. The international elements in *Farewell My Concubine, The Blue Kite,* and most of Zhang's films such as the danger of political dictatorship help viewers construe the image of China as a space with direct and indirect personal relevance to their own various cultural backgrounds. More specifically, the suffering of Chinese people under the repressive Confucian tradition and during Mao's reign may well have existed, or have been luckily prevented, elsewhere. Such cinematic elements can easily arouse sympathy and empathy among audiences of different cultures.

Aside from the structural strategies, post–New Wave also employed textual strategies finessed by Hollywood that have come to be associated in popular reception with the notion of "quality." In this sense, the globalization of post–New Wave is contingent on the globalization of what is taken as Hollywood-defined aesthetic qualities. Yet the Hollywood paradigm is not the product of inbreeding within Hollywood. The process of assimilation has always been a conscious choice for Hollywood. It is manifested in Hollywood's strategic appropriations of both talent and stylistic elements from European and Asian cinemas, as well as Hollywood's development of its own art cinemas dating back to the 1960s. However, even though various thematic and stylistic subtrends have been sustained throughout Hollywood's history, what has prevailed in *New Hollywood,* a term commonly applied to the American film industry since its financial crisis of the late 1960s and early 1970s, is a classical narrative gift wrapped with big-budget and high-tech. As argued by Kristin Thompson, New Hollywood's most important and typical narrative strategies are, in most respects, the same as those in use during the earlier studio era, that is, the classical era.[53] The globalization of Hollywood should thus be further defined as the globalization of the classical textual strategy that takes to its core the value of narrative clarity and coherence. The coherence and economy of narrative is complemented by Hollywood's star actors and directors and its commonly perceived superior technical aspects of acting, cinematography, mise-en-scène, editing, and so on. A point worth highlighting is that the relative worth of cultural products is determined only partially by comparative assessments of intrinsic features such as aesthetic qualities.[54] The salience of the (re)New(ed) Hollywood in a global market must be attributed in large measure to its economic, demographic, and geopolitical power as a major culture. Thus, the globalization of Chinese post–New Wave is, in

essence, a process of the economically, demographically, and geopolitically less powerful Fifth G's assimilation into the prevalent narrational
mode of the New Hollywood.

While recognizing the power dynamic involved in the globalization of
Hollywood, one must also acknowledge that cultural protection tied to
rules and laws cannot be equated with cultural survival or resistance
which are more related to historically formulated audience identities. Chinese spectators' taste was shaped, historically, by Hollywood-influenced
morally conscious melodrama with simple and clear moral implications
set up by a well-defined central conflict and delivered via contrived twists
and turns. The box-office success of post–New Wave could be attributed
partly to its reprising of such a cinematic strategy often associated with
quality in the popular psyche. Conversely, the box-office demise of New
Wave could be partially explained by the Hollywood-"affiliated" Chinese
spectators' indifference to alternative cinematic representations such as European art cinema, or for that matter, the historical materialist/socialist realist cinema. As such, the Fifth Generation's selective visual representation
and its appropriation of a classical narrative paradigm are motivated more
by the concerns of economic well-being than those of cultural identity.

Yet, in an ironic twist, post–New Wave's reprise of a classical narrative
actually connected the Fifth G with Chinese cinema's theatrical roots. The
classical narrative rejuvenated in New Hollywood is not necessarily
unique to the American film industry, since various cultures share a similar progression of narrative. In the case of Chinese cinema, its shadowplay
tradition genetically linked to traditional Chinese stage drama very much
resembled classical/New Hollywood. However, the Fifth G's renewed attention to feature films' theatrical repertoire is not a complete throwback
to shadowplay tradition that privileged cinema's dramaturgy. Rather,
post–New Wave took to its core motion picture's visual potency while
seeking to synthesize cinema's visuality with drama's theatricality. Thus,
the antagonistic relation between film's audiovisual parameter (cinema)
and theatricality (drama) under New Wave is transformed in post–New
Wave to a balanced unity. The ultimate goal of the newly realized honeymoon between the two was to fully extend the feature film's pictorial and
dramatic potential in order to compete not only with Hollywood but with
television and home video.

From experimental cinema to commercial cinema, it seems that the cinema of the Fifth G has retreated from an oppositional cinema to a mainstream cinema. However, while pressured by shifting economic and cultural
conditions, the stylistic evolution of the Fifth Generation from New Wave to
post–New Wave is also internal/organic, consistent with its cinematic experimentation dwelling on the border of modernist cinema and classical cinema. While de-emphasizing classical cinema's affinity to drama, New Wave
filmmaking never went so far as to incorporate modernist cinema's princi-

ple of reflexivity and disjunctive construction. Consequently, the cinematic techniques it experimented with were limited mostly to symbolic editing and composition, leaving out modernist cinema's ambiguous expression and narrative fragmentation achieved through abrupt and elliptical filming and editing. The New Wave ultimately operated under André Bazin's idea(l) of objectivity and photographic realism. In a sense, the cinema of the Fifth Generation has always been a "communicative" one that centers around the transmission of a definite message through the identification of a prior reality, as opposed to a "writing" one in which disjunctive montage generates a dynamic play of meanings.[55] As such, the Fifth Generation's cinematic revolution was never radical. Lastly, stylistic variations exist among the three Fifth G filmmakers. The classicism in Chen Kaige is an epic-style narrative with massive scale in terms of settings and extras. To the contrary, the classical narrative in Zhang Yimou is an intimate one with few settings and virtually no extras. On the other hand, Tian Zhuangzhuang's is the most restrained, understated, and naturalistic, contributing to Chinese cinema elements of the commonplace, ordinary people, and the dose of daily life long missing in the films of Mainland China.

The post–New Wave's international bent coupled with Hollywood's sweeping reentry into China's domestic market linked, for the Chinese critics, Chinese cinema with a global market. As a national framework gave way to a transnational framework, Chinese film criticism underwent a transformation, shifting from its focus on issues concerning national cinema as an isolated entity to issues concerning the relationship between national cinema and international cinema. Postcolonialist theory with its distinctly critical function was taken up by the Chinese critics as the continuation of an ideological criticism in the era of globalization. "Eurocentrism" became the key concept for the Chinese postcolonialist critics to challenge the myth of the Fifth Generation.[56] The Fifth G's post–New Wave films were challenged for their legitimacy in representing China and Chinese culture. The accusation said that what the post–New Wave depicted was a distorted version of China, a version influenced by Eurocentrism and catering to Western taste. Consequently, the terms *Americanization* or *Westernization* of Chinese cinema became the buzzwords of film discourse, raising the issue of Chinese cinema's cultural identity. At the center of the debate is the question of whether the commercialization and globalization of the Fifth G has resulted in the privation of post–New Wave's, indeed Chinese cinema's, cultural identity.

What sets Chinese cinema apart from others is its traces of traditional Chinese visual arts, chiefly, Chinese opera and classical painting, and its social and cultural references and relevance to both Chinese audiences and the establishment of Chinese cinema. The influence of traditional Chinese stage drama and classical Chinese painting is apparent in post–New Wave. Indeed, post–New Wave's retreat to the shadowplay tradition, or its reclaiming of cinema's theatrical roots, makes it more in line with the tradition of Chinese cinema than that of New Wave. Post–New Wave's thematic reference and relevance to the Chinese audience are rather obvious. *Farewell My Concubine* and *The Blue Kite* are about the Chinese Cultural Revolution. All Zhang Yimou's post–New Wave films dealt with the story and culture of the Chinese during various historical periods. The cultural identity of post–New Wave is, hence, discernible through its textual relation with an already established discourse of Chineseness and its production relation with China's political economic system and a global capitalist system that dictates the global flow of cultural products. While the latter propels post–New Wave toward adopting a universal cinematic style, the former poses constraints on how far such a global tendency can go and therefore turns the issue of cultural identity into the question of balance, the possibility of combining opaque, translatable, and international cinematic elements in one film. Such a leverage strategy was utilized by post–New Wave in its striving for global recognition and market share and its simultaneous desire for its films' domestic popularity.

Indeed, the Hollywoodization of post–New Wave has more to do with China's overall economic reorientation than with Hollywood. In terms of cultural relevance to the establishment of Chinese cinema, neither post–New Wave nor New Wave emphasized cinema's pedagogical function. While post–New Wave foregrounds film economy, New Wave focused on film art. In terms of formal parameters, Chinese cinema's patterns of staging, shot relations, editing, inserts, and so forth are the result of the confluence of both traditional Chinese arts and global cinematic heritage.

Interestingly, as Chinese cinema's economic reform gradually opens up new domestic revenue and attracts multiple domestic and international financiers, and as China's cultural, economic, and political atmosphere becomes more stable and relaxed (at least in the entertainment sector), post–New Wave has changed its cinematic strategy, turning to making films with a domestic bent. The Fifth G became less swayed by the critical discontent and more concerned with cultivating a friendly relationship with the state for its films' guaranteed domestic market. Chen's *Temptress Moon* and *The Emperor and the Assassin* and Zhang's *Staying Cool, Not One Less*, and *My Father, My Mother* (1999) all targeted the domestic market. While Chen still exercises a dual schema approach combining global and indigenous markets with relatively lightweight box-office returns in both markets, Zhang's "domesticated" films have consistently provided excellent box-office returns. On the other hand, Tian is involved in coming up with new story concepts and putting together marketable projects for the new generation filmmakers.

The post–New Wave's "reactionary"/retrospective style and culturally localized stories have made it less attractive in the international art film circle. Zhang himself suggested that films such as *Staying Cool* could not possibly be a hit on the international market, since it utilizes mostly the opaque cinematic elements such as Chinese slang, humor, and certain characteristics of interpersonal relations rooted in traditional culture flattering only the Chinese audience.[57] The post–New Wave's domestic bent suggests the immediate impact on the development of Chinese cinema of China's domestic political, cultural, and economic situation. Of course the domestic situation constantly responds and adjusts to any new direction in global trade and cultural exchange. The international art film circle is undergoing its own transformation, becoming increasingly commercialized and competitive and being increasingly dominated by films associated with Hollywood in their financing and distribution. The commercialization and mainstreaming of international art cinema have marginalized cinemas from minor cultures with less consistent global appeal than the commercial art films produced by Hollywood-led majors. Furthermore, the returning to a classical narrative is not a local phenomena but a global one, manifested in the films of new Hollywood. Both the changing domestic and global cinematic environments propelled Chen Kaige, Tian Zhuangzhuang, and Zhang Yimou to turn to producing popular films targeting mainly China's domestic market.

The transition from New Wave to post–New Wave was really the transition from experimental film to popular film, with the former focusing on art and the latter on economics. Indeed, post–New Wave has come to represent a particular mode of production involving international financing and distribution and domestic labor and equipment. In this regard, all contemporary mainland productions involving international financing and distribution can be subsumed under the rubric of post–New Wave. As such, the conception of the Fifth G as a distinctive group has become obsolete. Indeed, the style of the Fifth G during the era of post–New Wave no longer presents a unity. Stylistic diversity exists among Chen, Tian, and Zhang. The only common ground among the three up to the late 1990s was their avoidance of contemporary subjects. Yet the avoidance of contemporary subjects, too, is not distinctively Fifth G. Rather, it was a general trend among filmmakers who were shying away from any political implications of contemporary subjects. Being linked together only for their association with a particular film class, the disintegration of the Fifth G in the era of post–New Wave has led to the collapse of the generational paradigm as an efficient descriptive concept. Rather, Chinese cinema in the new era can be more productively addressed in terms of types of films than filmmakers.

By the mid-1990s, the Chinese film industry was producing four types of films: big-budget blockbusters often involving private investors, government-promoted and government-sponsored main-melody epics; middle-budget entertainment films; and offbeat low-budget urban dramas by the sixth generation filmmakers. The entertainment films had become the staple of Chinese cinema, with the commercialized main-melody picture and post–New Wave films getting shares of the mainstream market. The big-budget blockbusters included Chen and Zhang's post–New Wave films which often commanded sizable audiences. The main-melody pictures were able to draw audiences through either government-reinforced and government-sponsored screenings or the films own commercialized packaging. The sixth generation's small-scale films became the marginalized art cinema of the new era.

While the big-budget blockbusters, the main-melody propaganda pictures, and the sixth generation urban dramas were making the buzz, the majority of Chinese films were the middle-sized entertainment pictures, most of them mediocre genre films, including detective films such as *The Shadow in the Rose Building* (Qin Zhiyu, 1995) and *The Foggy House* (Huang Jaing Zhong, 1995), comedies such as *Living With You* (Huang Jun, 1995) and *Fool in Love* (Chen Guoxing, 1995), and kung fu films such as *Heaven and Dragon* (Qian Yongqiang, 1995), or films dealing with seasonal topics such as *Stock Fever* (Li Guoli, 1995).[58] Such genre films performed less well at the box office than their Hollywood and Hong Kong counterparts.

FROM POST–NEW WAVE TO POST-WAVE

From marginal to mainstream, the films of the Fifth G filmmakers have walked up or down a ladder, depending on one's perspective. Indeed, the critics of the Fifth G have shifted from a constellation of low-brow audiences and conservative critics and professionals during its New Wave era to that of high-brow audiences and liberal intellectuals and professionals in the mid-1990s.[59] Though the transition of the Fifth G paralleled Chinese cinema's and Chinese culture's general trend of commercialization promoted by the state's economic modernization project, the Fifth G's populist cinematic turn disappointed many of the New Wave champions who considered the transition vulgar. Indeed, by the mid-1990s, rapid commercialization had left many filmmakers and established writers unable to appeal to a wider audience. Prominent literary figures such as Liang Xiaosheng, Xiao Xialin, and Zhang Chenzhi expressed their dismay over the growth of a populist literary trend that catered mostly to the taste of a vernacular public.[60] The Fifth G's post–New Wave films became the consummate example of cultural vulgarization within the Chinese film circle.[61] The Fifth G was further faulted by its mentor Zheng Dongtian and the prominent cultural critic Dai Jing for its courting of popular taste at the expense of its early modernist aspiration.[62] Nonetheless, mainstream Chinese audiences embraced the transformed Fifth G. Most of Zhang's films found enthusiastic local audiences. While Chen's domestic popularity is less overwhelming than Zhang, *Temptress Moon* did relatively well at the

box office in comparison with other domestic films.[63] After many cuts demanded by the censor, *Farewell My Concubine* was screened in theaters to
popular praise. While the popular reception of *The Blue Kite* domestically
is still up in the air due to the prolonged ban, Chinese film practitioners
who watched the film on tape were generally positive about Tian's coming
to terms with a classical style more in line with the humanist spirit of early
Chinese cinema.

Regardless, by the mid- to late 1990s, the amount of critical attention the
Fifth G enjoyed from the mid-1980s to the mid-1990s has been overshadowed by the discourse concerning the film market. The Fifth G has become
history, with its remaining two giants Chen Kaige and Zhang Yimou joining the search for audiences, both domestically and globally. Chen and
Zhang's international bent was no longer a curse, as the Chinese film industry became ever more eager to break into a global market. In October
1993, for the first time in Mainland China, an international-oriented film
fair, the Shanghai Film Festival, emerged with major studios making their
sales pitches to overseas buyers.[64] "Get Connected with the International
Circuit" was the slogan for the festival. The festival confirmed that the
kinds of film desirable in the international film market were historical-cos-
tume entertainment films with an oriental flavor and art film reflecting
Chinese life and customs, especially those that had won international film
awards. Such confirmed the strategy of post–New Wave and encouraged
the adoption, by many studios and independent filmmakers, of such a
strategy comprising a popular narrative formula, international coproduction and distribution, and historical stories with distinctive Chinese flavor.
As such, tales of peasant atavism, Taoist mysticism, and stories of the wis-
dom of the East were aptly exploited by filmmakers attempting to make it
to an overseas market.

The political, economic, and cultural changes during the first half of the
1990s nurtured the transition of the Fifth G and Chinese cinema, in general.
The popularization of post–New Wave strategy made post–New Wave itself
a suprawave box-office formula. As such, Chinese cinema is no longer concerned with various art waves, since the only wave economically viable is
the entertainment one. Led by Chen and Zhang's post–New Wave films, the
entertainment wave has engaged an avalanche of reenergized fifth generation filmmakers such as He Ping (*The Swordsman in Double-Flag Town*, 1990)
and restless newcomers such as Jiang Wen (*In the Heat of the Sun*, 1995). Market forces have played such a decisive role in film production and criticism
that the old paradigm dividing films into art and entertainment or various
waves and isms by the established film critics was no longer sustainable.
Films were now being more snugly divided into the categories of *unmarketable*, *nonprofitable*, and *blockbuster* by the box-office-conscious industrial
practitioners.[65] To the policy makers, films, like any other cultural products,
were classified as *prohibited*, *tolerated*, and *supported*. Films that might

provoke censorship were now considered, by studios and individual film-makers, at best foolish and a nuisance and at worst marketing ploys that attempt to attract underground and overseas buyers. Both Chen and Zhang have avoided any real clash with the government. Zhang's withdrawal from Cannes due to the festival's very political interpretation of his current films might just be a gesture to reconcile with the state. The formerly underground filmmaker, Zhang Yuan, has surfaced, making apolitical films with popular appeal. Films that found a positive relationship with their social context might receive either critical or political endorsement. Yet only films with social relevance and that were, at the same time, popular among the audiences would be supported by both the policy makers and the critics. A state-subsidized biopic about a model Communist cadre, *Jiao Yulu* (Han Shanping, 1991), struck a chord with the public's nostalgia for an idealized moral past, contrasted with the market-corrupted present. Though the product of an unabashed ideological campaign, the film's impressive 420 prints, a record for a Chinese cinema, made it a commercial success.[66]

By the mid-1990s, while the big-budget entertainment pictures and historical epics were notable for their big box-office returns, the majority of the domestic commercial entertainment films, most of them thematically simplistic and stylistically formulaic genre films, continued to fail at the box office. Theaters had to rely on big imports to draw audiences. With the practice of the mandatory allocation of two-thirds of screen time being reserved for domestic pictures, theaters often complained about their sluggish business. Meanwhile, the lack of funding has resulted in the studios' low production capacity, which drastically reduced the number of domestic films available for screening. The shortage of not only quality features but the sheer number of films available for circulation discouraged the distributers–exihibitors, casting shadows on the future of Chinese cinema. While receptive to big imports, the domestic market proved rocky to the domestic pictures. The crisis of Chinese cinema was far from over during the second half of the 1990s; neither was Chinese cinema's prolonged economic reform. Film reform and the state of Chinese cinema during the second half of the 1990s will be the topic of my next chapter.

NOTES

1. See, for instance, Chen Muo, *On Zhang Yimou* (Zhang Yimou dianying Lu) (Beijing: China Film Press, 1995).

2. Zhang Yimou, "Sing a Song of Life" (Chang yiqu shenming de zhange), *Dangdai dianying* (Contemporary Film) 13, no. 2 (1988) 81–88.

3. Zhang rejects the categorization of cinema into mainstream and New Wave and considers *Red Sorghum* a bastard film. See ibid. See also Luo Xueying, *Red*

Sorghum: The Real Zhang Yimou (Zhang Yimou xiezheng) (Beijing: China Film Press, 1988), 49.

4. *Red Sorghum* was a major box-office success in China. Tickets in Beijing were twice as expensive as the average urban price and there was a brisk trade in black market tickets. See Chris Berry, "Market Forces: China's 'Fifth Generation' Faces the Bottom Line," in *Perspectives on Chinese Cinema*, ed. Chris Berry (London: BFI, 1991), 114–124.

5. The Chinese film critic Chen Muo, in his somewhat too-broad categorization of Chinese cinema, suggests that commercial cinema naturally comprises government-sponsored picture, art picture, and entertainment picture. See Chen Muo, *Anthology of Chen Muo's Film Criticism* (Chen Muo dianying pinylun ji) (Nanchang: Baihuazhou Art and Literature Press, 1997).

6. See Luo's interview with Zhang in her *Red Sorghum*, 62–63. The failure of *Codename Cougar* would unfortunately delay such an aspiration for another ten years—Zhang did not make another contemporary urban-setting film until 1997 with his comedy debut *Staying Cool*.

7. See Berry, "Market Forces."

8. Detailed textual analysis of *Jidou* is reserved for later in the chapter.

9. See Zhang's own words in Robert Sklar, "Becoming a Part of Life: An Interview with Zhang Yimou," *Cineaste* 2, no. 1(1993): 28.

10. Xu Lin and Zhang Hong, "The Crisis of Literature and the Humanist Spirit" (Wenxue de weiji yu renmen jingsheng), *Shanghai Wenxue* (Shanghai Literature) 6 (1993): 65–66.

11. See Stuart Klawan, "Zhang Yimou: Local Hero," *Film Comment* 31, no. 5 (1995): 11–16.

12. Ibid.

13. See Ying Xiong, "On *Shanghai Triad*" (Guanyi yaoayao yaodao wuaipuo-qiao), *Dianying yishu* (Film Art) 248, no. 3 (1996): 8–10.

14. As it turned out, Zhang was on the verge of breaking up with his Gong Li while shooting the film. *Shanghai Triad* became Zhang's final collaboration with Gong Li.

15. See Tony Rayns, "To Live," *Sight and Sound*, October 1994, 60–68. Zhang's disadvantaged family background might partially explain his disdain for elitism and his easier transition from New Wave to post–New Wave than the Fifth Generation's other two major figures, Chen Kaige and Tian Zhuangzhuang who came from privileged families.

16. Chen Yan, "Zhang Yimou on *Staying Cool*" (Zhang Yimou tan youhua hao-haoshuo), *Dianying yishu* 256, no. 5 (1997): 66–67.

17. Ibid.

18. Mette Hjort, "Danish Cinema and the Politics of Recognition," *Post-Theory: Reconstructing film studies*, ed. David Bordwell and Noel Carroll (Madison: University of Wisconsin Press, 1996), 528–531.

19. See Luo's interview with Zhang in *Red Sorghum*, 51.

20. Ibid.

21. Chen, *On Zhang Yimou*, 295.

22. J. Hoberman, "1975–1985: Ten Years That Shook the World," *American Film* (June 1985): 36.

23. Rey Chow, *Primitive Passion* (New York: Columbia University Press, 1995), 236.

24. See Zhang's own words about returning to classical after New Wave, in ibid., 153.

25. See Paul Pickowicz's discussion of Chinese cinema's melodramatic tradition in "Melodramatic Representation and the 'May Fourth' Tradition of Chinese Cinema," in *From May Fourth to June Fourth Fiction and Film in Twentieth-Century China*, ed. Ellen Widmer and David Der-Wei Wang (Cambridge: Harvard University Press, 1993), 295–326.

26. See Jenny Kwok Wah Lau, "An Experiment in Color and Portraiture in Chinese Cinema," in *Cinematic Landscape*, ed. David Desser (Austin: University of Texas, 1994), 127–148.

27. Ibid.

28. See Robert Sklar, "Becoming a Part of Life: An Interview with Zhang Yimou," *Cineaste* 2, no. 1 (1993): 28.

29. See the domestic picture box office chart of 1997 compiled by *Dianying yishu* 260, no. 3 (1998) 1–2.

30. Zhang Zhiyi went on to star in Ang Lee's *Crouching Tiger, Hidden Dragon* (2000) and a leading role in Zhang Yimou's film *Hero* (2002), a martial arts flick.

31. I include here Zhang Yimou's letter to Gilles Jacob concerning Zhang's withdrawal from the 1999 Cannes Film Festival. The text was posted on the internet by Dr. Dina Iordanova, Centre for Mass Communication Research, University of Leicester, 104 Regent Road, Leicester LE1 7LT, England. It is a translation from the Chinese originally posted in the Internet edition of the *Beijing Youth Daily*, 20 April 1999. The Web address for the Chinese text is http://www.bjyouth.com.cn/Bqb/1990420/GB/3858^D042001B30.htm.

Respected President,

I have decided to withdraw my films *Not One Less* and *The Road Home* from you and will not be taking part in this year's Cannes Film Festival. The reason is I feel you have seriously misunderstood these two films and it is a misunderstanding I cannot accept.

My two films both concern beloved themes. *Not One Less* expresses our deep love for children and this whole national cultural situation for us today and our concerns for the future. *The Road Home* sings the praises of the truth and purity of love between a man and a woman. These are feelings common to all mankind. Therefore it is surprising that you critique my films on "political" grounds. This is nothing but political or cultural prejudice.

For many years, I have been an enthusiastic and active participant of the Cannes Film Festival. Cannes has an important place in my heart, just as it does for every other director around the world. To be selected to take part in Cannes is a great honor for us. But today, I have decided to withdraw because my faith in the cherished artistic motives of the festival has been shaken. I am very sorry that this has happened.

Whether a film is good or bad, each person can have his or her own way of looking at it, this is only natural. But I cannot accept that when it comes to Chinese films, the West seems for a long time to have had just the one "political" reading: if it's not "against the government" then it's "for the government." The naiveté and lack of perspective (lit. "one-sidedness") of using so simple a concept to judge a film is obvious. With respect to the works of directors from America, France and Italy for example, I doubt you have the same point of view.

I hope this discrimination against Chinese films can be overcome in time. Otherwise it will not only be an injustice to me, but also to other Chinese directors, including the next generation of young directors and their works.

Yours Sincerely,
Zhang Yimou

32. *The Road Home* won the Silver Bear at the Berlin Film Festival in 2000.

33. Geremie Barme's book *In the Red* (New York: Columbia University Press, 1999) has some lively discussions about the Chinese state's new governing style.

34. Tian came from a privileged family. His father served as the head of Beijing Film Studio, and his mother the head of Children's Film Studio. Both of them were well-accomplished film actors.

35. Howard Feinstein, "Filmmaker Tian Zhuangzhuang Cuts Loose with 'Kite,'" *New York Newsday* 10 April 1994, E2.

36. Wang Zhihong, "Tian Zhuangzhuang with Messier Hair," *China Screen* 3 (1996): 20–21.

37. See Xia Shangzhou's interview with Tian published in *Dianying yishu* 266, no. 3 (1999): 17–20.

38. See an interview with Tian in 1994 by Philip Lopate in "Odd Man Out: Tian Zhuangzhuang," *Film Comment* 30, no. 4 (1994): 60.

39. Ibid. I include a few relevant passages here:

Tian: "But after I finished *Horse Thief*, there was a period when I didn't make any films; this had a lot to do with censorship issues. Anyway, I began to question my own films. I realized the kind of film I was making before could only create sensations in people by evoking a mood. At the time I was quite happy with this. But I gradually realized that there was something emotional lacking in *Horse Thief*. Perhaps it was the portrayal of humans—the humans are too simplified. See, when I first started making films I was interested in the ideological problems of China as a whole. Gradually I became more interested in the people surrounding me and their psychology.

Lopate: But, for instance, the camera seems more distanced in *Horse Thief*, and there are more shots that seem there just for their formal beauty. It's a more formalistic work. In *Blue Kite*, the camera is closer, more middle-distance, and every shot advances the story. Would you care to comment?

Tian: I can only say I agree with all the things you've said so far. It was only after I made *Horse Thief* that I came to an understanding of this problem. It's not a problem of myself only, but my whole generation. We were pursuing something that was on the surface. We were formalists. Looking for formal beauty. A beautiful story, a beautiful environment, very beautiful colors, beautiful sound. Almost like an exhibition.

40. Hong Kong made *Farewell My Concubine* its entry for the Oscar when the Chinese government refused to allow it to enter the competition.

41. Nicholas D. Kristof, "China Bans One of Its Own Films; Cannes Festival Gave It Top Prize," *New York Times*, 4 August 1993, E4.

42. For a detailed report on the making of *Farewell My Concubine*, see Jianying Zha, *China Pop* (New York: New Press, 1995).

43. Ibid.

44. Michael Dwyer, "Silent Movies," *Irish Times*, 29 January 1994, E5.

45. See "Chinese Revolution," *World Press Review* (March 1993): 47.

46. The last change was condemned by the critics in Hong Kong as Mainland China's usual denial of the colony's location as a space of new order. Yet being from Taiwan where traditional Chinese culture was even more carefully preserved than on the Mainland, I suspect that Hsu would be particularly concerned with Hong Kong's subject position under the British shadow.

47. John Stanley, "Director Chen Kaige's Big Step," *San Francisco Chronicle*, 24 October 1993, E2.

48. See "Chinese Revolution."

49. See Zha, *China Pop.*

50. Easter Yau, "Yellow Earth: Western Analysis and a Non-Western Text," in *Perspectives on Chinese Cinema*, ed. Chris Berry (London: BFI, 1991), 62–79.

51. Stephen Holden, "A Bloodthirsty Unification of China," *New York Times*, 17 December 1999, E2.

52. Michael Porter, *The Competitive Advantage of Nations* (New York: Free Press, 1990).

53. Kristin Thompson, *Storytelling in the New Hollywood* (Cambridge: Harvard University Press, 1999).

54. See Hjort, "Danish Cinema and the Politics of Recognition," 520–532.

55. See David Bordwell, *On the History of Film Style* (Cambridge: Harvard University Press, 1997) 89.

56. See Zhang Yiwu, "Zhang Yimou in the Global Postcolonial Discursive Environment" (Quanqiu houzhimin huajingzhong de Zhang Yimou), *Dangdai dianying* 54, no. 3 (1993): 18–25.

57. See Yie Dan's interview with Zhang Yimou in *China News Digest*, 7 April 1998, C3.

58. The titles are selected from a comprehensive list of film compiled by *China Screen* in 1994–1995.

59. Editorial Board of *Dianying yishu*, *On Zhang Yimou* (Beijing: China Film Press, 1994).

60. See Barme, *In the Red.*

61. See Chen Muo, "The Fifth Generation's Decline" (Diwudai de shuaitui), in *Anthology of Chen Muo's Film Criticism* (Chen Muo dianying pinglun xuanji) (Nanchang: Baihuazhou Press, 1997), 30–40.

62. Ibid.

63. The market share of *Shanghai Triad* was reported at 46 percent and *Temptress Moon* 6 percent. While the former figure is considered exceptionally good, the latter one is not bad, given the dismal box-office return of average Chinese films.

64. See a brief report on the festival in *China Screen* 2 (1994): 31–34.

65. The newly established trade magazine *Chinese Film Market* published by the China Film Corporation treats films exactly around this line.

66. The film's box-office record was partly sustained by government-organized and company-sponsored screenings. See the news item in the Shanghai *Wenhui bao* (Cultural Report), 10 February 1991, 5.

5

Post-Wave:
"It's the Economy, Stupid"

INTRODUCTION

This chapter addresses the state of Chinese cinema from the mid- to the late 1990s. It focuses on the film industry's institutional restructuring, reprising Hollywood's model of vertical and horizontal integration, as well as on the industry's concomitant, commercially oriented film trends. In affecting the general trend in film production and criticism, the marketization and decentralization of the film industry directly contributed to the surge of entertainment pictures during this period. Furthermore, the ongoing economic reform was accompanied by the rise of popular culture led by Hollywood imports, which further opened the floodgates to Chinese cinema's commercial entertainment wave, what I term *post-Wave*, the wave that has engulfed both propaganda and art cinemas. The cinematic trends addressed include films of the writer Wang Shuo, of popular genres, of the tamed Fifth Generation filmmakers, and of the commercialized sixth generation filmmakers. Such trends directly responded to the industry's marketization agenda.

CHINESE CINEMA IN THE LATE 1990s

Chinese cinema in the late 1990s witnessed a further downturn. The popularity of big-budget domestic pictures in 1995 belied the fact that the majority of Chinese films performed poorly at the box office. While the 10 domestic blockbusters accounted for 24.8 million yuan (US$3.1 million) at the box office in 1995, the remaining 135 Chinese films produced in the same year earned only an average of 120,000 yuan (US$15,000) each.[1] A further blow to the Chinese film industry came from the fact that foreign films accounted for a disproportionate percentage of box office nationwide even in 1995. The ten big imports (six from Hollywood), shown under a percentage rental arrangement, accounted for just 3.3 percent of the total of 269 films exhibited in Beijing in 1995 but took in 40 percent of Beijing's box-office receipts of 92.6 million yuan (US$11.5 million).[2] While average imports did not pose a real challenge to the domestic films, the "box-office-sharing" Hollywood films have consistently overshadowed Chinese domestic pictures. Hollywood blockbusters continued to dominate the Chinese market throughout the late 1990s, due largely to the performance of *Titanic* (James Cameron, 1997) and *Saving Private Ryan* (Steven Spielberg, 1998) which together accounted for about one-third of the total box office in Beijing and Shanghai. *Titanic*, the box-office record breaker in China, accounted for 21 percent of Shanghai's total (38 million yuan [US$4.75 million]) and 28 percent of Beijing's total (36 million yuan [US$4.5 million]). The success of *Titanic* was partly the result of the Party General Secretary Jiang Zheming's enthusiastic endorsement. Upon his return from a state visit to the United States, Jiang exhorted the Chinese film industry to study and emulate *Titanic*. He interpreted the film to be a moving depiction of class tensions and love, and its popularity among Chinese audiences proved that films of entertainment value could be pedagogical and vice versa.

Interestingly, Chinese theaters' bidding war on Hollywood's big production contributed to the "big import fever." China's first auction for first-run rights of a Hollywood blockbuster was held in Shanghai on October 12, 1998.[3] The auction, staged by Shanghai Paradise Company Ltd. and the Shanghai Auction Company, was for the rights to premiere the Polygram film *The Game* (David Fincher, 1997). The Grand Theatre was the top bidder, offering 360,000 yuan (US$45,000).[4] In total, the seven theaters owned by Grand Theatre paid 1.72 million yuan (US$215,000) for the right to screen the movie for the first eight days of its run in Shanghai. Due to the unrealistically high bidding prices, the margins were extremely low; the 1.72 million yuan was barely recovered from box-office receipts. Nonetheless, a Shanghai Paradise distribution executive suggested that the auction was beneficial for film distributors and exhibitors because it encouraged competition. Cinema managers generally agreed with Shanghai Paradise's view, suggesting that they would participate in future auctions but would be more fiscally cautious.[5]

To curb the downturn, the Ministry of Radio, Film, and Television and the Ministry of Culture issued a joint circular in the spring of 1997 to mandate the allocation of two-thirds of screen time to the exhibition of domestic films.[6] The Chinese Film Distribution and Exhibition Association responded by launching a national-level theater chain, China Theater Chain, consolidating three hundred theaters in big urban areas to guarantee quality domestic films the best and most screen time.[7] In May 1997, the China Film Bureau issued yet another measure to reinforce the simultaneous opening of quality domestic films nationally at first-run theaters. The Chinese Internal Revenue Service was also involved, relieving the film tax on exhibition income.[8] Meanwhile, in an attempt to produce quality pictures, the average budget for a domestic feature was increased from 1.3 million yuan (US$162,500) in 1991 to 3.5 million yuan (US$437,500) in 1997.

However, these protective measures did not curb Chinese cinema's downturn.[9] Shanghai, China's largest film market, saw a 23 percent drop in box-office revenue in 1997.[10] Attendance was off by 8.68 million. Box office for all of China in 1997 was 1.56 billion yuan (US$195 million). Beijing, second after Shanghai, saw only a small increase, registering receipts in 1997 of more than 118 million yuan (US$14.75 million), up from about 110 million yuan (US$13.75 million) in 1996. The total box-office revenue in 1997 was 1.56 billion yuan (US$195 million), but only 22 percent of that went to domestic movie producers.[11] Box-office revenue for Shanghai and Beijing remained flat for 1998.[12] Such a downturn was attributed in part to a huge fall in the number of Chinese films made in 1997, as well as to competition from alternative markets, chiefly, television and cable. A government survey of twelve major cities found that 76 percent of city residents listed watching television as their top way of spending leisure time. Going to the movies did not even make the top nine list.[13] Only one-third of residents paid to see movies in a theater in 1996.[14] Young audiences preferred Hollywood classics on cable to domestic new releases at the movie theaters.

Film attendance continued its decline over recent years. China's national box office in 1998 was 1.45 billion yuan (US$181 million).[15] The number of film screenings totaled 4.15 million, with attendance of 570 million, which means an average audience of 137 people per screen.[16] Revenue from overseas sales of 143 Chinese films was 10.3 million yuan (US$1.28 million), an average of 72,000 yuan (US$9,000) per film.[17] China produced 82 feature films in 1998, down from 88 in 1997, continuing a slide that has not stopped since 1992 when 170 films were made.[18] On the other hand, box office for the eleven revenue-sharing films in the same year was about 600 million yuan (US$75 million), or more than 40 percent of China's nationwide total of about 1.4 billion yuan (US$175 million).[19] Domestic films lost 1 million viewers to foreign productions from 1995 to 1998.

The importance of introducing more market forces into the production sector was emphasized at a conference attended by studio heads in May 1998.[20] At the conference, Culture Minister Shun Jiazheng, formerly the head of the Ministry of Radio, Film, and Television, forcefully argued that without a healthy supply of domestic films, the Chinese film industry would be reduced to salesmen for Hollywood films. The distribution and exhibition of domestic films must remain the Chinese film industry's priority. The State Bureau of Radio, Film and Television (SBRFT; the former Ministry of Radio, Film, and Television) and the Culture Ministry issued a circular in early 1998 which stated that three periods would be set aside each year during which only Chinese films could be shown.[21] The periods, ranging from fifteen days to one and one-half months were June 10 to July 31, September 25 to October 10, and December 1 to December 20. During these periods, theaters were allowed to screen only eight state-endorsed domestic pictures. China Film was barred from releasing any foreign films during the periods and was required to release the award-winning domestic films at its national theater chain. During the periods, theaters were also prohibited from doing publicity or promotion for foreign films. The circular further affirmed that two-thirds of all films shown in China each year must be domestic.

Not surprisingly, the protective measure did not boost the attendance for domestic pictures. Instead, it dragged down the overall revenue by reducing the profit margin of the big imports in 1998.[22] The box office for the periods during which only domestic films could be shown was the lowest of 1998. Doubts were expressed in the distribution–exhibition sector as to whether such an antimarket practice was feasible in the long run.

Nonetheless, the Film Bureau and the Film Distribution and Exhibition Association continued to restrict the release of Hollywood films in 1999.[23] The entire months of May, June, September, and October were blacked out. The reason for the decision was due to the tenth anniversary of the June 4, 1989, Tiananmen Square crackdown and the fiftieth anniversary of the founding of the People's Republic of China on October 1, 1949. An official decision was made that no foreign films could be released during those four months. The decision also stated that any Hollywood films released in 1999 would only be allowed to carry out "low-key" promotion, while distributors would be required to aggressively promote domestic films, particularly films made for the commemoration of the Republic's fiftieth anniversary. Hollywood films released in China in 1999 included *Rush Hour* (Brett Ratner, 1998), *Mulan* (Barry Cook, 1998), *Enemy of the State* (Tony Scott, 1998), *Shakespeare in Love* (John Madden, 1998), *The Truman Show* (Peter Weir, 1998), and *A Bug's Life* (John Lasseter, 1998).[24]

Clearly, the state's protective measures chiefly benefited the state-supported propaganda films, what the Chinese film community termed "main-melody films." The vast majority of domestic pictures, most of them mediocre entertainment pictures, were left to fend for themselves. Literally pushed against the wall, the film industry initiated a new round of vertical and horizontal consolidation to reorganize, indeed expand, the motion picture business.

Vertical and Horizontal Integration

Industrial integration continued in the late 1990s, following the model of New Hollywood and ushering the Chinese film industry into the age of conglomerates. Studios and other production companies either partnered with distributors and theater chains or were absorbed into burgeoning entertainment conglomerates or became conglomerates through diversification. The impetus behind this merger movement was to stabilize operations by creating alternative "profit centers" to protect against business downturns in a specific area. Studios and newly established production companies in major production centers such as Beijing, Shichuan, and Jiangshu provinces initiated collaboration with local theater chains.[25] In April 1997, the Beijing Municipal Distribution Company, Beijing TV, the Cultural and Art Publishing Company, and the Center for Television Art created a joint venture, the now-formidable Forbidden City Ltd. In early 1998, Jiangshu Yangtze Film Company, one of the largest regional film companies, wooed many first-tier theaters and county film distribution companies to join a partnership. In addition, the company acquired a new film and television production company, Yangtze Film and Television Production Center. New plans were finalized to set up the China Midwest Film and Television Shareholding Company Ltd. to pool the resources of Xian Film Studio and other film studios and companies in neighboring provinces, including Ermei Film Studio.[26] In a similiar move, the Pearl River Film Studio in southern China set up its second theater chain to cover the Pearl River Delta and the rest of Guangdong province. The Liaoning Northern Film Shareholding Company Ltd. was formed in early 1998 to consolidate film companies from eleven cities in northeastern China.[27] Since its establishment, the Liaoning has reduced its number of employees from more than 1,300 to 180. At the same time, its film distribution revenue has grown 16 percent since 1997.[28] The company is also investing in feature films. In addition, it has created the Northern Theater chain by bringing together the province's top sixty cinemas. By the end of 1998, many provincial-level distribution and exhibition companies had consolidated with local studios to form regional film groups. Such monopolistic practice is encouraged by both the state and the industry. Market oligopoly is seen as a plausible solution for the beleaguered film industry.

Meanwhile, the consolidation of the audiovisual industry, particularly the collaboration between film and television, continued and has benefited the film industry. The handover of studio management from the Ministry of Culture to the Ministry of Radio, Film, and Television in July 1986 gained the studios more than 10 million yuan (US$1.25 million) from television commercials. China Central Television's (CCTV's) film channel paid Chinese film studios 160 million yuan (US$20 million) alone in 1998 for purchasing the rights to broadcast feature films.[29] The film channel also invested 17 million yuan (US$2.1 million) in coproducing motion pictures with the studios. Carried by cable with subscription of an estimated 30 million households, CCTV-6 aired 389 foreign films (including films from Taiwan and Hong Kong) in 1998 and directly invested in the production of made-for-television films in 1999. In September 1998, CCTV-6 launched *A Date with Film Classics*, a program seen every Saturday at 8 P.M. that showcases outstanding foreign and Chinese films. It premiered with a sixth generation film, *This Is How Iron Is Made* (Gangtie shi zheyang liechende; Lu Xuechang, 1995). It has featured award-winning hits such as *The Fugitive* (Andrew Davis, 1993) and *Close Encounters of the Third Kind* (Steven Spielberg, 1977). China International Television Corpation (CITV), the investment arm of CCTV, is in discussions with Shanghai Paradise Company to set up a new film distribution company.[30] If such an alliance comes about, it would be a major step for CCTV in diversifying its business to include film and will offer Shanghai Paradise a national presence. CCTV also has taken a 10 percent stake in a recently formed film investment company spearheaded by Hengdian Group.

In early 1998, six film companies in Beijing agreed to create a massive new group company, China Film Group.[31] The group includes Beijing Film Studio, China Film, China Children's Film Studio, China Film Co-Production Corporation, China Film Equipment Corporation, and Beijing Film Processing Studio. The State Council officially approved the plan to set up the China Film Group by the end of 1998. The group promised to offer a consolidated audiovisual business dealing with film, television, and home video. It also promised to consolidate its production, distribution, and exhibition operations.

Institutional restructuring eventually brought in structural overhauls at the top level. In March 1998, China's parliament restructured its twelve ministries and put the former Ministry of Radio, Film, and Television under a new Ministry of Information Industry that includes the electronic industry, postal services, and telecommunications. This merger followed the general trend of transindustrial activities in the West, attempting to create synergy among the three sectors.

Lastly, a handful of nonmedia-related Chinese companies have entered television and film production. Their interest in audiovisual production was mostly motivated by efforts to promote their main business. Wanke, a company specializing in manufacturing scientific and educational equipment, established a film and television production subdivision in 1988. So far, Wanke has produced seven feature films and five television dramas. Ginwa, a company based in Xian, which has engaged in a variety of businesses, including medicine, commercial retail, and hotels, set up its telefilm production company in 1996. It produced a film, *Dog Days* (*Gouri*; Huang Jianxin, 1998), with Xian Film Studio. Baoan, a Canton-based electronics company, purchased a production quota from China Children's Film Studio and made a feature film, *Ink Stone* (Yanshi, Feng Xiaoning, 1996). The film's distribution rights were purchased by China Film, which sold European rights for the film to Twentieth Century Fox and executed a deal for Taiwan rights. The film became the first Chinese film to be purchased by a Hollywood studio. Zhejiang's Hengdian Group partnered with Beijing Film Studio in October 1998 to form a film investment company. Hengdian, which invested in Xie Jin's *Opium Wars* (Yapian zhanzheng, 1997) and Chen Kaige's *The Emperor and the Assassin* (Jinke Chi Qinwang, 1999), promises to invest at least 80 million yuan (US$10 million) each year for film production. The number of private companies interested in film production is likely to grow as the state continues to loosen its grip on film licensing.[32]

Overall, film reform in the late 1990s focused on the consolidation and reorganization of the motion picture business. The result was the emergence of a few media conglomerates that have monopolistic control over regional markets. The consolidation and reorganization was aided by the expansion and relaxation of film licensing, particularly the policy of licensing a single feature film issued in early 1998 that allows private companies to apply for film production and distribution permits on a case-by-case basis.[33] As a result, the majority of the feature films produced in 1998 were from the nonstate sector, leaving the state-run studios on the sidelines. The studios fought back, attempting to reenergize their production operations. In fact, a new circular issued in early 2002 practically allows any citizen with the financial means to apply for a permit to make films, although any films made will still require the censor's approval. The new regulation hopes to revive China's domestic production in the face of a sharp increase in foreign competition as World Trade Organization rules allow more foreign films into the domestic market.

My recent phone interview with Li Zhipu, a screenwriter and producer at Guangxi Film Studio, Chinese New Wave's birth studio, suggests that the Chinese filmmakers generally welcome such a symbolic step in the state's attempt to break the monopoly of state-run studios and to further open up the film industry. Over the past decade, a number of Chinese filmmakers have tried to set up their own production companies. But they could make films only in partnership with a state-run studio. The studios not only charged a fee but also took a cut of the film's royalties. Many filmmakers tried to bypass the system by shooting films independently and releasing them at festivals abroad, suffering the consequences of having their films banned in China. The new regulation hopes to encourage talented directors to make films in China at a time when China's entry into the World Trade Organization inevitably brings a sharp rise in the number of imports allowed into the domestic market. To give the state-run studios a boost, the new rules further permit the studios to directly seek investment from abroad.

In the distribution–exhibition sector, the dismantling of the state monopoly has not yet solved the problem of localized monopoly. Under the control of provincial and municipal administrations, local distribution–exhibition companies continue to cultivate a segmented market that has proven counterproductive to film marketing at a national level. Zhuo Shunguo, general manager of a newly established national film distribution chain, Beijing Forbidden City Sanlian Telefilm Distribution Company, suggested that the vast majority of film distribution companies in China were really localized theater chains that functioned to ensure the supply of film prints in regional markets.[34]

Under the mantle of the Beijing Film Studio, He Ping (*Red Firecrackers, Green Firecrackers* [Hongpaozhang, lanpaozhang], 1994) spearheaded an ambitious project in April 1997 to invest a total of 150 million yuan (almost US$18.75 million) on twelve prominent directors to produce thirty high-quality features in 1998.[35] Well-known filmmakers committed to the project included Zhang Jianya (*Shan Mao Joins the Army*, 1992), Feng Xiaogang (*Party A, Party B*, 1998), Wu Tianming (*Old Well*, 1987), and Tian Zhuangzhuang (*The Blue Kite*, 1993). Likewise, a group of young filmmakers from Shanghai Film Studio launched an initiative in 1999 to revitalize Chinese cinema by making "new mainstream films" (*xing zhuliu dianying*)—"innovative low-budget commercial films" exemplified by *The Trouble Shooters* (Mi Jiashan, 1988) and *Shan Mao Joins the Army*. The group analyzed the commercially successful low-budget, independent Hollywood films and promised to make moderate pictures in the tradition of classical continuity cinema.

The cultivation of rural markets has also become one of the policy maker's new priorities. The Chinese film industry has long neglected the vast rural market. In 1998, 70 percent of county-level film exhibition teams lost money; 29 percent of China's counties have no film exhibition teams; 26 percent of all villages do not see even one film per year. The Film Bureau unveiled a new "2131" plan in December 1998 to provide at least one film per village per month ("31") at the beginning of the twenty-first century ("21").[36] The goal of the program was to open new markets for Chinese film. Leading film distributors predicted that China's urban film market would sooner or later be dominated by Hollywood, making the rural market crucial to the future of Chinese cinema.

Last but not least, the film industry has attempted to introduce a legal system independent of political interventions. Zhao Shi, deputy head of the SBRFT in charge of the film industry, said in early 1999 that drafting has already started on the country's first film law.[37] The law is based on the Film Management Regulations issued in 1997, but will be far more comprehensive. It will regulate the film industry, curbing illegal film practices such as piracy, copyright violation, and false box-office reports. False box-office reports are particularly alarming at the present. Film producers and distributors are taking an increasingly aggressive position against this common practice. Taking the lead are several veterans in the industry, including Xie Jin, who estimates that his epic *Opium Wars* should have earned 140 million yuan (US$17.5 million) following its release in 1997.[38] Instead, the film reported box-office revenue of 70 million yuan (US$8.75 million); and the film's producers (Xie included) collected only a little over 20 million yuan (US$2.5 million). Film producers typically earn 30–35 percent of box-office revenue under the standard film distribution deal in China. But even that is nearly impossible to collect because of false reporting. Exhibitors rely on several different methods of doctoring their books. For example, they will sign a deal with a distributor to screen a film for one week, but actually start screenings a week earlier, so that by the time the contractual week arrives, most income from the film has already been earned. Or exhibitors will unilaterally increase the number of screenings per day and not report the extra income. Or they will simply report false attendance, say 30 percent instead of 50 percent. Short of dispatching monitors across the country to verify receipts, producers and distributors have little recourse to address the problem. Law enforcement in this area is notoriously weak. The problem should improve if more competition is allowed in the film market to break up existing distribution–exhibition monopolies and if modern theater chains with computerized ticketing systems are established. Industry executives have appealed for the SBRFT to promulgate new regulations to govern revenue-sharing film distribution (including defining penalties for any violation). The Film Bureau has mandated that the three hundred cinemas that are part of China Film's Zhonghua Theater chain will be required to use computerized ticketing. Any theater refusing to do so will no longer be allowed to screen revenue-sharing films.

Piracy is another problem that has plagued the industry, indeed causing many international disputes. China produced 39.2 million video compact discs (VCDs) in the first five months of 1997, already 2 million more than the total number produced in all of 1996. Demand is growing intensely, with production capacity falling behind. As a result, smuggling of pirated VCDs is on the rise. Authorities in Guangdong province announced the largest ever seizure of smuggled VCDs, uncovering a single shipment of 910,000 discs in Shantou. The government recently reallocated fifteen of the forty-nine production lines that had been closed for piracy to newly formed companies, with the hopes of creating production bases in Beijing, Shanghai, and Guangdong. The reallocation is expected to help alleviate the severe shortage of legitimate VCDs on the market.

Attempts have also been made to boost international coproduction. China Film Co-Production Corporation has made important concessions to allow two different prints for all coproductions, one for domestic release and one for international release.[39] The measure is significant because the former "one print" policy meant that coproductions were sanitized by Chinese censors largely because of domestic concerns over content, removing many internationally marketable elements. Overseas investors viewed this as a major impediment to recoup from overseas sales. Another change is to allow the processing of film prints to take place at several designated locations in Hong Kong in order to make the coproductions easier for Hong Kong and Taiwan studios, the largest investors in China's production sector. The China Film Co-Production Corporation (CFCC) has been trying to attract directors, producers, and writers from overseas to come to China and make films. CFCC officials boasted that joint ventures would allow American filmmakers to circumvent the law limiting American films to ten a year while entitling them to double the usual foreign film box office of about 16 percent. Talks have been underway with Disney to coproduce some dramas, action movies, and comedies for China. Thomas Leong, the Los Angeles representative for the Hong Kong–based CFCC, hinted that censorship can be navigated if a film company can stage its production in Hong Kong, which has more liberal media standards under provisions set up for China's takeover of the former British colony.[40] CFCC claims that the Chinese film industry is interested in coproducing any subject, even English-language films with Chinese themes, as long as it makes commercial sense. In commenting on the Disney animation film *Mulan*'s disappointing box-office receipts in China, Yang Buting, deputy director general of the Film Bureau suggested recently that if the picture had been a Sino–U.S. coproduction, it would have done better at the box office in China.[41] The Disney version of an ancient Chinese legend did not reflect the image of Mulan long-rooted in the Chinese peoples' imagination.

A new policy issued at the end of 1997 promised to give foreign companies that purchased Chinese films preferential consideration when submitting their films for import into China.[42] Warner Bros. and Twentieth Century Fox have enjoyed good relations with SBRFT by purchasing Chinese films. To encourage the internationalization of Chinese films, the SBRFT's Film Bureau has required all feature films to carry an English title in addition to a Chinese title.[43] Meanwhile, in his talks with senior Chinese cultural officials, Jack Valenti, chairman of the Motion Picture Association of America, made the offer of a film festival to promote Chinese-made films abroad. Valenti urged China to open its giant market not only to more American movies but also to American investment in studios, coproductions, and theaters.[44] He also urged Chinese policy makers to allow competition in film distribution and to reduce the heavy taxes on film revenue.

The poor state of movie theaters has always been blamed for the decline in movie attendance.[45] In response, SBRFT has come out in support of private investment in movie theaters. An SBRFT circular stated that corporate and private investment in renovating old, or building new, cinemas was good for the film industry.[46] The Zhonghua Theater chain is establishing a secondary chain that will screen domestic films only. Preferential treatment would be given to the theaters that join this chain. Beijing announced the classifications for the city's movie theaters, ranking them from one star to five stars.[47] The growing number of multiplex theaters in China is demonstrating the attraction of a comfortable and diverse filmviewing experience and is posting good results. Guangzhou now has four multiplexes with the recent opening of the six-screen Tianhe Film City. Following its renovation, Huanan Theater now has three multiplexes. In 1998, policy makers began to experiment with permitting foreign capital investment in film exhibition. Several companies have entered the Chinese market. Lark International has already launched a theater in Wuhan and built an eight-screen multiplex in the heart of Beijing that opened in early 1999. Studio City Cinema, a subsidiary of Lark International Entertainment, opened a six-plex in Shanghai, the company's third multiplex in China.[48] A fourth multiplex in downtown Beijing opened in the summer of 1999. The company's first two theaters, a five-plex in Wuhan and a six-plex in Chongqing, have performed well. Its Wuhan theater accounted for 20 percent of the city's total box office. Hong Kong's Golden Harvest is one of the first foreign companies to invest in China's fledgling multiplex business. Its Golden Cinema Haixing (a four-plex) opened in October 1997. Monthly box-office revenue reached 600,000 yuan (US$75,000) in December 1998. Total revenue for all of 1998 was more than 3 million yuan (US$375,000). The figure grew to 5 million yuan (US$625,600) in 1999. The cinema was expected to recoup its investment by 2000. A deal involving Japanese, Singapore, and Hong Kong investment of 60 million yuan (US$7.5 million) to renovate five theaters in Shanghai is also moving ahead. Singaporean money was also used to create an eight-screen multiplex in Guangzhou's Tianhe Square.[49] Universal Studios was allowed to open an entertainment complex in Beijing in September 1998, highlighting themes from some of the studios top films in recent years, including *Waterworld* (Kevin Reynolds, 1995) and *Jurassic Park* (Steven Spielberg, 1993). Likewise, Procter & Gamble has branded an activity in Guangdong province to screen feature films in rural areas.[50] The monthlong activity, called "Procter & Gamble Movie Night Market," held six hundred free movie screenings in at least four rural counties. Proctor & Gamble carried out promotional tie-ins for its products in tandem with the screenings. McDonald's and Universal Experience Beijing teamed up in 1999 to organize a "Secrets of Film" promotion.[51] The activity was held in more than forty McDonald's in Beijing, where film experts were invited to speak to middle school and elementary school students on the history and development of film, and the use of computer-generated effects in film.

Overall, film reforms in the late 1990s attempted to revitalize all three sectors of the motion picture business through the encouragement of further marketization and privatization. With the exception of films carrying out a propaganda function (in the name of pedagogy), the state conceived its film policy almost entirely in economic terms, failing to develop a nurturing system for the film industry to thrive. Indeed, the centralized studio system has long been dead to the commercial filmmakers, since it was able to finance only main-melody propaganda films. The moribund studios have been struggling to make ends meet by releasing independently made films, making television programs, and coproducing and cofinancing commercial films with either overseas or private domestic investors. The privatization of film production was already a reality by the end of the 1990s. The transformation of state-owned companies into shareholder companies is being carried out in the film distribution and exhibition sectors. The Chinese government has given overseas and domestic investors the green light to enter the distribution and exhibition sectors of the Chinese film industry. This new policy was made public in July 2000 in a circular entitled "Instructions on Deepening the Reform of China's Film Industry," issued by the Ministry of Culture and the SBRFT.[52]

Interestingly, the reluctance with which the state conceives of film policy in artistic and cultural terms has not discouraged it from constant intervention into the types of films made and distributed from a political standpoint. The Chinese film industry continues to be regulated by both the planned and the market economies. Under such a dual-track economic model, production targets and film licensing are administered according to the state's ideological concern while production investment and film promotion operate under the rule of the market. It is the odd combination of the postsocialist Chinese state's laissez-faire economic policy and its unrelenting political/ideological dictatorship that worships, simultaneously, a market freed of concerns for cultural values and a politics devoid of democracy and free expression that has impoverished Chinese cinema, resulting in the film industry's economic pragmatism and political cynicism which trumpets cinema's commercial value over all else. Indeed, as the economic reform deepened, the commercial entertainment wave has grown stronger. If Chinese cinema in the early 1990s still sought to fulfill film's triple functions of pedagogy/ideology/propaganda, art, and commerce, then, by the late 1990s, it attended only to film's commercial value. In their courting of popular appeal, both art and main-melody films have turned commercial. The market has become the dominant force in defining all types of Chinese film. As such, there exists only one wave in Chinese cinema at present, the commercial wave, what I call "post-Wave," since there is really no wave at all, only various types of films that cater to various audience demographics.

POST-WAVE

In the mid-1990s, commercial entertainment films occupied 75 percent of the annual production output, main-melody films 20 percent, and art films 5 percent.[53] Profit incentives began to erode the main-melody films in the second half of the 1990s. Though the ideological/pedagogical function of such films continued to be valued over their entertainment function, studios' concern for box-office return has pushed propaganda films toward adopting a commercial formula in film packaging and promotion. Likewise, art films have either gone underground/unnoticed or been packaged as erotic and exotic for certain niche markets. What became the staple of Chinese cinema in the late 1990s were popular genre films, particularly comedy and romance produced by the newly formed media conglomerates.[54] Beijing Forbidden City's comedy *Party A, Party B* (Jiafan, Yifan, 1998), a story about a group that runs a "Dream One-Day Tour" business, was one of the recent hit comedies. A romantic comedy produced by Xian Film Studio, *Spicy Love Soup* (Aiqing shuanlatang; Zhang Yang, 1998), was another recent box-office success. The film adopted a multilayered story line similar to that of Wang Kaiwei's *Chongking Express* (Congqing shenglin, 1994).[55] The film was popular among young moviegoers.

I will address a few cinematic subtrends within the general trend of post-Wave that are symptomatic and emblematic of the film industry, indeed Chinese society's uneasy march toward marketization and popular entertainment. Such subtrends include satirical films adapted from Wang Shuo's fiction, Zhang Jianyao's postmodern films, the commercialized younger generation films, and the Fifth Generation filmmakers' new cinematic turn.

From Wang Shuo's Black Humor to Feng Xiaogang's Urban Comedy

The satirical films adapted from the Beijing-based pop fiction writer Wang Shuo were influential to the development of Chinese cinema during the era of marketization. Born in 1958, Wang Shuo rose to prominence in the late 1980s owing to his playful and ironic novellas popular among urban readers in their twenties and thirties. Like characters in his fiction, Wang openly ridiculed Chinese intellectuals and the traditional and official notions of morality, decency, and integrity. Many of Wang's fiction featured antiheroes who mocked the pretentiousness of the intelligentsia as well as the absurdity of the official ideology. Most of his antiheroes were cynical city dwellers, some of them smart-aleck hooligans living on the social fringe and some of them self-serving young professionals who defied anything holy and serious. With their relentless pursuit of short-term pleasure yet at the same time claiming to be true to their own feelings and behavior, Wang's characters stood out as a unique group in China's literary scene. By talking about fame and money with open bravado traditionally forbidden in China, Wang's characters defied the hypocrisy of a traditional Chinese society. Fed up with all the talk of ideas/ideals, they had no faith in Communist ideology, since for them such an ideology was, at best, lies concocted to fool people. Traditional notions of order and morality were tossed aside as a smokescreen masking a servile and atrocious desire. Furthermore, the dialogue in Wang's roguish fiction was more lively and humorous than the fiction of the Chinese literary establishment, incorporating much slang popular among the young urban dwellers.

While Wang's antiheroes make arresting characters seldom seen in a Chinese film, the humorous urban slang, crispy dialogue, and wisecrack voice-over narration in his fiction made it particularly attractive for film adaptation. The well-known Wang Shuo films include *The Trouble Shooters* (Wan zhu; Mi Jiashan, 1988), *Half Flame, Half Brine* (Yiban shi huoyan, yiban shi haishui; Xia Gang, 1989), *Transmigration* (Lunhui; Huang Jianxing, 1988), *No One Cheers* (Wuren hechai; Xia Gang, 1993), and *In the Heat of the Sun* (Yangguang chanlan de rizhi; Jiang Wen, 1995). Wang also coscripted Chinese television's first major successful serial drama *Aspiration* (Kewang, 1990) and another hit serial *A Native of Beijing in New York* (Beijingren zhai niuyue, 1993). He also flexed his comic muscles on several hit sitcoms for Beijing TV, including *The Story of an Editorial Office* (Bangongshi de gushi, 1992) and *There's No Denying It's Love* (Aini meishangliang, 1993). Urban, anti-intellectual, irreverent, and sardonic have come to be the trademark of Wang Shuo's film/television. For a period of time, the popularity of Wang Shuo's fictions/films tackling serious social issues were deemed foolish, naive, and spurious.

Wang's satirical and, at times, farcical depiction of Chinese intelligentsia and its cultural tradition captured Chinese society's prevailing moral cynicism, political apathy, and existential anxiety on its march from socialism to commercialism. It also captured the dwindling influence of Chinese intellectual culture and the rising impact of a popular culture. Wang's popularity and his mockery of both the elite intellectuals and the pretense of literature as a form of high culture annoyed the Chinese literary establishment. Wang was dismissed by the self-proclaimed serious writers and critics as a literary "lightweight" and his work, at best, "popular fiction" and, at worst, "hooligan literature." Wang's works were attacked for their cynicism and moral decay. The defenders of Wang, on the other hand, suggested that the louts of Wang Shuo's fictional world were not themselves guilty of defying sacred ideals or social goodness.[56] Rather, it was life itself, the contemporary China, that had been polluted by the so-called sacred and good.[57] Furthermore, Wang was one of the few professional writers in China who were not supported by the state. Most Chinese writers work for various government-sponsored cultural organizations and receive monthly salaries. Wang's position as a nonsalaried writer thus made him something of an outcast. Wang was banned by the state in 1996–1997 as the result of the state's new round of ideological cleansing.

Directed by Xia Gang, a fifth generation filmmaker whose films have focused on contemporary urban life, Wang's *Half Flame, Half Brine* tells the story of the dark and disillusioned urban underground world and of the characters' renewed quest for identity during China's crisis-ridden reform era. The film centers around Zhang Ming, a charming ex-laborer/ex-convict who makes a living as a blackmailer. Zhang impersonates a policeman and extorts money from rich Hong Kong businessmen who pick up the women for whom Zhang and his friends pimp. As it happens, a naive yet venturous college girl, Wu Di, becomes attracted to Zhang and his freewheeling lifestyle and eventually falls in love with him. She enters his world, becomes a prostitute, and, still in love with him, though despairing at the realization that he may never have loved her at all, kills herself when the police detain them. Zhang is sent back to jail. At the end of the story, Zhang is released from jail and takes up with another girl who looks strikingly similiar to Wu Di. Xia Gang corroborated again with Wang Shuo in making another urban themed film, *No One Cheers*, a study on deteriorating relationships between urban couples. Both films enjoyed mild box-office success.

Directed by Mi Jiashan, *The Trouble Shooters* tells a story about a group of self-employed Chinese stuntmen who set up the "Three T Company" to sell their services to people in need of help. The name "Three T" (*santi* in Chinese), literally means "the three substitutes." Their own promotional line suggests that they are proxies who "get people out of difficulty, help people amuse themselves, and take the place of people in trouble."[58] One of their members, Yang Zhong, is sent to fill in for a man who cannot make a date with a young woman. Yang keeps the girl entertained by babbling about the meaning of life, touching on Nietzschean philosophy, Freud, and existentialism, the hot topics of Beijing's young pseudo-intellectuals. Yang is subjected to a mock Freudian analysis in the end. The girl asks, "I'm sure you really want to marry your mother?" Yang answers with a typical Wang Shuo-esque rant, "What I'm saying is that you'd like to be married to your mother but you can't because of your father unless your father was castrated, though that wouldn't really solve matters because of ethical considerations, so you agonize over it, and you can't fall for anyone else and only want to marry your mother but you can't because of your father; how come I'm talking in circles? Anyway, I don't know, but that's just the way it is, and in foreign books of quotations they say that the person you end up looking for as a partner is really your mother."[59] The film captured nicely Wang's tongue-in-cheek satire.

Adapted by Wang Shuo and directed by Huang Jianxing, a close associate of the fifth generation, *Transmigration* focuses on a group of disillusioned Beijing youths. It features Shi Bao, a smooth hustler whose empty and meaningless life has become quite bothersome even to himself. The son of a high-ranking official, Shi Bao has no faith in the Communist ideology. He and his friends with similar family backgrounds openly mock the socialist state and the party. Shi Bao is involved in an illegal business that brings him money but also threats. Some gang members power-drill screws into Shi Bao's leg and cripple him. His defiant girlfriend stands by his side and eventually marries him. But happiness remains elusive. Shi Bao's deep depression culminates in a shocking ritual suicide. His troubled and alienated soul presumably passes to his unborn son. As the epilogue rolls, we are told that the son is born several months later in a small black room. The film is clearly a darker version Wang Shuo film. The director Huang Jianxing's overwhelming sentimentality in *Transmigration* transformed Wang Shuo's cynicism into an exercise in critical realism, which makes the film the least Wang Shuo-esque.

Directed by the star actor and first-time director Jiang Wen, *In the Heat of the Sun* tells a story about a group of Beijing youths coming of age during the Cultural Revolution. It took an iconoclastic view of the Cultural Revolution, offering us a nostalgic account of the chaotic yet pleasurable years that happens to coincide with the main characters' sexual maturation and youthful dreams. The film opens with Ma Xiaojun, a mischievous son of an army officer whose job takes him away from his wife and son most of the time. Ma and other army kids form separate gangs, fighting each other. As the story progresses, Ma develops a habit of prying open all sorts of locks. He opens his father's locked drawer and damages a condom, which leads to the birth of his younger brother a year later. Then he ventures to break into people's apartments. One day, he breaks into a room as a pretty teenage girl unexpectedly returns. Ma hides under a bed, watching the girl changing clothes. Ma falls in love with the girl and introduces her to his friends. To Ma's distress, the girl is interested in one of his friends. Tension mounts between Ma and his friend. Ma beats up his friend at Ma's birthday party. As the film shows Ma beating his friend, his voice-over questioned whether the fight really happened: Was he brave enough to punch his friend who was bigger and older? Shot in black and white, the film's epilogue has the now adult Ma ride in a black limousine and comment on the new scenes of Beijing. *In the Heat of the Sun* was a huge box-office hit in 1995.

The popularity of Wang Shuo's films and television as well as his novels created a Wang Shuo phenomenon in China's literary scene from the late 1980s to the mid-1990s. Wang became a cult figure. In his most dramatic action to date, Wang published an anthology of his fiction in 1998, announcing his departure from the Chinese literary scene. In his preface to the anthology, he bemoaned that his years as a writer had turned him into the very thing that he most detested: an intellectual.

Covering China in transition since the late 1980s, Wang Shuo's films captured the impetuous, profit-seeking, and nihilist mentality of a Chinese society in which ideological systems and values were in a state of extreme flux. As such, Wang Shuo's films stand out as a thematic group. Stylistically, each individual filmmaker has brought to the films his own predilections. Wang's films also introduced irony to Chinese cinema burdened by

the high-minded cultural films of the Fifth Generation and the official propaganda films. The first writer since Mao to publish a four-volume *Selected
Works*, Wang became the consummate example of a new generation of Chinese with a knack for turning everything into a commodity. Wang's success
as an entrepreneurial author helped turn writing for television and film
into a lucrative enterprise, creating a generation of professional writers
who responded to the market rather than the party.

One protégé and cohort of Wang Shuo has been making a splash at the
box office since the late 1990s. Feng Xiaogang, a television soap opera
writer and director turned filmmaker whose three Wang Shuo-esque
"New Year pictures," shown during the New Year celebrations, topped the
domestic box office. Like Wang, Feng publicly claims that he seeks financial stardom, making films for the audience, not the critics.[60] In the early
1990s, Feng jump-started his career by collaborating with Wang on the
popular television serials *Aspiration* (Kewang, 1991) and *The Story of an Editorial Office* (Bangongshi de gushi, 1992). Feng came to real prominence
when he directed the popular serial *A Native of Bejing in New York* (*BNY*,
Beijingren zhai niuyue, 1993), a melodrama depicting a disheveled Beijing
artist's pursuit of a rosy American dream in New York City. The hero of
the show, Wang Qiming, competes with a white male for the possession of
both capital and women. America is portrayed as a place with a dog-eat-
dog mentality and American characters as brutish and greedy creatures
without humanity. Wang is forced to give up his avowedly wholesome
Chinese values to be successful in America. His victory on both battle-
grounds enthralled Chinese audiences, making the show a sensation during the course of its twenty-one-week run. *BNY* nicely tapped into the
"screw-you-America" mentality prevailing in China during the period of
moral confusion seen as the result of commercialization. The heavy-
handed (mis)representation of the United States validated a view of re-
formist China that the world created by a competitive market economy is
one in which there are no ground rules, no morality, a place where the
strong devour the weak.[61]

Yet as the Shanghai-based critic Xu Jilin points out, the hero was, in
fact, the television embodiment of Wang Shuo's ruffian or hooligan.
After amassing considerable wealth for himself, the hero projects an ex-
aggerated sense of greatness as well as deep hatred and aggressions toward America. In one scene, Wang is being entertained by a white
prostitute. He holds a large number of bills in his hand and forces the
half-naked prostitute to say "I love you." The last scene of the show happens at a street intersection in Atlantic City, New Jersey. After gambling
away his entire savings, Wang sticks out his middle finger and yells
"fuck you" to a white female driver who is yelling at him for blocking
traffic. Some critics suggested that *BNY* illustrated the ambitions and
frustrations of Chinese males in the 1990s.[62] Regardless, the show won

the applause of officials, everyday people, and a certain segment of the intelligentsia in China, establishing Feng Xiaogang as a formidable player in the Chinese media.

Feng began to direct motion pictures in the late 1990s, creating a series of commercially successful "Feng Xiaogang films." His three New Year's pictures—*Party A, Party B; Be There or Be Square* (Bujian bushan, 1998); and *There is No End* (Meiwan meiliao, 1999)—have topped the box-office returns consecutively from 1997 to 1999. All three films are urban comedies employing Wang Shuo-esque crispy dialogue with smart comic situations. Wang Shuo's black humor metamorphosized into Feng's lighthearted urban comedy exploiting the foibles of city folks in their daily lives. Feng is the reincarnation of Wang Shuo in the Chinese film industry but his films are a more gentle version of contemporary urban lives than those of Wang Shuo and those of Feng's television dramas. *Be There or Be Square* is a romantic comedy about Chinese emigrants trying to make it in a preposterously hostile Los Angeles. The Beijinger residing in Los Angeles is no longer the crisis-ridden Wang Qiming in *BNY* or the flamboyantly cynical characters in most of Wang Shuo's films. The lighthearted urban comedy has become one of the economically viable genres in the domestic market. Indeed, the cultivation of popular genre films has been a major market-oriented trend since the early 1990s.

Genre Film

Chinese films from the 1950s to the 1980s were typically divided into various types according to their subject matter. The most common types included films of rural themes, of urban themes, of war, and of historical figures/events. Studies of film genre began to take off in the early 1990s when the domestic market encountered more Western-genre films. Filmmakers began to exploit the notion of genre in project pitching and film marketing. Film critics soon followed the suit, beginning to (re)categorize Chinese films based on narrative archetype rather than subject matter. Major Chinese film genres include comedy, martial arts, action adventure, romance, detective, spy, historical epic, science fiction, horror, and musical; among these, the detective film is the most prolific genre in terms of production output.[63] Between 1977 and 1997, a total of 229 detective films were produced, an average of more than 10 pictures a year. The second most prolific genres are action adventure, romance, and martial arts, comprising a total of 150 pictures within twenty years. The least prolific domestic genres are disaster, science fiction, and horror; interestingly, such are the most popular genres of New Hollywood. Currently, the most popular domestic genre is comedy, a genre that is most culturally dependent and therefore less susceptible to Hollywood's penetration. Most of Wang

Shuo's films fall under the general category of comedy, though the typical mainstream Chinese comedies are rural slapsticks.

In the early 1990s, the comedies of Zhang Jianya such as *Shan Mao Joins the Army* and *Mr. Wang, Flames of Desire* (Wangxiansheng zhi yuhuo-chongsheng, 1993) also made a splash in Chinese cinema. Adapted from the well-known Shanghai cartoonist Zhang Leping's popular comic strip *Shan Mao Series*, which ran throughout the Sino–Japan War and the Chinese Civil War in the 1940s, the playful *Shan Mao Joins the Army* combined the cartoon character with its human impersonator and the documentary with fictionalized documentary. Shot in black and white, it radically borrowed and juxtaposed seemingly irrelevant musical notes from Western classics and Chinese revolutionary songs as well as film segments from both Western and Chinese classics, including the revolutionary model operas and the Fifth Generation films. *Mr. Wang, Flames of Desire* is based on another popular comic strip, *Mr. Wang*, by another well-known cartoonist, Ye Qianyi. Zhang deftly satirized Fifth G films by making references to and bringing together bits and pieces from Fifth G classics such as *Farewell My Concubine* (Chen Kaige, 1993), *Red Sorghum* (Zhang Yimou, 1987), and *Raise the Red Lantern* (Zhang Yimou, 1991). Mr. Wang's two dream sequences are particularly playful in their direct references to *Red Sorghum* and *Raise the Red Lantern*. The famous scene in *Red Sorghum* when the bride and her lover passionately made love in the sorghum field was mimicked almost shot by shot in *Mr. Wang* until the very last shot when the muscular lover on top of the bride is replaced by the skinny Wang. The contrast is visually stunning, creating a remarkable comic effect.

What is more, the sorghum crushed by the passionate lovers in *Red Sorghum* refused to stay down in the case of *Mr. Wang*; and his hat refuses to be thrown into the air. The sequence ends with the newly married Mr. Wang clumsily undressing himself as his bride waits impatiently, yearning. As it turns out, the sorghum field scene was just a daydream that occurred when the overeager Wang struggled to take off his long gown in front of his bride. Bored from the long wait, the bride sits up from a suggestive position in the sorghum scene and plays with grass to kill time. In another sequence, Wang has his legs beaten lightly for sexual stimulation, just as the main character does before her master arrives for the night in *Raise the Red Lantern*. In the case of Wang, his legs keep on bouncing back by the stimulation and, hence, the erotic moment in *Raise the Red Lantern* becomes comic in *Mr. Wang*. The self-conscious citing of various classical Fifth G sequences make Zhang's films parodies of Fifth G. It suggests how formulaic and clichéd the Fifth G films had become. The overwhelming irony and intertextuality and the elements of bricolage and eclecticism in Zhang's Shanghai-based urban satire has earned him the title of the Chinese postmodern filmmaker. His films received both critical and popular attention in the early 1990s. The emergence of Zhang

Jianya–style postmodern films further suggests the scale and effects of consumerism and media saturation in today's China.

While the comedies of Wang Shuo and Zhang Jianya attracted much critical attention, the majority of the genre films remained relatively obscure. Such films, however, are the main staples of Chinese cinema. The martial arts film, the most developed genre film in China, has consistently demonstrated its box-office appeal, though it continued to be undervalued by some high-minded mainland film practitioners. As a result, many Hong Kong–based filmmakers such as Tsui Hark and Jackie Chan have made inroads into China's martial arts film scene. At the same time, talented mainland martial arts filmmakers such as He Ping (*The Swordsman in Double-Flag Town* [Shuangqizheng daoke], 1990) are overshadowed by their Hong Kong counterparts. Indeed, most of Mainland China's martial arts films in the 1990s were coproduced with Hong Kong and Taiwan— utilizing Taiwan's investment and Hong Kong's technology and star actors and directors—and Mainland China's natural and human resources. A genre of Chinese origin, martial arts films have helped quite a few Hong Kong–based Chinese filmmakers to launch their Hollywood careers. With the crossover success of Jackie Chan and Jet Li into the U.S. film market, the Beijing Film Academy, in collaboration with Beijing Dalong Telefilm Center, has launched a new program bringing together martial arts skills and acting. China has an estimated ten thousand kung fu schools, but little opportunity for martial arts students after they complete their studies. The new film program hopes to tap this huge pool of talent. Interestingly, with his much-taunted *Crouching Tiger, Hidden Dragon* (2000), the Hollywood-based Ang Lee has made successful inroads into the arena of martial arts. The status Ang Lee brings to the genre has made it easier for mainland filmmakers to publicly endorse martial arts films. Indeed, Zhang Yimou's most recent feature project was the big-budget and star-studded martial arts epic *Hero* (2002).

The major players of genre films have been either the fourth generation filmmakers or the contemporaries of the Fifth Generation. As the latecomers of the fifth generation such as Zhang Jianya, Xia Gang, Huang Jianxing, and He Ping have attracted much critical and popular attention, the three giants of the fifth generation, Chen Kaige, Tian Zhuangzhuang, and Zhang Yimou, seem to have lost some of their creative edge and market appeal in the late 1990s. Indeed, the mid- to late 1990s witnessed the disintegration of the Fifth Generation as a group inspired by similiar personal ambitions and artistic visions. After his noisy flop, *Temptress Moon* (Fengyue, 1995), Chen upped the ante with the historical epic *The Emperor and the Assassin* (Jingke chi qingwan, 1999), an ambitious story of a botched assassination attempt of China's great unifier Emperor Qin. The film cast popular stars Gong Li, Zhang Fengyi, and Li Xuejian. The production tab ran up to 240 million yuan (US$30 million). Yet the film opened to a dismal box-office return. It received mixed reviews in China and even less favorable reviews at Cannes in 1999. Sony Classics distributed the picture in North America to little critical attention. The film had nowhere near the success of *Farewell My Concubine*, either critically or commercially. Discouraged by his unsuccessful flirting with China's domestic market, Chen teamed up with star Heather Graham to make his English-language directing debut on the erotic thriller *Killing Me Softly* (2000).[64] The film received little public and popular notice. Chen's recent project *Together* (Heni zhaiyiqi, 2002), a comedy about tangled domestic relationships, was a popular hit and a critical success domestically.[65] Tian Zhuangzhuang, on the other hand, has retreated to an earlier era, remaking Fei Mu's 1948 film *Spring in a Small Town*. Meanwhile, with *Not One Less* (1999) and *The Road Home* (1999), Zhang Yimou detoured during this period to make films with pedagogical values.

Zhang Yimou's Main-Melody Turn

Produced by Guangxi Film Studio, Zhang Yimou's *Not One Less* tells a story about a teenage girl working as a substitute teacher in a rural area who fights to get a local kid back to school. The film calls attention to the poor conditions of elementary education in rural China. The official press championed the film for its pedagogical value. Casting only nonprofessional actors, the film recalls, stylistically, Zhang's early feature *The Story of Qiuju* (1992).[66] The newly formed China Film Group paid 12 million yuan (US$1.5 million) for domestic distribution rights to the film. The film was released in more than one thousand of the Zhonghua Theater chain cinemas, including the three hundred top city cinemas. It marked the first time that a simultaneous national release was attempted. Yet the film opened in the spring of 1999 to disappointing box-office returns.[67] Its box-office receipts picked up after a top award from the Venice International Film Festival, ending up ranking number two in domestic film box-office receipts in 1999.[68] Yet the critics and audiences complained about the film's lack of a compelling central conflict and a clear character motivation.[69] In portraying the city as strange and the urban dwellers as insensitive, the film further reveals Zhang's ingrained rural nostalgia, a characteristic of Zhang seen by some critics as reactionary.[70]

Zhang's courting of state approval is a particularly interesting case. With solid critical and box-office records, Zhang seems to be more interested in fostering a constructive relationship with the state than in seeking approval from both the critics and the public. This points to the issue of freedom of expression in Chinese cinema. Ideologically, Chinese cinema still has a long way to go to achieve political and artistic independence. Economic liberalization has not so far led to much political and artistic freedom. The threat of the Taiwan experience, in which open politics and a free press has led to democratization on the island, pushed the concerned Party Secretary Jiang Zemin to start a new round of political movement in the mid-1990s to "talk up politics" in the hopes of forestalling ideological deviation. The movement led to criticism of spiritual pollution and renewed attempts to limit cultural autonomy in the name of regulating the cultural market. The state banned controversial films and books and closed down leading intellectual journals.

While the Chinese film *Devils on the Doorstep* (Guizhi jingchunle; Jiang Wen, 2000) won the Grand Prix Jury Prize at Cannes in 2001, the press in China, professional and popular, remained silent about the award. In a sign that the blackout was a calculated snub, the popular *Beijing Evening News* and *Beijing Youth Daily* newspapers both gave extensive coverage to Hong Kong star Tony Leung and Taiwanese director Edward Yang who won the best actor and best director awards at the festival. Jiang Wen's *Devils on the Doorstep* portrays the bloody massacre by Japanese troops of the inhabitants of a remote village in rural China during the war. Although the film is unsparing of the Japanese, it is also critical of China's tendency to blame others for its own problems. It portrays Chinese officials during the time in a less than favorable light. Commenting at the festival, Jiang took a swipe at his fellow Chinese by suggesting that they should take a closer look at themselves to explain some of the problems that have plagued China in recent years. Understandably, the film failed to please Chinese censors. Furthermore, the issue of Japan's wartime atrocities during the 1937–1945 Sino–Japan War became extremely sensitive at the moment when a constructive relationship between the two nation–states was desired by the Chinese government in its hopes for more capital investment from Japan. A letter was sent to Jiang from the Chinese Film Bureau, suggesting that the film should not show Japanese soldiers killing people and that Japanese soldiers should not be kept as prisoners.[71] Meanwhile, similar suggestions were offered by the film's Japanese producers who were afraid that the film would upset Japan's right-wingers.

As the state speeded up its marketization process in early 2000, it launched a new ideological campaign to keep liberal ideas at bay. Chinese film practitioners must carefully read the party's line to avoid having their films censored. As lamented by Tian Zhuangzhuang, filmmakers in Mainland China spend most of their time screening the scripts not to ensure quality but to secure the censor's approval. The combination of the fear of party censorship and the seduction of a potentially huge domestic market has pushed the Chinese filmmakers to adopt a pragmatic attitude, skirting sensitive issues and making efforts to conform. In the case of Zhang Yimou, perhaps aging has something to do with his mellowing. But young directors such as Jiang Wen have yet to choose whether to cooperate with the state or to be denied access to the domestic market. The Film Bureau, meanwhile, has never issued or followed straightforward guidelines for censorship. As Jiang puts it, "The biggest problem today for filmmakers in China is that there are no strict, apparent guidelines. One can only guess. This game is a black comedy in and of itself."[72]

Zhang Yimou's recent feature *The Road Home* recounts a love story between a couple from the perspective of their adult son.[73] The film begins with the death of the father and the son's returning to be with his mother at his father's funeral. The son then recounts the loving relationship between his mother and father when they were young. Half of the film was shot in black and white, which represented the present; the colored segments represented the past. The portrayal of the young mother has a romantic undertone, contrasting with the more realistic portrayals of the rest of the characters, including the mother in her old age.[74] The film minimized plot, foregrounding instead the structurally unrelated segments and details suggestive of the young mother's love toward the young father. Hailed as a potential art film classic and a film of value, *The Road Home* won official endorsement.[75] The film also won a Silver Bear award at the Berlin Film Festival in 2001. Yet both the official and the critical endorsement as well as Zhang's star reputation could not guarantee the film's market value. The audiences were not thrilled by a plotless recounting of an old-fashioned love story from a different era. The film fared at the box office no better than *Not One Less*.

To reestablish his box-office status, Zhang turned to making a large-scale martial arts film, *Hero*. Conceived by Zhang, *Hero* is a traditional tale set at the violent dawn of the Qing dynasty, circa 220 B.C. China's soon-to be first emperor is on the brink of conquering the war-torn land and three of his opponents are trying to assassinate him. The Emperor hires one man to stop them. In addition to Zhang Zhiyi, the star of *Crouching Tiger, Hidden Dragon*, the three top-billing Hong Kong stars Jet Li, Tony Leung, and Maggie Cheung are cast in the film's leading roles. Zhang was reported often to be at a loss when coming to shoot the action scenes.[76] *Hero* failed to top the critical box-office sensation of *Crouching Tiger, Hidden Dragon* in the United States.[77] Zhang's benevolent view of the notorious despot who slaughtered his opponents in the name of a unified Middle Kingdom was considered reactionary in the West.[78]

As the industry's march toward the market under the censor's nose continues, a younger generation of filmmakers, the sixth generation, has come to terms with the power of the market and the censor.

From the Sixth Generation and Beyond

Emerging in the early 1990s, the sixth generation filmmakers confronted contemporary social problems by examining the intimate moments of their protagonists' personal lives. Financed by overseas investment, the sixth generation's early films offered mostly personal accounts of their adolescent experiences. Such accounts were narrowly constructed, capable of striking a chord with only limited audience segments. Attempting to forge a distinctively different cinematic approach from the established conventions of earlier generations, the narrative technique of the sixth generation was more reflective of the so-called art cinema narration that featured a goal-bereft protagonist and employed an episodic structure. Films such as *Dirt* (Toufa luanle; Guan Hu, 1994), *The Days* (Zhangda chengreng; Wang Xiaoshuan, 1993), *Falling in Love* (Tanqing shuoai; Li Xin, 1995), *Rainclouds Over Wushan* (Wushan yunyu; Zhang Ming, 1995) have, to varying degrees, utilized the principles of art film narration and articulated a pervasive pessimism felt by many sixth generation directors. Stylistically, the sixth generation films were more cinematic than dramatic, relying heavily on voice-over narration to piece together an episodic narrative. The sixth generation's cinematic bent was often attributed to its more systematic cinematic training and less eventful life experience compared with previous generations. Though the sixth generation's early obsession with individual expression informed by certain types of European art cinema did not fit the domestic audiences' conception of "good narration," many of its films received critical acclaim at international film festivals. Only a handful of the sixth generation films were officially distributed in China, including *A Lady Left Behind* (Liushou Nushi; Hu Xueyang, 1991), *Dirt*, and *Rainclouds Over Wushan*. As such, the sixth generation has come to be regarded as representing underground/independent film in China.[79] The underground/independent filmmakers have exercised the marketing strategy of willful self-marginalization to promote their products globally. Following in the footsteps of the Fifth G, some of the sixth generation filmmakers attached to themselves political/ideological subversiveness as an economically exploitable trademark. After all, a government ban would guarantee international attention. As self-packaged dissidents, certain sixth generation directors became bankable for their ability to accrue market value in overseas art circles and on the domestic black market. The experience of one of the sixth generation directors, Zhang Yuan, serves as a perfect example in this regard.

After graduating from the Beijing Film Academy, Zhang rejected an official posting to an army studio in exchange for the life of an independent. He made his feature debut *Mama* (1991) with merely 10,400 yuan (US$1,300). With his success in making documentary and music videos for MTV in Hong Kong and the United States, Zhang collected enough money to make his second feature *Beijing Bastards* (Beijing zazhong, 1993), a movie featuring two preeminent rockers whose rebellious attitude caused them trouble with the authorities. The minimalist narrative revolved around a Beijing rock band that is driven out of its leased building and had difficulty finding another place to rehearse. Various film segments were connected by random street scenes of Beijing. The bulk of the film consisted of rock 'n' roll songs—footage of the rock singer Cui Jian's concert performances. With a sense of alienation and discontent expressed by the music, the film had enough attitude to make Zhang noticeable overseas and to establish him as a prominent alternative artist within China. Articles on Zhang and his film even appeared in the Hong Kong–based travel magazine *China Guide*.[80] The film was distributed overseas by Tomson, the Hong Kong–based company that produced Chen Kaige's *Farewell My Concubine*. The film won an award at the Tokyo Film Festival, but the "unofficial" screening of this film at the festival incited the Chinese censor. Zhang was banned by the government in 1994 from any future work on the mainland. The official censure attracted further international attention for Zhang. In 1996, his docudrama *Sons* (Erzhi) was acclaimed at the Rotterdam Film Festival. He used a Rockefeller Foundation grant to travel in the United States over the summer of 1996 and later made China's first "gay film," *East Palace, West Palace* (Donggong, xigong, 1997). Zhang was barred from leaving China to attend Cannes when the film was screened there.

As the overseas art market became more competitive, indeed mainstreamized, and at the same time a domestic market became more open to new talents, some self-exiled sixth generation directors began to make mainstream films, connecting themselves to a larger base of audiences at home. As suggested by Geremie Barme, politically, an increasing official tolerance has threatened to leave entrepreneurial cultural dissidents with nothing new to say and no particular harassment to lament.[81] The shifting political economy resulted in the emergence of some of the sixth generation filmmakers from underground. Zhang Yuan was back in the filmmaking business in 1999, making an officially endorsed film *Home for the New Year* (Huijia guonian), a story about the life of inmates in China's reform-through-labor camps. It remains to be seen whether Zhang's work is capable of striking a chord with mainstream audiences.

So far, the most successful commercial director among the sixth generation filmmakers is Zhang Yang, whose multilayered urban drama *Spicy Love Soup*, was a box-office hit.[82] The commercial success of *Spicy Love Soup* suggests that the sixth generation has broken out of their own trap to reach the public. Zhang Yang's second feature, *Shower* (Xizhao, 1999), was also a critical and popular success. Another commercially formidable director often associated with the sixth generation is Jiang Wen, who scored a box-office record with his Wang Shuo film *In the Heat of the Sun*. Meanwhile, Jin Chen directed a commercially successful contemporary romance, *Love in the Time of the Net* (Wangluo shidai de aiqing, 1999).[83] Other young directors have broken into the mainstream market with upbeat movies appealing to young moviegoers. Shi Runjui directed *A Beautiful New World* (Meili xingshijie, 1999), a film about a country bumpkin who arrives in Shanghai and succeeds in humbling the big city slickers with his perseverance and industry. *A Beautiful New World* was distributed in Taiwan, Japan, Austria, and Switzerland.[84]

Under the principle of niche marketing, the latest trend in China's regional market is to produce feature films in local dialects.[85] China's 1.3 billion people divide themselves into eight major dialect groups, but, with the exception of (Beijing, Cantonese, and Shaoxing) opera films, these dialects rarely appear on the big screen. Zhang Yimou experimented with the Shanxi dialect in *The Story of Qiuju* in the early 1990s. Only recently, a slew of new dialect films emerged, including Jia Zhangke's *Xiao Wu* (1997), Lu Yue's *Mr. Zhao* (Zhao xiansheng, 1998), Yang Yazhou's *A Tree in House* (Fangjianli de yikeshu, 1997), and Zhang Benshan's *The Man in Charge of Women* (Nan funu zhureng, 1999). The use of dialects not only adds a unique flavor but also commercial value to a film. Shot in the Tianjin dialect, *A Tree in House* had a run of more than thirty days in Tianjin, a cosmopolitan city neighboring Beijing with a population of over 10 million. Several of the recent films were shot in the Sichuan dialect, which is spoken by more than 100 million residents of Sichuan province. Despite having a guaranteed market locally, the films also attracted many curious nondialect speakers. Aware that a dialect film would not travel too well in other parts of China, producers of *Stock Craze* (Gufeng; Jia Hongyuan, 1994) made two prints, one in the official language of Mandarin and one in Shanghainese; the dialect print registered strong interest in Shanghai.

Despite various production adjustments in the late 1990s, domestic pictures continued to slide at the box office. The box-office return in 1999 dropped rapidly, a shortfall of more than 79 million yuan (US$9.9 million) from 1998, a 50 percent drop.[86] Particularly alarming is the box-office failure of two big-budget pictures, *The King of Lanling* (Lanling wang; Hu Xuehua, 1998) and *Red Lover* (Hongshe Lianren; Ye Ying, 1998). Studios and production companies began to reassess their investment strategy, shopping for small-scale pictures with good production values. As I mentioned earlier, a group of the sixth generation filmmakers in Shanghai set out to make new mainstream films, low-budget (between 150,0000 and 300,000 yuan [US$18,750 and US$37,500]) commercial films with originality and urban themes. Some argued against the proposal of scaling down the budget as the solution for the revival of Chinese cinema.[87] Hang Xiaolei suggests that low-budget might be feasible for a particular type of film; yet for large-scale films, sufficient investment is a necessity.[88] What is at stake is the diversification of a Chinese cinema that encourages the coexistence of various popular genre films, a few big-budget and high-tech blockbusters, a few government-sponsored main-melody pictures, and even a few not-profit-driven art films. Indeed, the recent trend has been moving toward the representation of the urban, the return to the everyday world, the divergence of film genres, and the fusion of the "art" film with popular genres such as the thriller, the Chinese western melodrama, and even martial arts. Various types of films have tried to create their own niche market and produce their own audiences.

With the reality of having a seat in the World Trade Organization sinking in, the Chinese film industry senses a momentous challenge from increasing film imports. China's entry in the World Trade Organization means that the state will have to allow foreign investment in film exhibition, provided that such investments do not exceed 49 percent of the overall investment. A quota of twenty revenue-sharing imports per year must be observed, overriding any potential protective measures against foreign imports. The foreseeable consequence would be the decisive dominance of Hollywood pictures in the Chinese market. The state, on the other hand, will not be allowed to intervene on behalf of the domestic film industry. With the decline of European and Japanese cinemas in the face of Hollywood, an "under-siege" mentality prevailed among the Chinese film practitioners. *Film Art*, the bimonthly journal published by the Chinese Film Artists' Association, ran a series of articles in its February 2000 issue discussing the ways Chinese cinema could effectively compete with Hollywood imports. The consensus was that the national/regional film industry would be able to maintain its market only by concentrating on the production of films with unique national/regional characteristics, including certain genres traditionally associated with Chinese culture. As such, only films of Chinese characteristics/identity, which Hollywood would not be capable of making, could compete with Hollywood for a domestic market share. The issue of Chinese cultural identity was revisited, albeit from an economic perspective. What counted as Chinese cultural identity remained vague; but traces of Chinese tradition, Chinese ways of thinking, and/or Chinese aesthetics were suggested to be essential in determining such an identity.

CHINESE CINEMA: FROM THE PRESENT TO THE PAST

The development of Chinese cinema's commercial entertainment trend from the mid- to late 1990s was both the result and the manifestation of the film industry's shifting economic and cultural orientations. The satirical and farcical nature of Wang Shuo–type films, on the one hand, captured Chinese society's prevailing cynicism, political apathy, and existential anxiety on its march from socialism to commercialism. On the other hand, such films introduced black humor into Chinese cinema, breaking Chinese cinema's dominant mood of righteous sentimentality. Zhang Jianya's comedies further flexed the muscle of humor, opening the floodgate to parody, irony, intertextuality, bricolage, and eclecticism emblematic of postmodern cinema. Feng Xiaogang's box-office-motivated urban comedies neutralized the political/ideological and stylistic controversies found in Wang and Zhang, making comedy the commercial staple since the late 1990s. The significance of the Wang Shuo phenomena further lies in the author's self-positioning as a financially successful cultural entrepreneur who openly suggested the nature of cultural production being economic rather than cultural. The prominence of Wang Shuo provided a certain degree of legitimacy to the market practice of many filmmakers who cultivated popular genre films. The commercialization of the fifth and sixth generation filmmakers at last attested to Chinese cinema's shifting orientation toward foregrounding cinema's economic function.

What further fostered the wave was the impact of Hollywood's second entry into China's domestic market. Hollywood's popularity among Chinese audiences propelled the Chinese film industry to adopt the narrative paradigm institutionalized by Hollywood and the industrial structure and market practices refined by Hollywood. Both Chinese cinema's institutional restructuring and entertainment wave in the late 1990s actively sought their paradigms from Hollywood. Indeed, film reform in the late 1990s focused on the consolidation and reorganization of the motion picture business, which ushered the Chinese film industry into the age of conglomerates, following the lead of Hollywood, which has shifted its economic strategy from vertical integration to horizontal integration in responding to globalization. In July 2001, the State Bureau of Radio, Film, and Television formally announced a plan to establish six regionally based film groups that would consolidate the production facilities and human resources of the existing provincial-level studios. The six big cinema groups include the Beijing Film Studio–based China Group, the Shanghai Film Studio–based Shanghai Group, the Canton-based Pearl River Group, the Changchun Group covering northeast China, the Ermei Group covering central China, and the Xian Group covering the southwest region.[89] All such structural maneuvers were motivated by a renewed sense of nationalism that urged the preservation and protection of a national film industry in the era of participation in the World Trade Organization. In a similiar vein, successful Hollywood films are perused by Chinese filmmakers to delineate a commercially viable narrative formula for emulation while retaining Chinese cinema's cultural relevance, or identity.

Interestingly, Chinese cinema's current search for structural and textual solutions from Hollywood has its parallel in the early development of Chinese cinema, especially from the mid-1920s to the early 1930s, another time when competition from Hollywood cast a shadow on the domestic screen. Both periods present similiar political, economic, and cultural constraints and promises. During both periods, commercialism and nationalism played significant roles in shaping the direction and duration of the entertainment wave and institutional restructuring. Particularly relevant is the role of a film culture characterized by traditionalism, populism, and pragmatism in the development of the entertainment wave and institutional restructuring. A look at Chinese cinema's early commercial practice and first entertainment wave should shed some light on Chinese cinema's current development, in particular, and on the development of regional cinemas under the shadow of Hollywood, in general. Such will be the task of the next chapter.

NOTES

1. Willie Brent, "China to Raze the Red Tape, Centralize Studios," *Variety*, 13 May–19 May 1996, 44.

2. Ibid.

3. From *China Entertainment Network News* (*CEN*; a trade magazine delivered on-line to its subscribers), November 1998.

4. The six other top bidders were Hengshan, Cathay, Guoji (International), Tianshan, Paradise, and Huaihai.

5. In a phone interview I conducted with Tang Zhengli, the manager of Chaoyang Cinema in southern China, he suggested that price was worth paying for stimulating the competition. The phone interview was conducted in the fall of 1999.

6. Fang Cheng, "The Aria of Cinema" (Dianying de yougtan) as reported in *Chinese Film Market* (August 1997): 10–11.

7. Ibid. The total number of theaters in China in 1997 is not available.

8. Ibid., 38.

9. See Shu Lang, "Film Market Report on the First Season of 1997," *Chinese Film Market* (May 1997): 4–5.

10. *CEN*, February 1998.

11. *CEN*, May 1998.

12. Shanghai earned 180 million yuan (US$22.5 million) in revenue, the same figure as 1997. Beijing earned a record 127 million yuan (US$15.8 million) in 1998, a small rise from 118 million yuan (US$14.75 million) in 1997. The highest grossing Chinese film in Beijing was Feng Xiaogang's *Party A, Party B*, which earned 11 million yuan (US$1.4 million). The biggest earner in Shanghai was the documentary *Zhou Enlai*, with reported revenue of 7 million yuan (US$875,000). See *CEN*, January 1999.

13. *CEN*, June 1998.

14. Zhang Tongdao, Liu Ningzhi, and Shong Juang, "A Report on the Relation between Film and Television" (Guangyu dianying yu dianshi guanxi de diaocha baogao), *Dianying yishu* (Film Art) 247, no. 2 (1996): 51–60.

15. *CEN*, March 1999.

16. A total of 221 titles were released, with 12,266 prints made. See *CEN*, March 1999.

17. From the Web site MUZI.NET (http://www.muzi.net), a Chinese and English on-line news and information service, 10 April 1998.

18. Of the eighty-two films, only six were coproductions, while Beijing Film Studio produced thirteen films, the most of any domestic studio.

19. *CEN*, February 1999. The films were: (1) *Titanic*, (2) *Who Am I?* (3) *Saving Private Ryan*, (4) *Deep Impact*, (5) *Home Alone 3*, (6) *Volcano*, (7) *Into the Eagle*, (8) *Daylight*, (9) *Once Upon A Time in the West*, (10) *Greedy Island*, and (11) *The Game*.

20. *CEN*, May 1998.

21. *CEN*, July 1998.

22. See Shu, "Film Market Report."

23. *CEN*, March 1999.

24. *CEN*, March 2000.

25. See Zhao Shi, "A Retrospective of Chinese Cinema during the Era of Reform in the Past Two Decades" (Chuangzhao huihuang pandeng gaofeng—gaige kaifang ershinian de zhongguo dianying huigu), *Dianying Yishu* 264, no. 1 (1999): 4–12.

26. *CEN*, March 1999.

27. *CEN*, June 1998.

28. *CEN*, July 1998.

29. *CEN*, February 1999.

30. *CEN*, March 1999.

31. *CEN*, February 1998.

32. *CEN*, March 1999.

33. *CEN*, February 1998.

34. *CEN*, January 2000.

35. *CEN*, December 1997.

36. *CEN*, December 1998.

37. *CEN*, January 1999.

38. *CEN*, September 1998.

39. *CEN*, July 1998.

40. Ibid.

41. See Willie Brent, "Murdoch Urges Respect for Chinese Culture," *Daily Variety*, 24 May 2000, 17.

42. *CEN*, December 1997.

43. *CEN*, February 1999.

44. Ibid.

45. *CEN*, June 1998.

46. *CEN*, September 1998.

47. *CEN*, February 2000.

48. *CEN*, February 1999.

49. *CEN*, January 2001.

50. *CEN*, September 1998.

51. *CEN*, March 1999.

52. Zhu Linyong, "Film Industry to Be Reformed" (Dianying gongyie youda gaige), *China Daily*, 11 July 2000, 4.

53. Li Yiming, "From the Fifth Generation to the Sixth Generation" (Chong diwudai dao diliudai—90 niandai qianqi zhongguo dalu dianying de yianbian), *Dianying yishu* 258, no. 1 (1998): 16–22.

54. The least favorites were disaster, tragedy, and industrial films. See *CEN*, December 1997.

55. *CEN*, March 1998.

56. See Rao Shuoguang, "On the Evolution of Cinematic Views from the Late 1980s to the Late 1990s" (Lu xingshiqi houshinian dianying shichaode yianjing), *Dangdai dianying* (Contemporary Film) 93, no. 6 (1999): 64–70.

57. See Ding Dong and Sun Ming, eds., *On Wang Meng Phenomenon* (Shiji Zhi jiaode chongzhuang—Wang Meng Xianxiang Zhengming Lu) (Beijing: Guangming Daily Press, 1996).

58. See Geremie Barme, *In the Red: On Contemporary Chinese Culture.* (New York: Columbia University Press, 1999), 74–75.

59. The English translation of the dialogue comes from Barme, *In the Red*, 74–75.

60. Feng's disdain for high-brow cinematic practice was unmistakable in my interview with him in Bejing in the summer of 1997.

61. For more discussion on the "screw-you-America" mentality and a series of television dramas representative of such a view, see Xu Jilin, "On A Native of Beijing in New York" (Wudu shi houde jiazhi anshi—zai shuo *Beijingren zhai niuyue*), *Wenhui bao* (Cultural Report), 13 November 1993, 3.

62. See, for example, Sheldon Lu, "Soap Opera in China: The Transnational Politics of Visuality, Sexuality, and Masculinity," *Cinema Journal* 40, no. 1 (2000): 25–47.

63. See Jia Leilei, "On Chinese Genre Film from 1977 to 1997" (Fengxing shuishang, jidong botao—zongguo ruixing yingpian 1977–1997 shuping), *Dianying yishu* 265, no. 2 (1999): 4–12.

64. Paul Duke, "Chen Makes a 'Killing' in English," *Daily Variety*, 30 May 2000: 1.

65. See Gu Zhi, "Chen Kaige and Chen Hong Together" (Chen Kaige and Chen Hong zhai yiqi), *Dianying zhazhi* (Film) 4 (2002): 36–37.

66. A local fourteen-year-old girl was cast in the leading role in *Not One Less*.

67. See Chao Baoping and Yi Ran, "Examining Film Narrative from *Not One Less*" (Cong *Yige dou bunen shao* kan dianying xushi), *Dianying yishu* 268, no. 5 (1999): 77–81.

68. See the domestic picture box-office chart compiled by *Dianying yishu* 272, no. 3 (2000): 4–5.

69. See Chao and Yi, "Examining Film Narrative from *Not One Less*." See also a group of articles discussing the film published in *Dangdai dianying* 89, no. 2 (1999): 4–26.

70. See Deng Guang, "Cinema Verite and the Cultural Imagination of the Popular Media" (Jishi yihuo dazhong chuanmei de wenhua xiangxiang—*Yige dou bunenshao* guanhou), *Dianying yishu* 268, no. 5 (1999): 82.

71. See Richard Corliss, "East Asian Films at Cannes," *Time* (June 2000): 22.

72. Ibid.

73. *CEN*, October 1998.

74. See Wang Xiaoming, "Thoughts on *The Road Home*" (Luge de xingban—guankan yingpian *Wuo de Fuqing Muqing* yougan), *Dianying dongxun* (Film Report) (January 2000): 62–63.

75. See Zhao Shi, "A Retrospective of Chinese Cinema during the Era of Reform in the Past Two Decades" (Chuangzhao huihuang pandeng gaofeng—gaige kaifang ershinian de zhongguo dianying huigu), *Dianying yishu* 264, no. 1 (1999): 4–12.

76. See Stephen Short and Susan Jakes, "The Making of *Hero*," *Time Asia on the Web* (January 2002), available at <http:www.time.com/time/asia/features/hero/story.html>.

77. The box-office return of *Crouching Tiger, Hidden Dragon* in China was rather unremarkable, due partially to the two Cantonese-speaking Hong Kong stars' broken Mandarin. To avoid the same mistake, Zhang has kept the dialogue in *Hero* to a minimum.

78. See Derek Elley's review of *Hero* posted on *Variety*'s on-line review (<http://www.variety.com>) of 3 January 2003.

79. See Chen Muo, *Anthology of Chen Muo's Film Criticism* (Nanchang: Baihuazhou Literature and Art Press, 1997), 26–34.

80. See Barme, *In the Red*, 191–192.

81. Ibid.

82. See Ying Hong, "Chinese Cinema in 1998" ('98 Zhongguo dianying beiwang lu), *Dangdai dianying* 88, no. 1 (1999): 28.

83. *CEN*, February 1999.

84. The sixth generation's continuing struggle with both the market and the censor was discussed in a round table conference on April 17, 2001, "Contemporary Chinese Cinema in China, Taiwan, and Hong Kong: A Collective Force in the Global Market," sponsored by the University of Texas at Austin's Center for Asian Studies and Department of Radio-Television-Film, and the Transnational China Project, Rice University. The on-line transcript is posted on <http://www.ruf.rice.edu/~tnchina/commentary/chiaoroundtable0401.html>.

85. *CEN*, February 1999.

86. See Shun Yiqing, "Urban Movie Theaters in 1999" (1999 Nian de dushi dianying) *Dianying dongxun* (January 2000): 23.

87. See Hang Xiaolei, "(The Sixth Generation's) Cultural Drift after Breaking Out of an Encirclement" (Tuweihou de wenhua piaoyi), *Dianying yishu* 268, no. 5 (1999): 58–65.

88. Ibid.

89. Wang Chuang, "Beijing Establishes Six Big Film Groups," *World Daily*, 28 July 2001, E1.

6

Shadowplay:
Early Chinese Cinema
in the Shadow of Hollywood

INTRODUCTION

This chapter explores the political, economic, and cultural factors conducive to the rise and fall of Chinese cinema's first popular entertainment wave and the film industry's first institutional restructuring. The two occurred almost simultaneously from the mid-1920s to the early 1930s, resembling Chinese cinema's current popular entertainment wave and the ongoing institutional restructuring since the late 1980s. Film distribution and exhibition are driven during both periods by the demand for Hollywood features. Both periods present similiar political, economic, and cultural constraints and promises. Politically, a repressive regulatory body under the control of either the Nationalist or the Communist government encourages Chinese cinema's apolitical tendency during the periods. Economically, a market-oriented system during both periods ensures free competition within the industry, which leads to a series of institutional overhauls. Culturally, a film discourse characterized by traditionalism, populism, and pragmatism during both periods favors the morally unequivocal and stylistically restrained classical films with popular appeal.

This chapter further explores the cultural and cinematic heritage of the leading popular entertainment genres from the late 1920s to the early 1930s, the costume and martial arts–ghost dramas. The stylistic components of the popular genres during the period have had a long-lasting impact on Chinese cinema. Overall, a look at Chinese cinema's first entertainment wave

A version of this chapter originally appeared in Ying Zhu, "Commercialism and Nationalism: Chinese Cinema's First Wave of Entertainment Films," *Cine Action* 47 (summer 1998): 56–66.

and institutional restructuring aims to provide a historical linkage and, therefore, analytic references to Chinese cinema's current entertainment wave and institutional restructuring. This exploration hopes to shed some light on the direction and duration of the current entertainment wave and institutional restructuring.

A NASCENT FILM INDUSTRY: CHINESE CINEMA FROM THE TURN OF THE CENTURY TO THE MID-1920s

Chinese national cinema had a long, difficult early development, co-inciding with one of the most disastrous periods of Chinese history. The motion picture was introduced to China in 1896, two years after China's defeat in the Sino–Japan War. China's defeat encouraged the Western powers to increase their entrenchment in their Chinese commercial concessions and treaty ports, backed up by military force.[1] The expansion grew more aggressive in 1900 after the defeat of the Boxer Uprising, which was an or-ganized armed peasant movement initially attempting to overthrow the Manchurian regime and later joining the Manchu government to fight for-eign aggressors. The humiliating defeats of both the Sino–Japan War and the Boxer Uprising had a profound impact on how the motion picture was perceived by the Chinese and how the development of China's national film industry would later be conceived.

Much like the development of the motion picture in most of the colo-nized/semicolonized Third World nation–states around the turn of the century, the development of early Chinese cinema occurred, to a great ex-tent, under the shadow of imports. Early films in China were imports from Europe, mostly from France, with foreign merchants acting as distributors. These merchants, further tempted by China's potential market, soon ven-tured into film exhibition in China's large cosmopolitan cities such as Shanghai and Beijing. The dominance of foreign distributors and imported films in the Chinese market was perceived as yet more proof of Western imperialism in China, provoking much nationalistic reaction. The nation-alistic reaction was evident in both the audience's resistance to film im-ports with unsympathetic portrayals of China and the Chinese and in the film practitioners' protective and defensive approach, in relation to the Hollywood-led foreign imports, toward the establishment of a national film industry. Closely related to the strong Nationalist sentiment, early Chinese filmmakers considered cinema a tool for social reform for a stronger China, inheriting the Confucian idea of entertainment for en-lightenment or pedagogical purposes. Cinema's pedagogical function of enlightening the masses to save the nation in crisis was considered as equally important as, and at times more vital than, cinema's economic function of making a profit. Such a conception of cinema would shape the future development of Chinese film industry.

On the economic front, both industrialization and privatization had not yet caught up with China when the motion picture was introduced to its coastal cities. Lack of domestic capital investment placed Chinese resources under indirect foreign control, since much of the finance stemmed from foreign banks, often branches of major Western financial firms head-quartered in the United States, Britain, France, Germany, Spain, and Portugal. In terms of cinema, before the fall of the Manchu dynasty in 1911, little domestic effort was made in venturing into such an entertainment sector.[2] Native exhibitors did not emerge until 1903 when a Chinese merchant, Lin Zhushan, screened films he brought back from the United States and Europe at a tea house in Beijing. The first Chinese film was made in Beijing in 1905 by a photo shop owner, Ren Qingtai.[3] Ironically, what propelled Ren's adventure into making his own films was his lack of capital for imports. The first real movie theater, Pingan Theater, was built in Beijing in 1907 by foreign merchants. It opened only to foreign patrons, reflecting the "No Dogs or Chinese Are Allowed" colonial mentality.

There were approximately one hundred theaters in China in 1927. The number reached 250 by 1930. Yet the rapid theater expansion was driven mostly by the demand for imports.[4] Of 250 theaters, only 50–60 showed Chinese films. The popularity of Hollywood imports forced Chinese native productions to accept high exhibition fees and low ticket prices. Meanwhile, theaters were forced to give away 30–50 percent of their revenue to foreign distributors, leaving them little money for expansion. Only a few big studios, notably Star (Mingxing) and Heaven (Tianyi), owned small theater chains. Lack of exhibition opportunities seriously hampered the capital circulation for Chinese filmmakers, further affecting the quality of native productions, a common excuse for the foreign-controlled distribution and exhibition network to reject domestic features.

The first production company in China, Asia Film Company, was founded in Shanghai in 1909 by an American merchant, Benjamin Brodsky. In 1912, Brodsky transferred his company's name and equipment to two American merchants, Essler and Lehrmann, in fear of the strong Nationalist sentiment in China.[5] In 1922, Essler and Lehrmann hired a local young man, the ambitious Zhang Shichuan who was fluent in English and who would later become one of the founders of the influential Mingxing Production Company (Bright Star; Star), to be Asia Film's Chinese representative in Shanghai.[6] Eager to make some profit out of the new production facility, Asia Film attempted to make a film adaptation of the then-popular stage play *Wronged Ghosts in an Opium Den*. Zhang Shichuan helped to line up the talent and negotiated with a theater for a possible production deal. The theater asked for more money than Asia

Film was willing to pay so the deal was aborted. In 1913, inspired by Asia Film's production effort, Zhang Shichuan contacted his theater friends, including Zheng Zhengqiu (who later became one of the cofounders of Star) and formed Xingming, a director-unit-style production company contracting with Asia Film. That same year Xingming produced *A Difficult Couple* (Zhang Shichuan and Zheng Zhengqiu), a narrative short. The film was a social satire portraying the absurdity of a feudal marriage. Another native production company, Huamei, was formed in the same year by the wealthy Li brothers in Hong Kong. Huamei produced *Zhuangzhi Tests His Wife* (Li Beihai) in 1913, another narrative short, also a social satire.[7] Both Xingming and Huamei were short-lived. The outbreak of World War I soon cut off the companies' supply of film stocks, shutting them down for good.[8]

Early Chinese films were mostly slapstick shorts. Since Hollywood-style feature-length film was becoming a global prototype for narrative films, Chinese film pioneers began to experiment with long narrative features in the early 1920s to compete with Hollywood for the domestic market.[9] In 1921, the Chinese Drama Research Association produced a plot-driven stage adaptation, *Yuang Ruisheng* (Ren Pennian and Xu Xingfu). The film, based on a real murder story, turned out to be a huge hit, breaking into the foreign-controlled theater, Olympic Cinema, for exhibition. Another popular feature produced in 1921 was *Beauty and Skeleton* (Guan Haifeng). Filmmaker Guan Haifeng shrewdly selected a pre-sold commodity—a popular stage play, itself based on a sensational murder case involving sex and money—applied a Hollywood-style detective plot structure, and spiced it up with Chinese martial arts. The box-office success of such entertainment-oriented features predicated the arrival of Chinese cinema's first commercial entertainment wave half a decade later, steering the film industry toward producing commercially viable films advocated by industrial entrepreneurs rather than socially responsible films advocated by both radical and conservative film pioneers. Most significantly, the success of both *Yuang Ruisheng* and *Beauty and Skeleton* triggered hopes that Chinese cinema might compete with Hollywood-led imports.

Early Chinese domestic films were mostly coproductions, dependent on foreign capital and technology. Consequently, the native film industry was limited to the treaty ports where such capital and technology were the most accessible. The establishment of a republic under the presidency of the foreign-educated Dr. Sun Yat-sen (Sun Zhongshan, 1866–1925) and the coming of World War I granted an opportunity for the nascent Chinese indigenous capitalist industry to develop. When the war-distracted European powers temporarily relaxed their profit-making activities in China, some wealthy Chinese theater lovers began to invest in film production. The economic recovery after the war freed up more domestic capital for film production. As the profitability of motion pictures grew, Chinese merchants became increasingly interested in venturing into film production, resulting in a surge of short-lived, small-scale independent production companies. The early 1920s thus saw several waves of speculative film financing in China, all of which struggled under the shadow of imports.

The production investment of Chinese cinema was nowhere near the scale of Hollywood. As cited by the Chinese historian Hong Shi, the average production cost for a domestic feature in the 1920s was between 5,000 and 20,000 yuan (US$625 and US$2,500) yet the average production cost for a Hollywood feature during the same period was between US$15,000 to US$20,000.[10] The film industry's short-term strategy of "small investment, fast production turnout, and marketable products" was detrimental to Chinese cinema's overall development because such a strategy downplayed the significance of production value, a quality often associated with Hollywood. To better compete with Hollywood imports, the Chinese filmmakers made an initial effort in the early to mid-1920s to consolidate capital and human resources.[11] As cited in Chen Jihua, in the 1921 boom, 140 companies were founded.[12] Yet by March 1922, only twelve were still in business. The 1925 upsurge was more durable, with 175 new companies operating at its peak and 40 companies still producing at least one film by the end of 1926.[13] The industrial consolidation reached its peak in 1927, reducing the number of production companies from well over one hundred to only thirty-two.

The consolidation in 1927 resulted in the oligopoly of three production companies—Mingxing (Bright Star; Star), Dazhonghua-Baihe (The Great China-Lily; GL), and Tianyi (First Under Heaven; Heaven)—and the Chinese national film industry took its initial shape. Among the big three, Star had the longest production history, the largest production capacity, and the best distribution network.[14] Established in Shanghai in March 1922, Star's early pictures were mostly melodramas that depicted the tragic lives of women and children in a feudal society. Star's chief founders, Zhang Shichuan and Zheng Zhengqiu, had their cinematic apprenticeship at the Asia Film Company but had different perspectives in their approaches to cinema. A businessman as well as a showman, Zhang approached film production from an investment perspective whereas Zheng, a prominent theater critic with experience in traditional stage drama, valued cinema's pedagogical potential. Combining both perspectives, Star strove to strike a balance between cinema's pedagogical and entertainment functions. The company's melodramas, while catering to the popular taste, preached the importance of and the value of traditional Chinese ethics and moral codes education in building a stronger China. The company's early productions included the Chinese classic *Orphan Rescues Grandfather* (Zhang Shichuan, 1923), a realist melodrama tackling contemporary social ills.

GL was established in 1925, the result of a joint venture between The Great China Film Company founded in 1923 and the Lily Film Company founded in 1924. The venture was aimed at consolidating the company's capital and talent. GL produced chiefly contemporary urban dramas, the most famous of which was *The Small Factory Owner* (Lu Jie, 1925). Its urban dramas imitated D. W. Griffith's melodramas then popular in China, including *Birth of a Nation* (1915), *Broken Blossoms* (1919), *Way Down East* (1920), and *Orphans of the Storm* (1921). In promoting women's rights and the right to choose one's own lover, GL's Westernized melodrama introduced to Chinese cinema some of the May Fourth modernization themes.[15] An antitradition cultural movement led by Chinese intellectuals from 1917 to 1920, May Fourth was a sociopolitical/intellectual revolution aiming at achieving national independence, individual emancipation, and the creation of a new culture through a critical and scientific reevaluation of the national heritage and selective acceptance of foreign civilization. GL's melodrama focused chiefly on the theme of individual emancipation. In terms of production scale and output, the company was second only to Star. Due to some internal management conflicts, GL suspended its operations in 1929. It later joined Lianhua (United China; UC), a formidable newcomer, in 1930. UC would replace GL as one of the big three from the late 1920s to the early 1930s.

Heaven, the predecessor of the powerful Shaw Brothers Studio in Hong Kong, was formed in Shanghai in 1925 by the financially adventurous yet culturally conservative Shaw brothers.[16] Disciples of Buddhism, the Shaw brothers looked to classical Buddhist literature for their cinematic inspiration. Heaven consequently cultivated its own signature genre, the historical drama, the forerunner of the more pronounced costume drama of the late 1920s. Heaven's historical drama competed head to head with Star's social realist melodrama and GL's westernized urban drama. Promoting traditional Chinese ethics, morality, and civilization, the historical drama was especially popular among the Chinese diaspora in Southeast Asia. The success of historical drama made it possible for Heaven to maintain a firm grip over Southeast Asia's film market. The dominance of Star, Great China-Lily, and Heaven would remain unchallenged throughout the second half of the 1920s.

COMMERCIAL WAVES AND INSTITUTIONAL RESTRUCTURING: CHINESE CINEMA FROM THE MID-1920s TO THE EARLY 1930s

Chinese cinema from the mid-1920s to the early 1930s witnessed, simultaneously, a commercial entertainment wave and a series of institutional restructurings. Building a profitable and nationalistic film industry became the two major themes during the period, resembling the struggle of Chinese cinema at the present.

The direction of Chinese cinema during the early period was closely related to the political situation at the time. China in the mid-1920s was anticipating a civil war between the newly established Communist Party and the Nationalist Party under Chiang Kai-shek's (Jiang Jieshi, 1887–1975) control. The two parties had a brief honeymoon in the early 1920s. Founded in 1921, the Soviet-inspired Chinese Communist Party advocated thorough political and cultural reform to revolutionize what it saw as a tradition-bound, semifeudal, and semicolonial society and re-unite the then-warlord-segregated nation. Meanwhile, eager to carry out its national reconstruction plan under the guidance of its founder, Dr. Sun Yat-sen, the reformed Nationalist Party began to draw arms and ad-vice from Soviet Russia and, in doing so, sought to work in collaboration with members of the Chinese Communist Party. The two parties launched a reunification campaign, the historic Northern Expedition, in the mid-1920s, to annihilate the warlords. The joint military force was led by Chiang Kai-shek, Dr. Sun's successor. The expedition began in 1926, moving northward from the Nationalist Party's base in Canton through Shanghai toward Beijing. As the armed forces swept northward, the Communist Party tried to mobilize the workers and peasants in Shanghai for a massive strike. Frightened by the threat of a Communist-led general strike, the business community in Shanghai sought to ally themselves with a moderate wing of the Nationalist Party. Jiang, who was then in the process of breaking with the left-wing Nationalists for his own conservative regime, appeared as a natural ally for Shanghai's merchants. At the same time, Jiang was eager to court Shanghai's ven-ture capitalists to secure financial support for his political ambition. The business leaders promised financial support if Jiang were to break with the communists to restore peace and order and to suppress labor move-ments in Shanghai. When the expedition forces reached Shanghai in March 1927, Jiang staged a bloody purge of the communists, formally breaching the pact with the Communist Party. As members of the Com-munist Party were being slaughtered, the nation came under the control of Jiang's Nanjing government in 1928.

The nationalist's extirpation of communists and other left-wing intellec-tuals, writers, and artists was partially intended to divert the urban popu-lace from radical social concerns. To maintain its one-party rule, Jiang's government appealed to Confucian values such as filial piety and loyalty to one's nation–state as an alternative to the Communist-advocated radi-cal cultural reform. The Communist movement was deliberately linked in righteous Nationalist propaganda with attacks on the Confucian family and with the advocacy and practice of free love deviant from Chinese tra-ditions. Jiang's concern over ideological dissension and political protest re-sulted in the Nanjing government's increased attention to censorial control of political opinions.[17] Jiang's government further censored the press to prevent criticism of Jiang's terrorism. By early 1931, criticizing the Nationalist Party in the press was decreed a crime against the state.

To further achieve his political and financial stability, in the ensuing years, Jiang not only set out to crack down on political dissidents but also turned the wave of terror against the business owners whose financial contributions fell short of his increasing demands. Severe pressure was put on business owners to make contributions to the Nationalist cause. Anti-Communist terrorism became a pretext to persecute business owners who dared to defy Jiang's demand for funds for his military. The wave of terror engulfed many merchants and affected the lives of everyday Chinese people. As such, the relatively loose political control the business community, intellectual community, and everyday people had together enjoyed in Shanghai for a decade prior to 1927 came to an abrupt halt.

Jiang's political terrorism and cultural conservatism discouraged Chinese cinema's social realist effort. The realist tendency was already on the wane in the early 1920s due to filmmakers' relentless pursuit of audiences who longed for escapist films during the era of civil war. The realist tendency was further diminished by the filmmakers' self-censorship in fear of possible political ramifications from films about contemporary subjects. Chinese filmmakers thus further steered the industry away from making contemporary melodramas and instead made strictly apolitical films for commercial entertainment. Understandably, few attempts were made during the period to depict the revolutionary wave of Chinese society.[18] The Nationalist's traditionalist cultural orientation further encouraged filmmakers to look for inspiration from Chinese literary classics, stage dramas, popular fairy tales, myths, and folklore.

On the economic front, after the initial hostility, the Nanjing government pursued a more cooperative economic policy toward the business community to encourage investment and industrialization. The consolidation of domestic transportation during and after the Northern Expedition boosted economic development and brought in substantial industrial investment to China's coastal cities. The cultural and linguistic barriers prevented foreign capital from venturing into local production, thus granting Chinese domestic production an opportunity to grow. With an oppressive political climate, a conservative cultural policy, an audience's escapist tendency, and a stable economic environment, the time was ripe for the surge of Chinese cinema's first wave of entertainment films.

Building a Profitable Industry: Chinese Cinema's First Entertainment Wave

The surge of Heaven-led costume drama in 1927–1928 signaled the arrival of Chinese cinema's first entertainment wave. The wave gained its momentum with the success of martial arts–ghost films led by Star from 1928 to

1931. More than half of the film output during the period fit one of the two popular genres.[19] Except for the first of the Chinese sound novelties, *The Singing Girl Red Peony* (Zhang Shichuan, 1930), all the financial successes during the period came from costume drama and martial arts–ghost drama. The films actively and effectively competed with Hollywood imports.

Costume Drama

Costume drama was launched in 1926 by Heaven as historical drama with semimodern and semitraditional costume. It was endorsed immediately by the critical and popular sentiment to subvert the modern urban drama's Westernization trend. The classical Chinese literature and popular folklore attacked during the May Fourth Westernization movement were making their way back to the literary scene in the early 1920s; and by the mid-1920s, films of Westernized contemporary urban themes had lost their connection with both the audiences and the critics.[20] Heaven saw the shrinking market for domestic films on contemporary subjects as a sign that the audiences were looking for something more Chinese. Heaven's founders, the tradition-minded Shaw brothers, themselves fans of classical Chinese literature and performing arts, considered Chinese literary classics and popular folk tales rich resources for films of Chinese characteristics.[21] The box-office success of imported historical films such as Cecil B. DeMille's *The Ten Commandments* (1923) and D. W. Griffith's historical epics also inspired the Shaw brothers to explore China's historical heritage and probe the possibility of reconciling the imported cinematic technology with a culturally specific narrative.

The early historical films did not pay close attention to the proper attire of the historical figures depicted, and some actors/actresses even wore modern clothing. The unexpected success of historical films in Heaven's Southeast Asian market propelled the company to expand its adaptation of classical novels to all kinds of Chinese literary classics and to seriously dress its characters in ancient Chinese attire. Historical drama soon evolved into the popular costume drama in 1927. Over two-thirds of China's domestic films made between 1927 and 1928 were costume dramas, and seventeen out of twenty-three studios, including Star and the Great China-Lily, were routinely involved in churning out such films. Heaven was the leader in the production of costume drama.[22]

Early costume dramas were mostly adapted from traditional Chinese performing arts, particularly Tanchi, a popular vocal entertainment format that consisted of chanted folk tales about tragic love in a repressive feudal society. Costume drama later ventured into literary adaptations of Chinese mythology, classic novels and poems, and period dramas based on historical events. Under the politically regressive and culturally conservative Nationalist rule, such a genre provided the film industry an alternative to the provocative social problem drama and the Western-style urban melodramas. The genre also spoke to its target audience's cultural taste. Early Chinese films catered mostly to socially and economically disadvantaged patrons, since well-off and better-educated Chinese patrons frequented only upper-scale theaters dominated by Hollywood films. The poor and the less-educated patrons grew up listening to Chinese operas and Tanchi. Screen renditions of such popular vocal narratives naturally appealed to them and to the Chinese residing in Hong Kong, Macao, and other parts of Southeast Asia. The cultural policies in Southeast Asia under colonial rule welcomed costume drama because such films bore no political relevance to colonial control, let alone challenging its legitimacy. Costume drama's popularity among overseas' Chinese was crucial for the Chinese film industry to make a profit and attract investments, since prosperous Southeast Asia promised both the market and the capital.

The literary resources of costume drama were generally divided into four types: folk tale, Tanchi, and unofficial historical events; Chinese mythology; canonized Chinese classical novels, traditional operas, and poems; and official historical events.[23] All four types of adaptation can be found in Heaven's popular productions such as *Liang Shanbuo and Zhu Yingtai* (Shaw Zhuiwen, 1926), a tale of faithful lovers; *The Tale of White Snake* (Shaw Zhuiwen, 1926), a Chinese myth; *Lady Meng Jiang* (Qiu Jixiang, 1926), a legend about a widow who sought revenge on the emperor who had killed her husband, an engineer on the Great Wall; *Monkey Fights Golden Leopard* (Shaw Zhuiwen, 1926), an episode from the classical novel by Wu Cheng-en, *Pilgrimage to the West*; and *Tang Bo-hu Burns the Incense/Marriage of Three Smiles* (Shaw Zhuiwen, 1926), a story of a Ming dynasty painter whose persistence won him the wife he wanted.[24] The Chinese Buddhist folk tale *Pilgrimage to the West* remained the favorite source, with historical novels such as *The Legend of Shuifu* and *Romance of the Three Kingdoms* delivering some of the most popular cinematic adaptations.

Character development and plot structure in costume drama mostly followed its literary origins. Audiences' familiarity with such popular characters and plots made the film adaptations less time-consuming and therefore more productive. While the themes of loyalty, heroism, and antioppression were common among the Chinese classics, costume drama frequently foregrounded the romance of "learned man and beautiful woman," or "hero and beauty." Comic elements were added to defuse such stories' melodramatic propensity. Costume drama strove to construct character archetypes rather than nuanced individuals, resembling classical Chinese painting's obsession for generalities. *Mei Ren Ji* (Shi Dongshan, 1927), a film hailed as one of the best costume dramas, portrayed six famous historical figures by casting only one salient dimension to each character and making them the representatives of cunning, filial piety, kindness, (sexual) purity, personal loyalty, and justice.

The style of costume drama was more theatrical than cinematic in terms of framing and editing. Cinematic movements including character/event development, camera movement, and cutting were all kept to a minimum. Both the filmmakers' affinity to stage drama and their limited knowledge of cinematic techniques and technology contributed to costume drama's minimal cinematic motion and dramatic tension. Particularly restricted was the camera mobility, which left the burden of movement to the performers and other mobile objects/subjects. Plot progression was slow, lacking dramatic momentum, which resulted in early Chinese film's characteristically prolonged scenes. The filmmakers' limited understanding of the more sophisticated editing techniques and the impact of montage might have contributed to the slow pace of most Chinese films during the period. It was further suggested that the Chinese people's lack of exposure to automobiles, airplanes, trains, and so on during the time was responsible for the relative immobility of early Chinese cinema that emphasized "picture" over "motion."[25]

In general, like most silent films during the time, the style of costume drama emphasized theatrical clarity over cinematic intensity and pictorial stability over mobility. Lighting was designed mainly for illumination rather than for dramatic tension. Long shots and medium-to-medium long shots were utilized to make the scene intelligible in the most efficient way. Both low- and high-angle shots that would otherwise dramatize characters and events were seldom employed. Likewise, editing was used to mostly clarify, rather than intensify, plots and character relations. As such, the shot/reverse shot was infrequently applied, even in the intense fighting scenes. Parallel editing was also minimized for fear of audiences' presumed inability to comprehend complex spatial and temporal relations. Close-ups reflective of character emotions and relations were also kept to a minimum. The relative spatial stability made it necessary to rely on temporal mobility for character development and plot advancement, yet the plot progression was basically linear, following a chronological order. Flashbacks were infrequently used to avoid perceived audience confusion. To offset the limits of a confined cinematic space and motion, coincidence and misunderstanding became the most frequently deployed theatrical devices for plot and character complication.

Early Chinese cinema's scarce use of close-ups and shot/reverse shot was influenced by traditional Chinese painting that emphasized a distant, communal point of view transcendent of the views of individuals. While putting the major elements in the geometrical center of the composition, the distant framing left much empty space above and on the right and left corners of the frame, further reducing the shot's dramatic energy. Some scholars suggested that the need for Chinese filmmakers to present the relations between characters within one frame/shot rather than with multiple shots was closely related to the need of the Chinese to immediately clarify power dynamics between/among the characters.[26] Supposedly, the power dynamic presented within one frame through character blocking and conversing was easier to identify than between multiple cuts.

The framing of costume drama is also influenced by Chinese stage drama. The frontality of stage drama contributed to the costume drama's affinity to lateral blocking and the shallow staging (lateral staging perpendicular to the lens). Both the lateral blocking and shallow staging strove to make certain aspects of the image salient for the viewers to direct their attention to the front- and center-staged character(s) and event(s) that were most likely the main character(s) and major event(s). Further, following the tradition of Chinese opera, props were simplified, striving not for realism but for symbolism. Chinese stage drama had traditionally relied on few symbolic props and blocking evocative of real surroundings and movements. Unlike the Western notion of realism that stressed verisimilitude, the Chinese view of realism focused on the evocation rather than the representation of reality. What is important is the feeling of the real but not the imitation of the real. Such symbolic realism was also rooted in classical Chinese paintings and literature. Some suggested that the Chinese film critics' and audiences' collective apprehension of early Western imports' depiction of the ugly side of Chinese reality such as foot binding and opium addiction had contributed to their nearly stubborn neglect of cinema's penchant and capacity for verisimilitude during the period.[27]

There were exceptions to the costume drama's tendency of frontality and immobility. For instance, *The Tale of the West Wing* (Hou Jue, 1927), a romantic love story adapted from a classic Chinese novel, utilized many cinematic techniques to depict characters' nuanced emotion and relationship. The camera was mobilized to depict the same scene/event from multiple angles and points of view. Massive blocking, at times five hundred people, was coupled with six cameras simultaneously shooting the scene. There were also shot variations. An extreme long shot was used to depict the danger of an approaching army, which showed the movements of troops in the mountains resembling that of a snake. Overhead and high-angle shots were utilized to depict the fighting scenes. Editing was smooth, with controlled change of pace, demonstrating a patterned rhythm. Superimposition was employed to combine various weapons in fighting so as to emphasize the severity of the battle. Special effects were used to depict the dream sequence. All such cinematic devices were orchestrated confidently by the veteran director Hou Jue who, prior to making costume drama, specialized in the Westernized social-problem drama.

The profitability of costume dramas attracted many small-scale production companies who were eager to make a few quick bucks. Yet the majority of such companies lacked sufficient budgets, talent, and technology for the production of quality costume drama with originality. The costumes and props used were mostly based on availability not on historical accuracy, which further reduced the authenticity of such drama. The proliferation of cheap knockoffs tarnished the reputation of domestic pictures, further steering middle-class patrons away from Chinese cinema. Once again, the survival of Chinese cinema became a hot issue among the critics and the filmmakers. Costume drama was criticized, resulting in the genre's metamorphosis in 1928 to the martial arts–ghost drama.

Martial Arts–Ghost Drama

As suggested by the Chinese film historians Li Shuyuan and Hu Jushan, martial arts–ghost drama was really the combination of martial arts and ghost dramas.[28] Emerging as separate subgenres of costume drama, the two soon found strength in each other. Depicting the lives of kung fu legend, martial arts stories were typically formulaic, combining heroic themes with predictable plot structure and characterization. The martial arts picture had fought for its niche market since 1927, amid the costume drama craze. The martial arts story had been a popular genre long before it was adapted to the big screen. The newspaper adventure serial and its derivative, picture books, had regularly featured stories of kung fu masters. Martial arts stories were also popular resources for various traditional Chinese stage performances such as were presented at Pingshu, Quyi, and other local operas houses. Furthermore, the martial arts novel as a literary genre occupied a special position in the history of Chinese literature. The popularity of kung fu stories made martial arts films easily accessible. Indeed, kung fu film was praised for its demonstration of Chinese people's physical ability, countering the stereotypical perceptions of Chinese as the "patients of East Asia." The sentimental urban melodrama, on the other hand, was criticized for its portrayal of neurotic characters with weak physiques. The Chinese critic Lu Mengshu publicly advocated martial arts drama for its embodiment of his "new heroism" ideal that called for a new kind of national hero who defied oppressive forces and elevated the public.[29] Other critics echoed his call, and "the new heroism cinema" became a slogan in the mid-1920s.[30] The popularity of imported historical tales such as Robin Hood and The Three Musketeers further influenced such a trend. The valuation of martial arts drama was also moralistic, praising the genre's egalitarian themes of helping the poor and the weak and its Confucian themes of filial loyalty and the loyalty to one's country.[31] The prevailing public and critical apprehension of melodrama during the period further benefited the ascendancy of martial arts–ghost drama. The devaluation of melodrama was nationalistic, as one critic during the period claimed that the endorsement of the martial arts film responded to the public's need for heroes during the time of ongoing national crises.[32]

Martial arts film received a boost after it absorbed supernatural elements from ghost stories. The combination of kung fu and ghost stories resulted in martial arts–ghost drama in which the kung fu legends, with their raw physical power, were granted a supernatural capacity. Old Buddhist temples were added to the kung fu drama's signature settings of barren mountains and remote countryside. Naked women and men wearing macabre masks were also added to create a mysterious atmosphere. Special effects were utilized to create the illusion of flying and disappearance of the characters. The popularity of martial arts and ghost stories in the 1920s made them lucrative pre-sold commodities for film adaptation. Meanwhile, new special effects technology made the production of such physically demanding films possible. Indeed, what mattered most to martial arts–ghost drama was not its originality of plot structure and characterization but the visualization of the already familiar story and characters. Star's *Burning of the Red Lotus Temple* (Zhang Shichuan) in 1928 started the strong wave of martial arts–ghost drama. In promoting traditional Chinese ethics, it also carried on the legacy of costume drama. From 1928 to 1931, martial arts–ghost drama swamped the domestic and overseas Chinese markets, prolonging the commercial entertainment trend.

Overall, martial arts–ghost drama had a much narrower, yet arguably more creative, focus than costume drama in terms of its literary resources and its themes. While a small amount of martial arts–ghost drama was adopted from classical novels, traditional operas, and folklore, most of the scenarios were the filmmaker's own creation. The heroes of martial arts–ghost drama were all chivalrous swordsmen/women with super martial arts skills. Physically capable and appealing, such heroes/heroines always attracted attention from the opposite sex. But such explicit love interest served merely to tease the audience since it never amounted to anything substantial, because the Buddhist heroes/heroines' celibate vows prohibited any possibility of consummation.[33] Like costume drama, most martial arts–ghost drama was made on shoestring budgets in a short period of time, ranging from a few months to just ten days. Outdoor settings with limited props and natural daylight were utilized under such production conditions. Actors' martial arts talent was emphasized over their acting skill; and with the aid of special visual effects for the aura of mystery and the supernatural, kung fu legends' physical ability was emphasized over their psychological complexity.

The four common story types of martial arts–ghost drama were rebellion against tyranny, revenge, martial arts competition, and treasure hunting, with the competition between opposing kung fu schools being the most popular one. *Burning of the Red Lotus Temple* zeroed in exactly on the theme of fractional strife among various kung fu schools. It was a story about the fight against a group of evil kung fu Buddhists who occupied the Red Lotus Temple for their murderous deeds. At the end of the first episode, after the furious battle involving martial arts skill and supernatural power between the evil kung fu masters and four chivalrous kung fu masters from outside the temple, the Red Lotus Temple was burned. But the three leaders of the temple escaped. The following seventeen installments focused on the battle and competition among various kung fu schools led by the three escapists and the four kung fu masters, all of them possessing superior fist-fighting and sword-brandishing skills as well as the power of witchcraft. Special effects such as front and rear projections, glass shot, and the Schufftan process were applied to create the illusions of magic. The actors' martial arts skills were mostly conjured up through special effects and editing.

Overall, martial arts–ghost drama had evolved from costume drama's character-driven story structure to a plot-driven structure. The narrative no longer traced the rise and fall of its main character(s) but followed the victories and defeats of kung fu battles. The depiction of complex characters gave way to the construction of contrived plot. Since multiple and complex plots were favored over a single and simple plot, the narrative's causal relation was less clear, which made the narrative enigma(s) all the more intriguing. Close-ups and tracking shots were more frequently utilized in martial arts–ghost drama than in costume drama. Numerous fighting scenes also demanded a faster pace and multiple angles. Editing was used to evoke magic and at the same time conceal the actors' somewhat inadequate kung fu ability. Though lacking advanced cinematic technology, filmmakers strove to create the illusion of magic, using some of the most primitive methods. One actress recorded her memory of the production of martial arts–ghost drama:

At that time there was no special photographic technique for filming unusual feats of daring. When I had to fly through the air, a rope was tied around my waist and I was hoisted up high above the floor. The shaky ceiling of the studio threatened to fall and there was no safety net to catch me.

For the fighting scenes, the studio hired ricksha pullers, pole-carriers and others who had never had any training in either sword-fighting or picture-making. Brandishing wooden broadswords and spears, they would strike blindly at me. I emerged from every shooting covered with bruises.[34]

Such primitive cinematic tricks worked well with relatively unsophisticated audiences during the time.

With its 1928 premier of *Burning of the Red Lotus Temple*, Star became the innovator and the leader in producing martial arts–ghost drama. Star's old specialties, the social problem drama and the urban melodrama, were not faring well since the ascendancy of the costume drama. The company was undergoing financial difficulties. Anxious to regain its strength, Star turned to making martial arts drama, the only commercially viable alternative to cheap knockoffs of Heaven's costume dramas, which were already waning by 1928.

Zhang, Star's business-savvy pioneer, settled on the then popular kung fu novel, *The Tales of Kongfu Legend*. Zhang suggested to his cofounder, Zheng, that they flesh out a screenplay based on this novel. The novel's screen adaptation, *Burning of the Red Lotus Temple*, was a huge hit. With its supernatural elements inherited from the novel, the film became the debut of the martial arts–ghost genre. Star's in-house actors were not famous for their martial arts training so Zhang introduced supernatural elements to mask his stars' insufficient kung fu skills. Supernatural power aided the film's leading lady, the popular female icon Butterfly (Hudie), in her portrayal of a female kung fu legend. The success of *Burning of the Red Lotus Temple* encouraged Zhang to make eighteen series from 1928 to 1930, generating enough revenue for the company to recover from its financial problems and to further expand its production operation. The movie's success also triggered a series of "Burning" films made by small production companies who merely imitated Star's formula. These films included *Burning of the Black Dragon Temple* (1929), *Burning of the White Flower Terrace* (1929), and *Burning of the Sword-Peak Fortress* (1930).

The success of *Burning of the Red Lotus Temple* further promoted some medium-level companies such as You Lian, The Great China-Lily, and The Great Wall Picture to follow Star's lead, creating the wave of martial arts–ghost pictures. Soon many small production companies joined suit, hoping to make a quick profit out of the new trend. Such productions were severely underbudgeted, seriously hurting the quality and, hence, the reputation of martial arts–ghost drama. The production of martial arts–ghost films reached its height in 1929, with an annual output of eighty-five pictures. The replication of Star's successful formula resulted in an oversaturated market, contributing to the demise of the martial arts–ghost trend. By the early 1930s, the quality of martial arts–ghost drama had seriously deteriorated. The low quality and high quantity gave the distributors from Southeast Asia leverage to cut the price, draining studios' production investment. It also gave the foreign-controlled theater chains in big cities an excuse to further reject Chinese native productions. Finally, the furious competition and the rising cost of production resulted in the bankruptcy of many production companies, even medium-sized ones. Meanwhile, the genre's superstitious elements had attracted much derision from the critics, resulting in an outcry for the banning of martial arts–ghost pictures. The Nationalist government banned martial arts–ghost film in 1931, officially ending Chinese cinema's first wave of entertainment films.

Building a National Industry: Chinese Cinema's First Institutional Restructurings

At the time the film industry witnessed its first entertainment wave, it also underwent a series of institutional restructurings. The institutional restructurings were the direct result of the film industry's spontaneous effort to foster Chinese native production and exhibition. Both the entertainment wave and the institutional restructurings shared the same goal in their attempt to compete with Hollywood for the Chinese market. Hollywood's dominance in the Chinese market continued throughout the second half of the 1920s, occupying 90 percent of the screen time.[35] Overall, foreign capital had actively monopolized the distribution and exhibition sectors. Film exhibition in the 1920s and 1930s adhered to the two-tiered colonial structure. While some crudely equipped theaters were built in the hinterlands and small towns, many well-equipped theaters were built in big cosmopolitan cities such as Shanghai and Beijing. Upscale theaters all had exclusive contracts with Hollywood. Heavy fines were imposed when such theaters screened Chinese films. The fine was also applied to some middle-scale theaters. Most of the small production companies were intimidated by the foreign-controlled theaters.

Chinese film practitioners were keenly aware of the necessity of establishing their own theater chains. Battles were waged against the Western monopoly over film distribution and exhibition. Star took the lead in cultivating a market for domestic productions. Imitating Hollywood's vertically integrated studio system, the company founded its own distribution network. Star also built its own theater chains. Its Central Theater in Shanghai became a palace for domestic films. Star further sought to buy out the foreign-run distribution–exhibition networks, initiating cooperation with other local companies to establish a united exhibition network—United Film Exchange (UFE)—exclusively screening films made by the affiliated companies.[36] Heaven was the only big studio that did not cooperate with UFE. By cultivating its own signature genre, the costume drama, Heaven competed head to head with UFE, provoking severe retaliation from UFE. Heaven's ample output of popular costume drama posed a direct threat to UFE, who responded by publicly advocating national cinema with better quality, an unambiguous shot at costume drama films, many of them cheap knockoffs of an established formula. Heaven's market share had become larger than UFE from 1927 to 1928. Fearful of Heaven's further market expansion, UFE demanded its contracting distribution companies not to purchase films from Heaven. From 1928 to 1929, UFE also published a fan magazine, Film Monthly (Dianying yuebao), to promote its pictures. Zhou Jianyun, one of Star's founders who also maintained carte blanche authority at UFE, wrote columns for Film Monthly, explicitly attacking costume drama led by Heaven.[37] Such is Chinese cinema's first distribution war, the infamous "United Film Exchange encircling Heaven." Heaven lost part of its market share in Shanghai as the result of UFE's monopolistic control, experiencing temporary financial crisis. Heaven soon changed its strategy, focusing instead on cultivating and expanding its Southeast Asian theater chains. Heaven was able to maintain a solid monopoly over the Southeast

Asian market during the period. As suggested by the Chinese historians Li Shuyuan and Hu Jushan, the competition, however furious between UFE and Heaven, was kept low key.[38] UFE was particularly cautious in avoiding any comparison of its monopolistic control to Hollywood's market dominance in China. However, the Star-controlled UFE's aggressive marketing maneuvers did alienate many film practitioners. Star's self-serving distribution policy deserted its alliances within UFE, resulting in a series of internal power struggles, which eroded the company's financial strength, finally triggering its shutdown in July 1929. After that, UFE's former theater chains went their own ways, forming various small production companies. The furious competition among the small independent companies created chaos in the domestic film market, inciting the call for an integrated national film industry. Institutional restructuring was thus seen as the route toward a united Chinese national cinema.

The institutional restructuring during this period was driven by both the industry's concern for its economic survival and its patriotic practitioners' aspiration to build a stronger national cinema at the service of a nation in crisis. A latecomer, Lianhua (United China; UC) emerged as a formidable production company that would lead the way toward the revival of Chinese national cinema. UC was formed in 1930, the outcome of a series of vertical and horizontal integrations initiated by the patriotic Luo Mingyou, the owner of a chain of theaters located in northern cities. Luo came from a wealthy merchant family in southern China. The family was well-connected with the Nationalist government and the prosperous Hong Kong business community. Luo ventured into film exhibition by building the Zhen Guang Theater in Beijing in 1918. A decade later, he founded Northern China Film Company to expand his theater chain. By 1930, his company was managing over twenty theaters spread all over northeast China. Like most theaters at the time, Luo also relied on imports to attract affluent patrons. However, he considered the penetration of foreign imports an "invasion of foreign culture," regarded by the Chinese as disgraceful and humiliating.[39] Luo was determined to rescue Chinese cinema from the shadow of Hollywood. He was one of the first Chinese film practitioners who realized the importance of the vertically and horizontally integrated institutional structure and practice that were responsible for Hollywood's global success. According to him, the three maladies of Chinese cinema were poor production quality; the separation of production, distribution, and exhibition; and the destructive competition among production companies.[40] The coming of sound granted Luo an opportunity to venture into film production.[41] Due to the language barrier, foreign "talkies" did not fare as well as their silent predecessors. After the initial excitement and curiosity, Chinese audiences were losing their interest in imported talkies. Meanwhile, Hollywood had stopped exporting silent pictures, leaving many theaters scrounging for screening material.

Envisioning the inevitable demand for domestic pictures, Luo entered film production by courting existing production companies for a possible consolidation. His goal was to bring all the studios and film companies together in one huge vertically integrated enterprise. He courted various production companies, including The Great China-Lily, Star, Shanghai Cinema and Theater Company, and Hong Kong Film Company, for a possible consolidation under the new name United China Film Company. With strong financial support from his family and friends, he acquired shares of these companies by purchasing their equipment and signing contracts with them for exclusive screening of their films in his theater chains. He advocated constructive cooperation instead of destructive competition among studios. He also encouraged studios to support theaters showing Chinese films by supplying theaters with first-run quality films. Finally, he advised theater owners to consolidate their chains and to liquidate foreign-run theaters.

With Star, The Great China-Lily, Shanghai Cinema and Theater Company, and Hong Kong Film Company under its wing, United China Film Company was officially founded in March 1930. UC set up its general manager's office in Hong Kong. A management branch was also set up in Shanghai, overseeing three studios. Luo further consolidated theaters in Hong Kong, Shanghai, Guangzhou, and northeast China to establish a distribution–exhibition network. He scouted locations in coastal cities for additional theaters. Finally, he started a technicians' training group in Beijing and a song-and-dance class in Shanghai. UC's nationalistic aspirations and professional management skills attracted many of the top talents in Shanghai, boosting the company's image as a place for quality productions. UC's fast ascendance soon made it an equal of Star and Heaven, forming a new oligopoly of Chinese cinema during the period.

Cinema to Luo was first and foremost a vehicle for nationalistic pedagogy. UC produced twelve silent pictures in 1930 and 1931, most of them socially conscious melodramas directed by the famous directors Sun Yu and Shi Dongshan. Its debut, *Spring Dream in an Ancient City* (Sun Yu), a well-crafted social drama catering to better educated patrons, was an instant hit in 1930. Directed by the American-educated Sun Yu, the film dealt with government corruption and moral decay, a refreshing alternative to the martial arts–ghost pictures. The film was also critical of Chinese intellectuals' complacency toward government corruption. The film's box-office return during its premier in Shanghai, Hong Kong, and Beijing equaled that of an average Chinese film's full run. It signaled the beginning of the revival of Chinese national cinema. Influenced by Alexandre Dumas fil's play *Camille* (1852) and Frank Borzage's film *Seventh Heaven* (1927), UC's second feature *Wild Grass Leisure Flowers* (Sun Yu, 1928) was a melodrama about the courtship between a wealthy young musician and a flower girl with singing talent. After many twists and turns, the young lovers, separated by the young man's family, eventually get together. Like *Camille*, *Wild Grass Leisure Flowers* was a "problem film," a middle-class realistic drama addressing some contemporary ill and offering suggestions for its remedy. The film attacked the hypocrisy of Chinese society and championed for the young lovers' pursuit of unprejudiced love. It was a hit among urban youth and intellectuals, demonstrating the ability of quality domestic films to compete with Hollywood imports. The actress in both films was Ruan Linyu, a Chinese screen icon at the time.

From 1932 to 1934, UC went through a period of crisis brought on by both external and internal pressures. Externally, the Japanese invasion in 1931 interrupted Luo's vertically integrated operation. Luo's theater chain in northeast China was lost to Japan's occupation, and his studio in Shanghai was badly damaged by Japanese bombing. Domestically, the Chinese economy went through a difficult period, draining financial resources for film production. Internationally, the world economy was going through a similar slump, collapsing Luo's overseas' connections. UC's policy of emphasizing quality pictures not only slowed down production output but also raised budgets. The discrepancy between quality and quantity put UC at a disadvantage in competing with the big-two's popular entertainment pictures. Meanwhile, UC had some internal management problems, which further contributed to the company's financial crisis. The continuous expansion in building new studios had overextended the company's financial and human resources. Also, the problems of inefficiency and overbudgeting at its formerly independent studios persisted after the formation of UC. Finally, Luo's Hong Kong branch was not making a profit either. UC managed to overcome its financial crisis by injecting new talent into its production team, including the left-wing filmmakers such as Tian Han (*Three Modern Women*, 1933) and Sun Yu (*Wild Rose*, 1932) who made critically acclaimed and publicly endorsed social realist films at the time.

With the success of *Burning of the Red Lotus Temple* in 1928, Star, on the other hand, was able to expand its production in the second half of 1928 by moving to a larger lot and upgrading production facilities. The company's organization also went through a series of restructurings. It streamlined its production operation by establishing departments of directing, promotion, animation, and technical support. It also recruited new talent for writing, directing, and acting. Overall, Star came out of this period of reconfiguration and restructuring in a stronger position. Its number one position would not be challenged until late 1930 and early 1931 by UC. Star competed with UC by venturing into sound production, returning to quality pictures, consolidating its distribution–exhibition network, and cultivating its star system.

Heaven continued to cultivate its southeast market. Its number one position in southeast China more than offset its domestic box-office loss.

Heaven was also the first production company that ventured into sound production. In the early 1930s when domestic sound films were rare, Heaven's productions attracted audiences who were eager to try out sound films. Heaven later began to produce Cantonese-dialect films to further maintain its market grip in the southeast where the majority of Chinese spoke Cantonese.

Japan's 1932 bombing and burning of Shanghai destroyed much of the film industry's physical resources, forcing thirty small companies out of business. Sixteen out of thirty-nine theaters in Shanghai were also destroyed in the bombing, most of them theaters screening Chinese films. The Japanese invasion incited renewed patriotic spirit and lifted morale in the film industry. The remaining companies, including the big three and a few small-scale studios, began to make patriotic films. Some employees of Star and UC collected money for a "Save the Country Group" and helped to boycott Japanese goods. Meanwhile, led by underground Communist Party members, a left-wing film team started their systematic penetration into the financially ailing film industry. UC was one of the studios penetrated by the film team, which introduced to Chinese cinema the Marxist revolutionary theme of class struggle. The Nationalist-controlled government tried to crack down on communist influence and threatened to sabotage any production that promoted class difference. Luo tried to distance UC from the left-wingers. Yet left-wing filmmakers within UC circumvented him. Hence, UC paradoxically produced both Shanghai's most reactionary and most progressive films from 1934 to 1935.[42] UC stopped production after the official outbreak of the war against Japan in 1937. During its eight-year history, UC produced a total of ninety-four features, including some of the most well-known films in Chinese history.

The Influence of Film Culture

From the socially conscious melodrama to the box-office-conscious costume and martial arts–ghost pictures, Chinese cinema went from a cinema of enlightenment to a cinema of entertainment. The recognition of film production as a profitable financial investment promoted such a transition. The concurrent institutional restructuring during the period further foregrounded the recognition of cinema's economic function. The impending Sino–Japan War in the early 1930s interrupted Chinese cinema's entertainment wave, renewing discussion of cinema's pedagogical/cultural function of enlightening the masses to serve the nation in crisis. The late 1920s, particularly, saw a surge of critical discourse concerning the crisis of Chinese cinema in terms of its withering emphasis on its pedagogical function. While entertainment films lured the public to domestic pictures, such pictures were sharply criticized by the socially conscious film critics, most of them film practitioners, for their lack of pedagogical value and production quality. What formed the nucleus of socially conscious film critics was a constellation of playwrights-turned-filmmakers such as Zheng Zhengqiu and Tian Han, influential film directors and producers such as Zhou Jianyun and Luo Mingyou, prominent literary figures such as Yu Dafu and Mao Dun, and newspaper and magazine columnists such as Tang Na and Jing Chao.[43]

Yet the competition with imported entertainment pictures gave certain legitimacy to the cultivation of domestic entertainment pictures. As such, prior to the Sino–Japan War, the harsh view of a cinema of entertainment was muffled by the industry's anxiety over Chinese cinema's difficult struggle under the shadow of Hollywood. Paradoxically, the outcry for a stronger national cinema, for example, a socially conscious cinema, contributed to the arrival of the entertainment wave. Indeed, Chinese cinema's first entertainment wave was the result of a traditionalist cultural movement in the 1920s. As a kindred spirit, a populist cinematic tendency further endorsed a cinema with public appeal.

A Traditionalist and Populist Film Culture

The impact of film culture on the film industry can be better understood by examining the characteristics of Chinese film criticism during the time.[44] The early 1920s to early 1930s saw the motion picture being transformed into a popular and therefore influential visual format. Considered as part of art and literature with significant social impact, film began to be taken seriously by the Chinese cultural critics. Some of the critics were directly involved in film production by writing and directing films. Conversely, many filmmakers participated in film criticism by writing articles for newspapers and magazines. The close tie between film criticism and film production made the two mutually dependent, casting a practical angle on the critics' approach toward film criticism.

Overall, what characterized Chinese film criticism during the period was moralism, nationalism, and pragmatism. Early Chinese film criticism had a strong ethical/moralistic overtone. In fact, a Chinese film scholar coined the term *ethical/moral criticism* to characterize film criticism from 1921 to 1932.[45] Such criticism focused mainly on evaluating film texts from either a Confucian moral/ethical standpoint or a Western liberal standpoint. Textual analyses of film "content"—that is, film theme and its social impact—dominated, obscuring concerns for film style and technology. Promoting education, patriotism, universal love, and eradicating greed and improper treatment of women were listed as the proper thematic components of Chinese film.[46] In general, early Chinese film criticism was concerned not so much with the ontological issue of what cinema is, but with the social function of cinema from a moralistic standpoint. Indeed, adhering to traditional Chinese morality was one of the regulations inscribed in Chinese film policy during the time.

Chinese cinema's moralism was closely related to its patriotism/nationalism. The goal of producing morally righteous and uplifting films was to continue the glory of Chinese civilization and to strengthen the Chinese state. The endless civil war coupled with foreign military and economic aggression during the turn of the century made Chinese nationalism an ever urgent theme among the Chinese film practitioners. The nationalistic tendency of Chinese film criticism was reflected mainly in its outcry for quality domestic films to boost the image of Chinese cinema and ultimately to build a strong national film industry capable of competing with Western imports. In his heartfelt article, "Please Leave Room for Chinese Cinema," Zheng Zhengqiu begged film practitioners to take seriously their professional and social responsibilities by making quality films if only for the sake of creating a good name for Chinese cinema.[47] Zheng considered low-quality films responsible for the bad reputation Chinese cinema had among the elite Chinese and argued that filmmakers' commercial concerns should not overtake their social concerns. Production values aside, quality films also meant films of pedagogical function.[48] Cinema's pedagogical function was considered mandatory, as essential as military buildup, in strengthening China. The mission of Chinese cinema was ultimately to rescue China in crisis.

Pragmatism was the third characteristic of Chinese film criticism. It was rooted in the cross-fertilization of film production and criticism in terms of the crossover of filmmakers and film critics. The close tie between production and criticism resulted in the centrality to Chinese film criticism of finding solutions to the immediate and practical problems of film production. From the mid-1920s to the early 1930s, many articles were written from an institutional perspective, assessing the structural and marketing problems of Chinese cinema and suggesting immediate solutions to such problems. Such articles appeared in all major Chinese film magazines such as *Ying xing* (Silver Star), *Dianying yuebao* (Film Monthly), and *Zhongguo dianying zhazhi* (Chinese Film Magazine). Individual production companies also published special issues of their fan magazines to diagnose the industry's institutional and marketing problems. A few major problems were identified by various film practitioners, including

1. lack of collaboration within the film community and between film practitioners and other literary practitioners;
2. insufficient promotion before and after the release of a new film;
3. inadequate professional training;
4. an undercultivated star system and distribution–exhibition channels;
5. vicious competition among production companies;

6. lack of quality scripts with fresh concepts;
7. the unfair treatment of Chinese pictures by foreign-controlled theaters;
8. the demography of Chinese patrons being under- or uneducated, which impeded the exploration of more sophisticated cinematic techniques and more intelligent films.[49]

Structural overhaul in the form of vertical and horizontal integration and professional overhaul in the forms of streamlining responsibility, more professional division, and better training were offered as the solutions to the problems. The coming of sound was perceived as an opportunity for the industry to compete with imports by exploiting the Chinese native tongue.[50] Regarding the audience demography for Chinese cinema, film companies were advised to actively educate the public for more sophisticated cinematic taste.[51] Also, more and better educated patrons were encouraged to see Chinese films, and watching domestic pictures was equated with patriotism.[52] From a pragmatic perspective, Zhou Jianyun, one of Star's founders, even argued as early as in 1925 that the internationalizing of Chinese cinema was the solution and that the development of the Chinese film industry must follow the suit of Western cinemas by moving beyond the boundaries of a nation–state.[53]

Chinese film criticism's moralism, patriotism, and pragmatism were closely related, indeed codependent. Pragmatic considerations of building a strong national film industry were mandated in the name of nationalism and moralism. Nationalism and moralism, on the other hand, could only be realized with a strong national film industry under the guidance of pragmatic institutional and marketing suggestions. As articulated by Wei Yaoqing, "Promoting national cinema is essential to a stronger China." As a popular entertainment format, cinema had become an important educational tool for the dissemination of moralistic and nationalistic messages among the public, fulfilling the failed duty of educational institutions.[54] The more popular the domestic pictures, the more easily they would reach the masses. So a strong national film industry was absolutely essential to the nation's much needed massive campaign of moralism and nationalism. Indeed, many articles discussing the structural problems of Chinese film industry were written from the perspective of nationalism and moralism. The profit-minded opportunists were warned that they had no business in film production because film production was a serious financial investment with considerable social implications and, hence, sacred responsibilities.[55] Cinema was considered an important cultural investment and merited special social and moral responsibility. Interestingly enough, competition regulated solely by the free market was not considered the solution to a healthy development of Chinese cinema. Chinese film critics were mostly self-proclaimed intellectuals and patriotic filmmakers themselves. Their suspicion of the wholesale embracing of a film industry checked only by market force reflected exactly their concern that such competition would discourage more socially responsible films. Finally, while moralism, nationalism, and pragmatism essentially encompassed the politics and economy of Chinese cinema, early film criticism was by no means systematic but rather discursive, lacking theoretical rigidity. It was in essence film *criticism* instead of *theory*, a tradition influential to future inquiries on film in China.

The combination of moralism, nationalism, and pragmatism ultimately determined early Chinese film criticism's preoccupation with cinema's function, be it pedagogical or economic. It is helpful to briefly recap the somewhat antagonistic approaches toward film production between Star's two major founders Zheng Zhengqiu and Zhang Shichuan. The conflict between the two in terms of Star's production policy was the result of their different functional priorities, with Zheng representing the pedagogy school and Zhang the entertainment school. Born to a family of learned aristocracy, Zheng's perception of film was deeply rooted in traditional Chinese stage drama, which emphasized drama's ability to enlighten the masses.[56] Hence, Zheng's signature films during his early tenure at Star were all morally uplifting and socially responsible melodramas. Zhang, on the other hand, came from a Western-influenced merchant family, and approached film from a business perspective. To Zhang, film was first and foremost a commercial venture and must take into consideration market demand.[57] Their disagreement over Star's production priority resulted in Zheng's temporary withdrawal from Star in the early 1920s. The two reconciled in the late 1920s to early 1930s in a joint effort to revive the financially beleaguered Star by making martial arts–ghost dramas. Zhang's valuation of cinema's entertainment function did not exclude him from taking into consideration both its pedagogical and artistic functions; but these considerations were de-emphasized when they conflicted with Star's commercial interest. Zhang was more than happy to comply with Zheng's political and artistic considerations, provided that such considerations would not cloud a film's profit potential. On the other hand, Zheng had to face the economic reality of film production. Such was the basis for Zheng and Zhang's prolonged second partnership in the late 1920s to the early 1930s. Because the two founding fathers had different priorities, Star paradoxically produced Zheng Zhengqiu's socially responsible melodramas such as *Orphan Rescues Grandfather* (1923) and Zhang Shichuan's pure entertainment dramas such as *Burning of the Red Lotus Temple* (1928).[58] Clearly, due to various reasons I have discussed so far, the financial concern outweighed all other concerns from the mid-1920s to the early 1930s.

A traditionalist and populist film culture evolved concurrently with the wave of entertainment pictures and the building of a national film industry. The traditionalist cultural movement was a direct response to the new cultural movement in vogue in the late 1910s and early 1920s. Attacking conservatism and traditionalism, chiefly Confucianism, the new cultural movement culminated in the historical May Fourth Westernization movement in 1918, which primarily succeeded in introducing Western thought. In condemning Chinese Confucian tradition, it fell short of creating new systems of thought and new schools of philosophy. A split occurred in the mid-1920s among Chinese intellectuals who turned to Marxist socialism for solutions and those who turned to Chinese spiritualism as an antidote to Western materialism.

In their disillusionment with Western civilizations, which they saw as the cause of Western aggression, the traditionalists attempted to rediscover Chinese national heritage by calling for the revival of classical Chinese literature and Confucian ethics. The veteran advocate of the new cultural movement, Hu Shi, retreated from his early radical cultural view and looked to Chinese literary classics for inspiration, delving into ancient Chinese history. In his effort to preserve Chinese cultural heritage, he started the Sifting National Heritage movement in 1923, encouraging college students to peruse Chinese classics instead of participating in any radical political movement. Quite a few notable literary figures such as Xu Zhimo, Liang Shiqiu, and Chen Xiying publicly endorsed Hu, so did the Shaw brothers from the film community. Other filmmakers with backgrounds in traditional Chinese stage drama also welcomed traditionalists' apolitical but pro-classical approach. The disillusioned film practitioners attacked early urban melodramas for their imitations of Western lifestyle and considered the Chinese literary resources the saviors of Chinese cinema. Their sentiment also echoed the audiences' waning interest in westernized urban melodrama. The Shaw brothers were the most adamant supporters of the Sifting National Heritage movement in the film industry. "Paying attention to traditional Chinese moral and ethical values, promoting Chinese civilization, and avoiding Westernization" became Heaven's motto and catchphrase for its production of historical and, later, costume dramas.[59]

Echoed by the film community, the traditionalist cultural movement thus foresaw the wave of costume drama and the martial arts–ghost drama, since most of them were adaptations of Chinese literary classics and popular folk tales. Chinese audience besieged by a rapidly changing society apparently found films of traditional resources and values comforting, and their familiarity with classical stories made the film adaptation of Chinese classics easily acceptable, both further encouraging the traditionalist film practice. The beleaguered state of China in the early twentieth century further steered both the filmmakers and the audiences away from films of contemporary subjects.[60] Chinese cinema's first commercial entertainment wave thus became the natural extension of a traditionalist cultural movement.

To further legitimate their commercial practices, the traditionalist film practitioners embraced a populist cinematic view that appropriated the Confucian motto "educating via entertaining" in film practice. The motto emphasized the importance of cinema's accessibility to the public. As such, to educate the public, films must first appeal to them by addressing their needs and catering to their tastes. Early Chinese filmmakers considered cinema a popular art format and embraced its potential to become the art of the popular as opposed to the art of the elite.[61] The populist cinematic view was in vogue in the mid- to late 1920s among the critics. An article, "Cinemas of the Underclass," published in 1926 by Sun Shiyi was particularly illuminating of such a view.[62] Sun divided the evolution of European drama into four phases: mythological drama, aristocratic drama, bourgeois drama, and democratic drama. Democratic drama is the one centered around the popular by depicting the lives of the working class. In criticizing the bourgeois and aristocratic tendencies of the urban melodrama, Sun considered democratic drama the progressive drama and the model for Chinese cinema. Though not directly championing either costume or martial arts–ghost drama, Sun's advocacy of a popular cinema that served the proletarian, the majority of the population, was conducive to the development of both costume and martial arts–ghost dramas. Another film critic, Fu Yie, pointed to imports such as *Seventh Heaven* (Frank Borzage, 1927), *Metropolis* (Fritz Lang, 1926), and *Sunrise* (F.W. Murnau, 1927) as good examples of popular films addressing the concerns of the working class.[63] Charlie Chaplain's portrayal of the lives of the underclass was taken as the key to the popularity of his films. Other critics also wrote articles to echo such a populist cinematic view.[64] Both Heaven and Star actively and selectively combined the populist and traditionalist fashion during the period to legitimize their cultivation of popular entertainment genres.

However, some of the advocates of a populist cinema were left-wing filmmakers influenced by Marxism. Their ideal of a populist cinema called for a cinema reflective of the unequal social reality. The Communist-led left-wing filmmakers gradually penetrated major production companies, pushing to change the direction of Chinese cinema. The Marxist social realist tendency of the populist cinematic view would eventually contribute to the demise of both costume drama and martial arts–ghost dramas. The dissatisfaction with martial arts–ghost drama was not at all a sudden phenomenon, only that the criticism became more pronounced in the early 1930s, in the face of Japanese invasion.[65] The film practitioners' sense of duty in the face of Japanese military aggression called for a cinema more reflective of the nationalistic sentiment during the period. Consequently, the outcry for elevating national pictures, while granting an opportunity for the ascendancy of costume and martial arts–ghost dramas, eventually brought their demise.

Meanwhile, the government's changing film policy also played a role in the demise of the martial arts–ghost trend. The Nationalist government, under the pressure of the increasingly critical view of the commercial entertainment wave, banned the production and exhibition of martial arts–ghost drama in 1931. The entertainment wave eventually phased out by 1933, replaced by left-wing social realist film. It is necessary to examine the role of film policy, or the lack of it, in the development of Chinese cinema during this period.

The Role of Film Policy

The Nationalist government's film policy from the late 1920s to the early 1930s was driven first and foremost by the anti-imperialist sentiment during the time among the cultural critics, film practitioners, and the general public. The effort to censor foreign films, especially Hollywood films, originated from the popular and professional sentiments against the negative portrayal of China and the Chinese people.[66] Rooted in the medieval fear of "yellow peril," Hollywood's early depiction of Asia and Asian people either eroticized or demonized the land and the occupants.[67] The stereotypical Chinese in Hollywood films during the time were opium smokers, gamblers, servants, or thieves. Likewise, the settings for scenes involving Chinese people were mostly chop-suey houses and the opium dens of Chinatown.[68] Understandably, Chinese patrons were not at all amused by such derogatory caricatures of their own. Letters from general audiences and articles from film practitioners protesting offensive foreign films appeared in movie magazines and newspapers film columns throughout the 1920s.[69] The ever-growing outcry for obtaining national sovereignty from foreign aggressors propelled the Nationalist government to apply aggressive censorship over film imports and foreign companies' production attempts within China.

Up until 1928, the Chinese government had basically adopted a "no interference, no support" policy toward film production and distribution in China. In 1928, in responding to the public and the industrial practitioners' outcry against the lack of a protective film policy, the Ministry of Internal Affairs of the newly established Nationalist government issued "Thirteen Regulations on Film," banning films offensive to China and Chinese people's dignity.[70] The Ministry of Education later joined the Ministry of Interior in issuing another set of regulations with a similar clause on offensive foreign films. Finally in the 1930s, the first film censorship law in China was carved out to legally prohibit films offensive to the Chinese public. The National Film Censorship Committee (NFCC) was formed a year after to carry out the law.[71] NFCC not only effectively outlawed individual films offensive to the Chinese sensibility but also punished foreign studios producing such films by threatening to suspend the importation of all their films.[72]

The tough stand against offensive foreign films was extended to foreign studios' monopolistic film practice in China that had long delayed the buildup of China's domestic production, distribution, and exhibition network. The NFCC's tough stand thus responded directly to the film industry's demand for government intervention in protecting domestic production and market. Chinese film practitioners urged the Nationalist government to abolish the tax-free treaty coerced on the Manchu government by the Japanese and the European armed forces. Zhou Jianyun, Star's business manager, published an article urging the government to levy a tax on film imports.[73] Other film critics such as Ying Dou also voiced their concern about the lack of taxation on foreign films.[74] The NFCC subsequently adopted a series of measurements to safeguard the film industry's best interests. It forbade distribution companies from subtitling foreign talkies to protect China's own sound films. It charged foreign films reviewing fees but either completely exempted Chinese films from such charges or significantly lowered the fees applied to Chinese films.[75] Also, "problematic" Chinese films were treated with more lenience than "problematic" imports.[76] Chinese censorship's protective measurements, while conducive to the development of a national film industry, effectively greenlighted the wave of Chinese commercial entertainment films, most of them with lesser production values than the foreign imports. Film censorship toward imports and the lack of it toward domestic pictures had an impact on the outlook of Chinese cinema during the period. While the tough censorship applied to imports reduced, or at least delayed, the exhibition of popular foreign hits, the lack of tough control over the commercialized domestic productions in conjunction with the Nationalist ideological grip, on the other hand, created a window of opportunity for Chinese cinema's first apolitical, commercial entertainment wave.

The Nationalist government's effort to protect Chinese screens and Chinese native production was partially motivated by its political interest in rallying popular support. As Zhiwei Xiao succinctly puts it, "[B]oth the film industry and the government censors exploited the rhetoric of nationalism in their public claims. The industry exploited this rhetoric so that it could enlist the government's help and public sympathy in its competition with foreign rivals. The government made political gains by playing the protective role. In so doing, it won the film industry's cooperation and rallied popular support."[77] What he does not point out is that the Nationalist government's protective policy toward domestic productions was selective, applying only to domestic pictures that did not challenge the Nationalist political legitimacy. Consequently, film policy makers encouraged only the production of entertainment films with no immediate social and political relevance. As such, the government's lack of censorship toward domestic production fostered Chinese cinema's entertainment wave led by the cultural traditionalists but not the social problem melodramas in vogue prior to the establishment of the Nanjing government. The harmonious courtship between the policy makers and the filmmakers would be challenged in the ensuing period when the Nationalist government sabotaged many domestic productions by the Communist-influenced filmmakers.[78]

THE ENTERTAINMENT WAVE: FROM PAST TO PRESENT

The political, economic, and cultural factors from the mid-1920s to the early 1930s augured the arrival of Chinese cinema's first entertainment wave. A culturally conservative regulatory body under the control of the politically repressive Nationalist government encouraged Chinese cinema's apolitical tendency by steering it away from the realist films of a decade earlier. The relatively stable political environment brought economic prosperity into China's coastal cities, ensuring a steady capital flow for the production and exhibition of domestic pictures. The combination of a populist, a traditionalist, and a pragmatic film culture favored films with distinctive Chinese characteristics that were easily accessible to the majority of Chinese patrons, the lower- and middle-class urban dwellers. Thus the arrival of Chinese cinema's first entertainment wave, the costume and martial arts–ghost films.

The development of Chinese cinema's first entertainment wave has much in common with the development of the current entertainment wave. Both had their slow and difficult starts under the shadow of Hollywood imports. The film industry's desire to compete with imported films promoted both the pioneers of Chinese cinema and the contemporary filmmakers to turn to making popular genre films and to Hollywood's vertically integrated institutional structure and horizontally integrated marketing practice. During both periods, nationalism and pragmatism played a crucial role in the ascendance of a popular entertainment wave. While nationalism demanded a strong national film industry, pragmatism provided practical textual and structural solutions. In terms of textual strategies, while the pioneers looked to Chinese classics for an alternative cinematic inspiration, the contemporary filmmakers looked to Hollywood blockbusters and genre films for box-office success. The current entertainment wave is more eclectic, ranging from comedies to Hollywood-style big-budget and high-tech pictures.

In terms of structural strategies, the film industry's current consolidation and marketization very much follow the lead of United China's cultivation of a Hollywood-style institutional structure and marketing practice in the early era.[79] However, the current institutional reform is more difficult than the earlier one because of the deadweight of years of a centralized and noncommercial film practice. A private and commercial industry in its infancy and throughout its adolescence, the Chinese film industry spent much of its adulthood getting cozy with a centralized industrial structure that considered film financing, production, and distribution–exhibition an ideological rather than a commercial practice. The industry has yet to undo the deadweight of a state-monopolized film infrastructure and to get reacquainted with a commercialized film practice. Though the dominance and control of foreign capital in distribution and exhibition are no longer the major concerns for the new era, film policy must address the issue of film practice at a transnational level. In this regard, a nationalism motivated by the film pioneers' cultural desire to carry on the glory of Chinese civilization is overshadowed by the contemporary film practitioners' economic anxiety over a globalized financing and marketing practice. A nationalism with a moralistic tone and within the confines of a nation–state is superseded in the new era by a capitalism without cultural boundaries and with no regard for pedagogy, craving entertainment instead. The pragmatism of Chinese film criticism during both periods foregrounded an institutional approach, producing a formidable body of film discourse concerning film economy. While institutional criticism during the early era zeroed in on building a vertically and horizontally integrated film infrastructure in however a fractured fashion, such a criticism during the new era has to dwell on decentralization, commercialization, and globalization.

NOTES

1. The Western powers were led by Britain, France, Germany, and Russia.

2. The Manchu dynasty was China's last traditional feudal empire.

3. The film he made was a recorded version of a Beijing opera performed by a popular opera singer. Ren screened his film at a tea house–style exhibition site.

4. Film distribution and exhibition in today's China very much resembles the earlier period, driven by the demand for Hollywood features.

5. As recorded in Jay Leyda's book *Dianying: An Account of Films and the Film Audience in China* (Cambridge: MIT Press, 1972), 22, the nationalistic sentiment was so strong in China in the early 1910s that when a cowboy from one of Brodsky's American films cocked his gun at the camera (audience) on screen, the angry Chinese spectators shouted "white devil" and burned the theater.

6. See He Xiujun (Zhang Shichuan's wife), "Chang Shichuan and the Star Production Company" (Zhang Shichuan he Mingxing dianying gongshi), in *Chinese Silent Cinema* (Zhongguo wusheng dianying), ed. Dai Xiaolan (Beijing: China Film Press, 1996), 1517–1548.

7. The film was a popular hit and became the first Chinese export—introduced to the United States by Benjamin Brodsky.

8. Film stocks were later imported to China from the United States. World War I made it possible for Hollywood to replace Europe as the dominant force in the Chinese film market.

9. The emergence of long narrative is considered by Chinese film historians as Chinese cinema's real dawn.

10. Hong Shi, "The First Wave" (Diyichi langchao), *Dangdai dianying* (Contemporary Film) 65, no. 2 (1995): 5–9.

11. See Ouyang Yuqian, *Since I Started My Acting Career* (Wuode yanyi shengya) (Beijing: China Drama Press, 1959).

12. Chen Jihua, ed., *The History of Chinese Cinema* (Zhongguo dianying fazhanshi) (Beijing: China Film Press, 1980) 53–54.

13. Ibid.

14. However, all three became veteran Chinese filmmakers.

15. For more detailed discussions on the May Fourth theme in the early films, see Zheng Jungli, *A Brief History of Modern Chinese Cinema* (Zhongguo xiandai dianying jianshi) (Shanghai: Liangyou Press, 1936), 38–39; and Paul Pickowicz, "Melodramatic Representation and the 'May Fourth' Tradition of Chinese Cinema," in *From May Fourth to June Fourth Fiction and Film in Twentieth-Century China*, ed. Ellen Widmer and David Der-Wei Wang (Cambridge: Harvard University Press, 1993) 295–326.

16. They later moved to Hong Kong and became the founding fathers of the Hong Kong film industry.

17. For a more detailed account see Frederic Wakeman Jr., *Policing Shanghai: 1927–1937* (Berkeley and Los Angeles: University of California Press, 1995), 132–163.

18. Only a few documentary films were made depicting the revolutionary efforts. Chen Jihua mentioned "The May 31 Shanghai Wave" (Wusha huchao) and "The Nationalist Revolution" (Guoming gemingjun hailukong dazhanji) in his book *The History of Chinese Cinema*.

19. See Li Shuyuan and Hu Jushan, *The History of Chinese Silent Cinema* (Zhongguo wusheng dianying) (Beijing: China Film Press, 1996).

20. I will discuss this more in the last section of this chapter.

21. See First Under Heaven, *Chinese Film Year Book* (Zhongguo jiaoyu dianying weiyuanhui) (Nanjing: China Educational Council Press, 1934), 241–247.

22. See Li and Hu, *The History of Chinese Silent Cinema*.

23. Ibid., 214–219.

24. See First Under Heaven, *Chinese Film Year Book*, 241–247.

25. Ibid.

26. See Hu Ke, "Understanding Chinese Silent Cinema from Multiple Perspectives" (Chong duojiaodu lijie zhongguo dianying), *Dangdai dianying* 74, no. 5 (1996) 57.

27. See Hu Ke, "Chinese Social Film Theory in the 1920s" (Ershi niandai zhongguo shihui diaying lilun), *Dianying yishu* (Film Art) 246, no. 1 (1996): 14–19.

28. Li and Hu, *The History of Chinese Silent Cinema*, 222–243.

29. Lu Mengshu, "New Heroism" (Xing yingxiong zhuyi), 736, and "National and Chinese Cinema" (Mingzhu zhiyi he zhongguo dianying), 755, in *Chinese Silent Cinema* (Zhongguo wusheng dianying), ed. China Film Archive (Beijing: China Film Press, 1996). In his call for new heroes, Lu made an interesting comparison between the Chinese notion of hero and the Western notion of hero: Female beauty in a Western film was represented not only by the actress's attractive face but also by her strong, athletic physique and active disposition, unlike Chinese actresses who were usually weak and inactive.

30. See articles reprinted in *Chinese Silent Cinema*, 736–760.

31. Yao Gengchen, "On Martial Arts Films" (Lun wuxia pian), in *Chinese Silent Cinema*, ed. China Film Archive (Beijing: China Film Press, 1996), 668.

32. Zhou Shuya, "On Martial Arts Drama" (Guanyu wuxia ju), in *Chinese Silent Cinema*, ed. China Film Archive (Beijing: China Film Press, 1996), 670.

33. Ang Lee's *Crouching Tiger, Hidden Dragon* (2000) very much worked within such a genre convention.

34. See Leyda, *Dianying*, 63.

35. Ibid.

36. See "The Opening Statement of United Film Exchange" (Lianhua xuanyan) published in the special edition of *The Evening of Shanghai* (Shenzhou gongshi Shanghai zhiye) 4 (1926): 39.

37. Zhou Jianyun, "The Future of Chinese Cinema" (Zhongguo yingpian zhi qiantu), in *Chinese Silent Cinema*, ed. China Film Archive (Beijing: China Film Press, 1996), 720.

38. Li and Hu, *The History of Chinese Silent Cinema*, 209.

39. Luo Mingyou, "To My Colleagues about the Issue of Reviving Chinese Cinema" (Wei guopie fuxing wenti jinggao tongye shu), in *Chinese Silent Cinema*, ed. China Film Archive (Beijing: China Film Press, 1996), 768.

40. Ibid. See also United China, "Four Years of United China" (Lianhua yingpian gongshi shinian jingli shi), in *Chinese Silent Cinema*, ed. China Film Archive (Beijing: China Film Press, 1996), 72. See also Li and Hu's discussion in *The History of Chinese Silent Cinema*, 199.

41. The first sound film was introduced to China from the United States in 1929.

42. See Leyda, *Dianying*, 93.

43. A collection of their critical articles can be found in *Chinese Silent Cinema*, 411–1310.

44. Early critical articles on film were published in film magazines such as *Yingxii chongbao* (1921/1922 first issue), and *Yingxi zhazhi* (first published in 1921) and newspapers such as *Shen bao*.

45. See Li Daoxing, "Building the History of Chinese Film Criticism" (Jiangou zhongguo dianying pipingshi), *Dianying yishu* 261, no. 4 (1998): 5–10.

46. Chao Yuankai, "The Essentials of Chinese Screenplay" (Zhongguo dianying juben yingjun de yaoshu), in *Chinese Silent Cinema*, ed. China Film Archive (Beijing: China Film Press, 1996), 836.

47. Zheng Zhenggiu, "Please Leave Room for Chinese Cinema" (Qing wei zhongguo yingxi liu qudi), in *Chinese Silent Cinema*, ed. China Film Archive (Beijing: China Film Press, 1996), 681.

48. See Shi Heng, "The Mandatory Mission of Chinese Film Community" (Wuoguo dianyingjie yinggai fuqi de shiming), in *Chinese Silent Cinema*, ed. China Film Archive (Beijing: China Film Press, 1996), 745.

49. See the following, all in *Chinese Silent Cinema*, ed. China Film Archive (Bejing: China Film Press, 1996): Lian Xiaochi, "Contemporary Chinese Cinema Has Gone Astray" (Xiejing zhongguo yingju zhi qilu), 692; Li Jianhong, "On the Dangerous Future of Domestic Productions and Its Remedy" (Lun guochan yingpian qiantu zhi weixian jiqi bujiu), 690; Lu Zhiyung, "The Necessity of Establishing a Filmmakers' Union" (Sheli dianying gonghui zhi biyao), 104; Xu Liuru, "The Development of Film Management" (Yingpian yingye de fazhan), 106; Chen Xianmo, "My Economic View of Cinema" (Wuo zhi dianying shangxueguan), 109; Lu Chubao, "Production

and Promotion (Zhipian yu tuixiao), 111; and Mr. Ma Er, "The Desired Quantity of Chinese Films" (Zhongguo yingpain zhi xuyaoliang), 101.

50. See Huang Yichuo, "The Revival of National Cinema" (Guopian zhi fuxing), in *Chinese Silent Cinema*, ed. China Film Archive (Beijing: China Film Press, 1996), 770; and Luo, "To My Colleagues on Reviving Our National Cinema," 768.

51. Zheng Zhengqiu, "The Big Headquarters of Collaboration" (Hezhu de dabengying), in *Chinese Silent Cinema*, ed. China Film Archive (Beijing: China Film Press, 1996), 113.

52. Fung Er, "The Audiences' Responsibility in Reviving Our National Cinema" (Zhongguo dianying guangzhong duiyu guopian fuxing yungdong yingjin de zheren), in *Chinese Silent Cinema*, ed. China Film Archive (Beijing: China Film Press, 1996), 780.

53. Zhou Jianyun, "The Chinese Film Community after the Tragic May 30" (Wusha chanan zhihou de zhongguo dianyingjie), in *Chinese Silent Cinema*, ed. China Film Archive (Beijing: China Film Press, 1996), 683.

54. Wei Yaoging, "Promoting National Cinema Is Essential to a Stronger China" (Tichang guochan wei jingri jiugu zhi lianji), in *Chinese Silent Cinema*, ed. China Film Archive (Beijing: China Film Press, 1996), 685.

55. See Feng Xizhui, "Film Production Companies and Stock Exchange Companies" (Yingpian gongshi yu jiaoyishuo), in *Chinese Silent Cinema*, ed. China Film Archive (Beijing: China Film Press, 1996), 97.

56. Ma Debo, "The Circle of Cinematic Movement: The Debate between Pedagogy and Entertainment for the Past Ninety Years" (Yingyun Huanliu: Jiushi nianjian zhaidao yu yure zhizheng), *Dianying yishu* 242, no. 3 (1995): 29–35.

57. See Chen Jihua, *The History of Chinese Cinema* (Beijing: China Film Press, 1963), 58.

58. *Orphan* was a sentimental and moralistic melodrama about a widow and her son being wrongfully stripped of their right to inherit the family wealth and eventually regaining their rightful status. See Leyda, *Dianying*, 38.

59. See First Under Heaven, "Ten Years of Heaven" (Tianyi Gongshi shinian jingli shi), in *Chinese Silent Cinema*, ed. China Film Archive (Beijing: China Film Press, 1996), 52.

60. Incidentally, the Chinese entertainment community has been shying away from contemporary subjects since the Tiananmen tragedy. The popular television dramas in China are predominantly historical, drawing resources from historical figures and events. The new costume dramas are particularly well-accepted by overseas Chinese.

61. See the following, all in *Chinese Silent Cinema*, ed. China Film Archive (Beijing: China Film Press, 1996): Tian Han, "The Silver Dream" (Yingshe de meng), 442; Yu Dafu, "Film and Literature and Art" (Dianying yu wenyi), 447; and Jing Chao, "Chinese Cinema and Art" (Zhongguo dianying he yishu), 455.

62. Sun Shiyi, "Cinemas of the Underclass" (Wang xiacheng de yingju), in *Chinese Silent Cinema*, ed. China Film Archive (Beijing: China Film Press, 1996), 761.

63. Fu Yie, "The Popularization of Cinema" (Dianying de mingzhonghua) in *Chinese Silent Cinema*, ed. China Film Archive (Beijing: China Film Press, 1996), 764.

64. See various articles in *Chinese Silent Cinema*, ed. China Film Archive (Beijing: China Film Press, 1996), 764–767, 1015–1027, 1037, 1039.

65. See the following, all in *Chinese Silent Cinema*, ed. China Film Archive (Beijing: China Film Press, 1996): Mao Dun, "The Feudal Literature and Art of Urban Petty Bourgeois" (Fengjian de xiaoshiming wunyi), 1039; Li Chushen, "Building a Nationalistic Cinema" (Jianshe guopian), 750; and Huang Yichai, "The Revival of a National Cinema" (Guopian de fuxing), 770.

66. For a detailed account, see Zhiwei Xiao, "Anti-Imperialism and Film Censorship during the Nanjing Decade, 1927–1937," in *Transnational Chinese Cinema*, ed. Sheldon Hsiao-peng Lu (Honolulu: University of Hawaii Press, 1996), 35.

67. For a detailed study, see G. Marchetti, *Romance and the "Yellow Peril"* (Berkeley and Los Angeles: University of California Press, 1993).

68. See Paul K. Whang, "Boycotting of Harold Lloyd's *Welcome Danger*," *China Weekly Review*, 8 March 1930.

69. See the following in in *Chinese Silent Cinema*, ed. China Film Archive (Beijing: China Film Press, 1996), Zhou Jianyun, "On the Issue of Film Censorship" (Guanyu dianying shengcha) 151; and Mong Xia, "Understanding Film Censorship" (Lijie dianying shengcha), 153.

70. See "The Regulations for Film Censorship Issued by the Department of Internal Affairs" (Neizheng bu gongbu dianying pian jiancha guize), *Shen Bao*, 6 September 1928, 16.

71. For a more detailed account of film censorship, see Zhiwei Xiao's finely detailed "Film Censorship in China, 1927–1937," (Ph.D. diss., University of California, 1994).

72. Ibid.

73. Zhou Jianyun, "Tax Independence and Chinese Cinema" (Guanshui zhizhu yu zhongguo yingpian), in *Chinese Silent Cinema*, ed. China Film Archive (Beijing: China Film Press, 1996), 116.

74. Ying Dou, "Production Companies Should Pay Attention to This Issue" (Yingpian gongshi ying jiqi zhuyi zhege wunti), in *Chinese Silent Cinema*, ed. China Film Archive (Beijing: China Film Press, 1996), 117.

75. For a detailed account, see Zhiwei, "Film Censorship in China, 1927–1937."

76. See Zhiwei, "Anti-Imperialism and Film Censorship during the Nanjing Decade, 1927–1937," 35.

77. Ibid., 52.

78. See Li Shaobai, "On a Low Ebb" (Chuyu diguzhong), *Dangdai dianying* 72, no. 3 (1996): 59–85.

79. Another patriotic company was The Great Wall Picture, a small production company formed by overseas Chinese and employing Chinese students returning from the United States. It issued a letter to the Chinese government advocating banning foreign films that harmed the image of the Chinese. It also actively sought a united front with other domestic production companies to develop the Chinese national cinema.

7

Chinese Cinema: A Cultural or an Economic Issue?

This book has demonstrated that the rise of Chinese cinema's art and popular entertainment waves and the commercialization of Chinese cinema since the late 1980s are both the result and the manifestation of China's shifting political, economic, and cultural orientations. It has situated the course of Chinese cinema during its post-Mao era against the backdrop of China's overall modernization project. It is one of the few studies on Chinese cinema that provides a historical overview of the evolution of China's film reform from the modernization of film styles to that of institutional structures and market practices. It highlights not only the role of film policy and economy but also the role of new cinematic ideas, of knowledge-bearing Chinese intellectuals, literary and film practitioners, and of knowledge-generating institutions such as the film schools and various film journals in pushing for the modernization of Chinese cinema.

This book has also built a case that the development of Chinese cinema's prolonged commercial entertainment wave has gone from the semiconscious stage driven by individual filmmakers' survival instinct in the 1980s to the conscious stage guided by the state's marketization agenda and the film industry's economic reform strategy in the 1990s. In foregrounding the role of film policy in shaping the direction of Chinese cinema, it provides the first systematic inventory of the key film reform measures carried out during the period and their impact on the commercialization of Chinese cinema. In this regard, it becomes the first institutional study of Chinese cinema during the era of China's ongoing economic reform.

Economic reform in the form of decentralization, privatization, conglomeration, and globalization has equipped the Chinese film industry with a modern economic lexicon but has not helped it obtain its independence from state intervention. Chinese cinema has yet to achieve its political/ideological and artistic independence. On the other hand, the survival of Chinese cinema in the face of transnational Hollywood will depend on the extent to which the state is able to provide sensible protective measures.

As such, the relationship between the state and the film industry will no doubt be a complex one. Even more complex, though, is the relationship between Chinese cinema and Chinese audiences. Plausible policies aside, the survival of Chinese cinema in the foreseeable future of China's membership in the World Trade Organization ultimately depends on Chinese audiences. Chinese cinema has yet to connect with its home-based audiences. In this regard, the cultural relevance/identity of Chinese cinema will become crucial.

In documenting the key film reform measures and addressing their impact on the changing direction of Chinese cinema, this book has so far grounded the discussion of culture within the realm of economics. Indeed, as the development of Chinese cinema moved from the modernization of film art in the late 1980s to the modernization of film economy in the late 1990s, the issue of cultural identity has shifted from a cultural one to an economic one. However, the issue of Chinese cinema's cultural identity is an important one and merits attention in its own right. The notion of Chinese cultural identity suggests that there exists a stable set of meanings/customs that can be derived from shared beliefs about Chinese culture. For the sake of focused argument, I use *culture* to mean the customary beliefs, social forms, and traits of a racial, religious, or social group. Specifically, Chinese culture here refers to the set of shared attitudes, values, goals, and practices that characterize what we conventionally perceive as Chinese. Culture defined as such is inherently unstable, an ongoing process of dynamic (re)interpretation and (re)definition over time and across space. That is, what comprises culture is a coherent but not necessarily cohesive universe of meanings, a universe that constantly strives to make sense out of persistent ambiguities and contradictions without pretense to a final solution.

Three aspects of culture are foregrounded by this definition. First, cultures are distinguished only by variables such as customary beliefs, social forms, shared attitudes, values, goals, and practices. It is not meaningful to categorize culture in terms of the degree of backwardness or forwardness— the old dichotomy between tradition and modernity is ideologically biased and logically flawed. What is at stake is the foregrounding—at different times and as a result of different power dynamics—of different elements of tradition as the central principle(s) of a culture. Tradition here refers to an inherited, established, or customary pattern of thought, action, or behavior, as well as a certain continuity in social attitudes, customs, and institutions.

Second, the central principles of a culture are themselves ambiguous and unstable, subject to constant reinterpretation and redefinition by the ever shifting economic and political ethos, both domestically and internationally. The social formations that develop in different civilizations are not attributable to "fixed" tendencies of a culture. The rise of new forms of social organization and activities entails new interpretations of traditional beliefs and institutional premises. These new interpretations may significantly transform antecedent tenets and institutions of a culture.

Third, cultural beliefs or visions become constitutive elements of a social order by the transformation of their basic premises into a system of rules that address the basic problems of social order.[1] These premises are a distinct and crucial analytical aspect of culture. The premise of Chinese tradition is principally Confucian.

A few provisos need to be added here to avoid oversimplification. First, by designating Confucian culture as the dominant principle of Chinese culture, I run the risk of suppressing Chinese culture's internal contradictions. Indeed the search for a coherent cultural identity more often than not results in the suppression of internal differences, tensions, and contradictions. The process of identification is thus invariably a homogenizing, mythologizing one, involving both the production and the assignation of a particular set of meanings, and the attempt to contain, or prevent, the potential proliferation of other meanings. Yet Chinese culture, like any culture, is neither monolithic nor static. Other cosmological ideals such as Daoism and Maoism do exist and have historically challenged Confucian thought and institutions. But the reign of Confucianism as the official national ideology from the second century A.D. to the early twentieth century and the late Qing dynasty made Confucianism the most influential and dominant source of Chinese cultural principles.[2] Even the anti-Confucian movements during both the May Fourth Westernization movement and the Cultural Revolution did not radically alter Chinese society's psychologically internalized cosmological thought derived for the most part from Confucianism. The commonly acknowledged principal Confucian orientations include avoidance of conflict, a vertical system of order that emphasizes social hierarchy and values seniority and patriarchy, belief in sage leadership that locates safeguards against the abuse of government not in political institutions but in the moral commitment of political leaders, anti-commercial attitude that disparages trading for profit emphasizing moderation in the pursuit of all forms of human pleasure which subjugates entertainment to moral enlightenment, and, finally, the notion of *"ren"* (humanity) that assumes human nature to be essentially benevolent.[3] Such principal orientations are externalized as a sociopolitical system and institution and internalized as people's psychological and behavioral patterns.

However, traditional values and their preservation are subject to change. Despite their persuasiveness and persistence, the principal Confucian orientations do not give rise to a static, integrated, and closed system. They do not produce perfect harmony but produce ongoing problematics. The rise of new forms of social organization and activities entailed new interpretations of many of the traditional beliefs and institutional premises. These new interpretations greatly transformed many of the antecedent basic tenets and institutions of Chinese civilization. In sum, cultures constantly appropriate current development into their core elements. At present, the rise of a consumer society has challenged many of the Confucian doctrines. The emergence of a wealthy consumer class and the rise of popular culture have ushered in a set of values often associated with the notion of "modern." Modernity celebrates industrialization, urbanization, bureaucratization, democratization, universal education, fast communication, and mass consumption. Such modern ideas have been absorbed into contemporary Chinese society and become part of the Chinese cultural identity.

Reflected in Chinese cinema, cultural identity comprises both tradition and modernity. Indeed, any tradition has to be understood as a selective version of the past filtered through the aspirations, experiences, and concerns of the present. In the sense that the majority of Chinese films in the era of post-Wave foreground film's commercial value over pedagogical value, Chinese cinema since the late 1980s has been less tradition-bound, a tendency emblematic of the Chinese society, in general. Ironically, it is the industry's concern for film's market value that has highlighted the imperative of Chinese cultural identity in film. The issue becomes how to reflect cultural identity in a cinematic representation. Since the Hollywood-finessed narrative structure and institutional practices have become part of the Chinese cinematic tradition, Chinese cinema's cultural identity can no longer be determined by the economy and technology of filmmaking or by a film's overriding dramatic structure and stylistic predilection alone, but by the story the film narrates and certain cultural orientation the story reflects. I am not dismissing all together the notion of Chinese aesthetics; rather, I am suggesting that stylistic elements of Chinese traditional painting and stage drama in a film are not sufficient to convey the sense of Chinese cultural identity since many of the stylistic elements exist in, or have been appropriated by, films of other cultures.[4] What is difficult to capture by a cultural outsider is certain contemporary (social) issues rooted within a unique cultural tradition. As such, a film addressing Chinese issues, contemporary or historical, from the perspective of Chinese cultural values is more recognizable as a film with Chinese cultural identity than a film that applies certain stylistic elements of Chinese traditional arts. Furthermore, a film of Chinese identity does not have to be produced in China. While film industries in many parts of the world today remain strongly national in character, the business of filmmaking and filmviewing have long been transnational in nature. In many cases today, deciding where exactly a film is "from" and to whom it is addressed has become increasingly problematic. I must emphasize that the question of production origin(s) of a film is not identical with the question of a film's cultural identity, though the origin of a film might partially determine its cultural identity. Lastly, the evaluation of cultural identity in a cinematic text is always a subjective process, depending on one's personal experience and perspective.

Empirical claims of cultural identity in a particular film may help to illuminate the issue of cultural identity. Since I have extensively covered the evolution of the Fifth Generation, it is imperative that I should zero in on one of the Fifth G's current films, *Not One Less* (Zhang Yimou, 1999), to examine the evaluation of cultural identity in a particular film. Zhang's film tackled the problem of rural illiteracy in China's culturally and financially deprived countryside. The subject matter does not necessarily attribute to the film's Chinese identity, as this problem exists in many developing countries. The film's contemporary Chinese setting grounds the problem on a concrete Chinese soil that brings to the film much of its Chinese characteristics, or Chinese identity. As a cinematic contribution to the "Hope Project," a nationwide project raising money as well as people's awareness for elementary education in poor rural areas, the theme of *Not One Less* can easily pass as a main-melody film. With its measured pedagogical/ideological impact characteristic of the main melody, the film's (official) Chinese identity is recognizable. As the story opens, a thirteen-year-old village girl, Wei, is selected to be a substitute teacher at a local elementary school when the real teacher, Gao, is on a weeklong sick leave. Wei accepts the job after the head of the village promises her 50 yuan (US$6.25) pay. Wei is further promised an additional 10 yuan (US$1.25) if she can keep the students in school, a difficult task given the fact that so many rural kids have withdrawn from the school. After the first turning point, a boy, Zhang, drops out of the school to work in the city. Informed that Zhang has gone to the city to help his father to raise the family, Wei is determined to find the boy, which sets in motion her searching for him in the big city, act two of the film. With the help of a local television station manager, Wei finally locates Zhang after many mishaps in the city.

As mentioned in the previous chapter, the film is ambivalent about Wei's motivation. It is never clear whether Wei's determination to bring Zhang back to the school is propelled by the promised cash reward or by some lofty ideal. During test screenings, many viewers expressed their dissatisfaction with the film's lack of psychological and narrative closure caused by the film's ambiguity about Wei's motivation. Critics have suggested that Zhang's desire to reconcile with the state and a Chinese cultural tradition has confined him to the main-melody formula that highlights, indeed allows, only the sublime human aspects to shine in a cinematic representation. The aspect of human desire and activities related to money is frowned on by classical Confucian principles. The acknowledgment of Wei's search mission being motivated by money might have triggered official criticism for trivializing Wei's altruistic behavior and therefore detract from the film's pedagogical value. With the local station manager, a Communist cadre, acting as a savior who helps Wei find the lost student, the film's resolution further confirms the main-melody formula and Confucian principles that locate the solution to all problems in the moral commitment of political leaders. The film's contemporary Chinese story and its marked conflict between the Confucian and the modern capitalist value systems made it an unmistakably Chinese film. The contest between Confucian moral tradition and the Mainland Chinese's newly discovered economic freedom in a postsocialist society captures well the ambiguous and unstable cultural identity of contemporary China, an identity that has struggled to balance between tradition and modernity.

The film received mixed reviews. At least three themes emerged from the critical responses to the film. Positive reviews touted Zhang Yimou for his brave cinematic turn away from the commercial entertainment wave, which symbolizes the triumph of Chinese cultural tradition. Negative reviews faulted Zhang for his compromised cinematic turn toward the main-melody formula that has resulted in the distorted representation of China and the Chinese in a postsocialist state. Zhang's main-melody turn promoted much criticism among the young cultural critics. The more neutral reviews suggested that the film's inability to come to a narrative resolution, on the one hand, reflected the filmmaker's own inner conflict and, on the other hand, captured well a Chinese society and culture in transition. In other words, political motivations aside, Zhang's moralization might reflect his own ambivalence toward Chinese society's changed values. Though the conclusions vary, all three critical perspectives linked the film to the general issue of cultural identity. This attests to my earlier suggestion that the evaluation of cultural identity in a cinematic text is always a subjective process in which diverse ideas compete with one another for interpretative legitimacy. The exercise of identity identification inevitably involves the assigning of a particular set of meanings and the attempt to contain or prevent the potential proliferation of other meanings. To the critics of *Not One Less*, the film's being out of touch with the Chinese cultural reality is partially blamed for its failure at the box office. To the champions of *Not One Less*, the film's aggressively cinema-verité style unfortunately distanced itself from the popular narrative formula that has become part of Chinese cinema's cultural heritage. That is, the deployment of narrative techniques often associated with Hollywood has become a precondition for a Chinese film to claim its Chinese identity and to survive the market.

As suggested by Michael Walsh, the success of the Hollywood formula lies mostly on its demonstration of quality, cosmopolitanism, and modernity.[5] Defined as a unitary standard of aesthetic value, the singular form of quality immediately excludes any alternative stylistic principles that would otherwise suggest qualities based on multiple standards. What counts as quality are narrational coherence and economy, the use of stars and, in some cases, high tech achieved through a big budget. Hollywood's cosmopolitanism derives from the globalization of U.S. popular culture. As the consummate specimen of the always cutting-edge American popular culture, Hollywood naturally comes to be associated with the cosmopolitan. In other words, Hollywood has eliminated much of its own cultural origin and has instead presented itself as an international cinema transcending cultural boundaries. Cinematic modernity refers to the belief that the Hollywood-style production operation represents the advanced film operation, the only kind commercially viable. The belief has been subscribed to by many national/regional film industries who have strived to adopt such an institutional modernism.

In the case of Chinese cinema, given its continued failure to gain a strong foothold in its own domestic market, film practitioners have more or less concluded that Chinese cinema has yet to attain sufficient quality and modernity. While modernizing film economy and technology, the Hollywood-style cosmopolitanism has to be replaced with films of Chinese cultural identity. The successful formula to the Chinese film industry comes down to a story of Chinese characteristics delivered through the narrative structure of a classical continuity cinema and produced and marketed with the modern industrial strategy perfected by Hollywood. As such, *Not One Less*'s box-office failure is caused by either the film's poor narrative quality or its inability to comprehend and therefore present, realistically, the changing face of Chinese culture.

The discussions on *Not One Less*'s cultural identity has been framed in terms of a marketing strategy; consequently, the issue of cultural identity becomes less a cultural than an economic one. That is, the pursuit of a unique cultural identity in a cinematic representation is seen as a marketing strategy but not a desire of a culture to express itself. Indeed, culture seems to have lost its value without being associated with economics. Such falls into the trap of classical liberal trade theories which argue that a nation–state should concentrate on producing commodities for which it enjoys certain competitive advantages. Thus, film production can be organized more efficiently around the areas of specialization, genre-wise, resource-wise, language-wise, and culture-wise. In breaking free of the stultifying rule of state socialism, the Chinese film industry is susceptible to falling prey to the machinations of the international market and the logic of global capitalism based on the premise of liberal trade theories.

The logic of the global capitalism subordinates not only culture but also morality and politics to the primary consideration of economics. As China recovered from the trauma of 1989, the collective project in which the Chinese public is invited to participate by the postsocialist state is not a political utopia of any sort but the making of an egalitarian consumer society that encourages public participation in the consumption of popular culture.[6] Associated with the popular, culture now parts ways with ideology and is turned into capital itself. There is, indeed, a contested but nonetheless widely shared conviction at the present moment that cinema and other forms of art or literature, simply as esthetic objects, no longer have a self-evident claim on our attention, and that their true significance is, therefore, to be sought in their connections with aspects of social, political, and economic life, which are felt to be more clearly urgent.[7] Is the discussion of cultural identity in a cinematic representation legitimate only when it serves to shed light on the survival of the Chinese film industry as a commercially sustainable entity? In a broader scope, has the discussion of culture become valuable only insofar as it illustrates social, political, and economic issues at large? Does culture matter in China's prolonged march toward economic modernization? What is the ultimate goal of economic empowerment?

I would argue that China's prolonged modernization project is propelled by the crisis of cultural identity and that economic empowerment is the means to the end but not the end itself. The end is the need for cultural empowerment. After all, to live is more than just to sustain life—it is to enrich and to be enriched by life. The drive for economic development will not occur without the desire of a culture to assert its pride in being what it is and being recognized as such. Cultural identity conceived as such has a moral implication as it suggests that cultures can flourish only to the extent that they are recognized. Thus, cultural identity is defined from this perspective by the commitments and identifications that provide the frame or horizon within which a culture can try to determine from case to case what is good, or valuable, or what ought to be done, or what it endorses or opposes. It is the horizon within which a culture is capable of taking a stand. Of course, identities can dissolve when horizons themselves clash.

The existence of a variety of cultures is not a mere accident but is meant to bring about a greater harmony.[8] It is reasonable to suppose that cultures that have provided the horizon of meaning for a large number of human beings, of diverse characters and temperaments, over a long period of time are almost certain to have something that deserves our admiration and respect, even if it is accompanied by much that we abhor and reject. What is required above all is an admission that we are very far away from that ultimate horizon from which the relative worth of different cultures might be evident. As such, it is imperative for different cultures to demand recognition of their equal value and the acknowledgment of their equal worth. In sum, culture matters in its own right and the expression of cultural identity in a cinematic representation is not merely an economic strategy suggested by the economically instrumental logic. Otherwise we would have no nations, no cultural differences, no ethnicity except differences in physical appearance. Indeed, we would have no "peoples" at all, just billions of individual workers/consumers in a morally undifferentiated, politically borderless global society (morally undifferentiated because differences of taste and lifestyle would flourish, but would contain no meanings other than as momentary expressions of sensorial preference). The reality contests otherwise. In a world of global flows of wealth, power, and images, the search for identity, collective or individual, ascribed or constructed, becomes the fundamental source of social meaning. People increasingly organize their meaning not around what they do but on the basis of what they are. This is not a new trend, since identity, and particularly religious and ethnic identity, have been at the roots of meaning since the dawn of human society. At present, the Chinese film industry's anxiety over its economic survival might overshadow its concern over cinema's cultural value. Sooner or later, the industry will have to come to terms with the cultural imperative of cultural identity in a cinematic representation. The limitations of a liberal economic analysis with its pragmatic bias that subjugates the discussion of culture to economics will then become apparent. In short, the long-term survival of Chinese cinema is possible only when its practitioners recognize the significance of preserving its cultural identity from the standpoints of both the film industry and the Chinese culture at large.

Future research on Chinese cinema will benefit from a comparative approach to relate the development of Chinese cinema with cinemas of other postsocialist states to further examine the role of such states and their institutions in shaping the course of their cultural industries. In this regard, three areas of literature will provide useful theoretical and empirical references. One is rooted in the intellectual tradition of comparative political sociology that stretches from Max Weber to Barrington Moore and to the works of Peter Evans. Closely related are works that recognize the importance of ideas and ideological production to the history of bureaucratized modernity and its social policies. As lamented by Theda Skocpol, most scholarship on the origins of modern social policy has "focused almost exclusively on class and political conflicts, de-emphasizing the equally important contributions of ideas, of knowledge-bearing groups, and of knowledge-generating institutions."[9] In the case of Chinese cinema, the characteristics and roles of salaried state filmmakers and critics in shaping the course of Chinese cinema needs to be addressed, which leads to the third area of literature.[10] The third includes writings from former Soviet bloc nation–states concerning characteristics of a (post)socialist culture. Nurtured after the 1920s by similar ideals and conditioned by like practices, Chinese cultural practitioners share many common traits with their counterparts in eastern Europe. Miklos Haraszti's *The Velvet Prison*, particularly, provides a useful analytic paradigm with which the complex relationship between the postsocialist states and their artists can be charted.[11]

NOTES

1. See Schmuel Eisenstadt, "Some Observations on Relations between Confucianism, Development, and Modernization," in *Confucianism and the Modernization*

of China, ed. Silke Krieger and Rolf Trauzettel (Hamburg, Ger.: Hase and Koehler Verlag, 1991), 83.

2. See Ian Philip McGreal, ed., *Great Thinkers of the Eastern World* (New York: Routledge, 1995).

3. See Silke Krieger and Rolf Trauzettle, eds., *Confucianism and the Modernization of China* (Hamburg, Ger.: Hase and Koehler Verlag, 1991), 74.

4. See Hector Rodriguez, "Questions of Chinese Aesthetics: Film Form and Narrative Space in the Cinema of King Hu," *Cinema Journal* 38, no. 1 (1998): 73.

5. Michael Walsh, "Fighting the American Invasion with Cricket, Roses, and Marmalade for Breakfast," *The Velvet Light Trap* 40 (1997): 40.

6. See Jing Wang, "Public Culture and Popular Culture: Urban China at the Turn of the New Century" (paper presented at the Popular Culture in the Age of Mass Media in Korea and Neighboring Countries Conference, University of Texas–Austin, February 1998).

7. See Andrew Low, "The Ethics of Modernism: The Contribution and Limitations of Charles Taylor," *Mosaic* 29, no. 2 (1996): 111–126.

8. See Charles Taylor, *Multiculturalism and the "Politics of Identification,"* (Princeton, N.J.: Princeton University Press, 1994).

9. Theda Skocpol, ed., *States, Social Knowledge, and the Origins of Modern Social Policies* (Princeton, N.J.: Princeton University Press, 1996), 3.

10. Paul Clark's *Chinese Cinema* (Cambridge: Cambridge University Press, 1987) is one of the few books that has approached Chinese cinema from this perspective.

11. Miklos Haraszti, *The Velvet Prison* (New York: Noonday Press, 1987).

Index

ABOUT THE AUTHOR

YING ZHU is Assistant Professor of Media Culture at the College of Staten Island, City University of New York.